UPBEAT

The Story of the National Youth Orchestra of Iraq

PAUL MACALINDIN

Foreword by Sir Peter Maxwell Davies

SANDSTONEPRESS
HIGHLAND | SCOTLAND

First published in Great Britain and the United States of America
Sandstone Press Ltd
Dochcarty Road
Dingwall
Ross-shire
IV15 9UG
Scotland

www.sandstonepress.com

The publisher acknowledges support from Creative Scotland towards publication of this volume.

ISBN: 978-1-910985-09-0
ISBNe: 978-1-910985-10-6

Jacket design by Mark Swan
Typesetting and plate sections by Raspberry Creative Type, Edinburgh
Printed by CPI Group (UK) Ltd, Croydon, CR0 4YY

To the brave young musicians of Iraq

Contents

List of Illustrations

SECTION TWO

Acknowledgements

Majid Al Azzawi

Du'aa Al Azzawi

Osama Abdulrasol

Ali Alghabban

Khyam Allami

Waleed Ahmed Assi

Ali Authman

Shwan Aziz

Samir Baseem

Chris Bowers

Robert Davidson at Sandstone Press

Sir Peter Maxwell Davies

Tara Jasmine Dewan

Mark Edwards

Mohammed Amin Ezzat

Barbara Frommann

Sheena Gordon

Tariq and Hassan Hassoon

Louis Hermiz

Saman Hiwa

Tara Jaff

Rezhwan Jalal

Bettina Kolb, Rim Najmi and Naomi Conrad at Deutsche Welle

Becca Lawrence

Heather Macpherson at Raspberry Creative Type

Gordon McPherson

Rachel Maley and Randal Swiggum at Elgin Youth Symphony
Orchestra

Annie Melconian

Frand Nashat

New Moon magazine for girls

Balen Qader

Alan and Daroon Rasheed

Firman Saeed

Tilman Schlomp at Beethovenfest
Bashdar Sdiq
Erin Sullivan at Friends of British Council USA
Hellgurd Sultan
Zuhal Sultan
Eliahu Sussman at School Band and Orchestra magazine
Tuqa al Waeli
Julian Lloyd Webber
Michael White at The Telegraph
Georg Witteler
Christian Wulff, former President of Germany
Boran Zaza

Foreword

When the great Western powers, led by the United States of America and the United Kingdom, committed to the 2003 invasion of Iraq there was widespread indignation and anger throughout both countries and elsewhere in the world. Countless thousands took to the streets and I was among them. Our protests were to no avail and the invasion began on 19th March of that year.

No avail that is, unless we count the galvanising of peoples behind a commonly held moral repugnance, and a gradual rethinking on how we are governed and by whom. The *New Statesman* quoted me at the time in the following manner: 'I've often thought that democracy would be a good idea in the United Kingdom, but one sees no evidence yet of it being implemented. As a composer what can you do about it? You have to bear witness.'

The invasion ended, the old leadership of Saddam Hussein was deposed, and the occupation began, but where the war's architects might have believed that a boil had been lanced and healing might begin, if anything things got worse.

Expression for me continued in my work, especially the third string quartet in the series that had been commissioned by the Naxos classical music group. Spontaneous, with martial references, ultimately bleak; such was my testimony. It seemed impossible that compassion and humanity in Iraq could survive, having given way to tribalism, torture and fear, but it so happens that the human spirit is made of stronger stuff. Throughout Iraq, and across the nation's ethnic division of Arab and Kurd, what W.H.Auden described as 'ironic points of light' did indeed 'flash out' and the Just 'exchanged their messages'.

In this case the Just were the young classical musicians of Iraq and the 'flashing out' was done through the internet. Their love of classical music and their aspirations to learn had not been, indeed could not be destroyed. They took their lessons remotely from teachers in the United States and Europe. They learned by ear from compact discs. They tended and maintained their instruments as best they could in a dry climate. Mostly though, they remained more or less isolated.

Isolated that is, until a remarkable young woman named Zuhal Sultan came up with an idea and determined to form the first National Youth Orchestra of Iraq.

Again by means of the internet, Zuhal made a series of outreaches which led to an unlikely series of connections, eventually coming to the attention, in even less likely fashion, of musician and conductor Paul MacAlindin. So unlikely was this that, for those with religious leanings, it must be hard not to suspect divine intervention. However it came to pass though, the right message went to the right man, at the right time in his life, in words that could not but inspire him.

Highly energised, Paul set about making his own connections: some current, some new, some revived. As an old and close friend he called me at my home here in Orkney. My reaction was immediate and positive. Such a story, even so far as it had then unfolded, could not but make my heart sing. Not only was it a musical response to the disaster, but its origination with, and involvement of, the young musicians of Iraq continued and extended my own, lifelong, commitment to young people and music.

Transcendence is too easily coined a word, too easily appropriated by the born-again brigades, purveyors of conversion cures, and single-step salvationists. Transcendence exists though, a necessary agent of change, and music is one of its means as has been shown time and again. For the National Youth Orchestra of Iraq it began between those solitary students and their remote tutors. With the advent of the Youth Orchestra it bonded them to their new leadership, the new tutors who arrived to work directly with them, and their new maestro. Eventually it took them to the music loving audiences of Germany, where Paul MacAlindin has made his home, Great Britain and France, and to a strong, but finally thwarted American connection.

It was my privilege to become the orchestra's composer in residence and I donated a seven- minute piece, *Reel of Spindrift, Sky*, intended to stretch without breaking the technical abilities of the young musicians and also, to some extent, to present the very different climate and culture of Orkney.

The task of building the orchestra was by no means simple or safe. The physical dangers to the musicians and their families should not be underestimated. Nor was it easy to continue year on year and to manage change. It is to Paul MacAlindin's great credit that he makes little of his own straitened circumstances while he gave his every waking hour, all of his mental and spiritual energy, and no doubt most of his dreamtime to this wonderful project.

The great adventure of the National Youth Orchestra of Iraq deserves not only to be recorded for posterity but also to serve as an example of how the essential can survive catastrophe. Within it, joy was made where there had been misery. From chaos, order was formed. Out of many losses a new, living thing was born. Friendships were made across cultures and unforgettable experiences shared. If some of the future Iraq's leaders began their formation here, as seems likely, the seeds of cooperation, consensus and order were planted deeply and well.

Paul MacAlindin has wisely chosen to title his book *Upbeat*. It recounts the history of the orchestra and describes the characters and experiences of the musicians, their tutors and supporters. Together they make a shining light, but another great character shines beside them in this accessible and entertaining account. It is that of the author himself who will surely, now, come into the public eye not only as a musical director with strength and determination as well as a musician of sensitivity and knowledge, but also as an author with a clear and unmistakeable voice.

The National Youth Orchestra of Iraq lives on in these pages but here I pause, urging you to continue with Paul MacAlindin. It is time for him to bear witness.

Sir Peter Maxwell Davies CH CBE
Sanday, Orkney

As this book was in the final stages of production in March 2016, Sir Peter Maxwell Davies died at his home on Sanday, aged 81. He will be greatly missed throughout the world of music and across the whole community in Orkney.

Introduction

The Egyptian author, Taha Hussein, once famously pointed out, 'Egyptians write, Lebanese publish, Iraqis read'. By the mid-20th century, Baghdad had become a veritable hub of artists and intellectuals, hungry to learn, discuss and create. Iraqi Jews led the thriving Arab music scene. In 1958, the Iraqi National Symphony Orchestra was founded in Baghdad, a first for the Middle East, followed shortly after by the Baghdad School of Music and Ballet. Although, fresh out of the spoils of World War One, Britain had invented this country to reflect its oil interests, Iraqis went on to forge an identity of their own. Behind them lay thousands of years of culture dating back to the cradle of civilisation, the Sumerians. Their writing system, cuneiform on clay tablets, recorded the world's first great work of literature, the Epic of Gilgamesh.

Some 4000 years on, lying alone at night in her Baghdad home, a teenage pianist from the Iraqi National Symphony Orchestra, Zuhal Sultan, had an idea. Out of the ashes of the Iraq war, a national youth orchestra would rise like a phoenix, a beacon of reconciliation and hope for the future, and a lifeline for young musicians across Iraq. What followed could hardly compete with King Gilgamesh in terms of fame or testosterone, but did turn out to be every bit as raw, epic and transformative. I suspect he would have grudgingly approved.

In the summer of 2009, the National Youth Orchestra of Iraq kicked off its first fortnight-long music camp in the Kurdish Iraqi town of Suleymaniyah. We followed this in 2010 with another fortnight in the oil capital of Erbil. As for 2011, we not only nailed two more weeks in Erbil but mounted our magic carpets, courtesy of Lufthansa, and flew to Germany at the invitation of Beethovenfest. When 2012 came round, our British roots pulled us out of Iraq and landed us amid the Edinburgh Festival and South Bank Centre for three weeks. In 2013, it seemed nothing could go wrong, and we organised a ten-day tour of masterclasses through three Kurdish towns, a summer course in Aix-en-Provence and a chamber orchestra collaboration with the Morgenland Festival in Erbil and Osnabrück Youth Choir.

Year after year, our platoon of players stormed onto stage to wage peace, love and reconciliation through composers such as Mendelssohn, Mohammed Amin Ezzat, Beethoven and Karzan Mahmood. However, Zuhal, every bit the Arab princess, soon found herself exiled to the darkest recesses of Glasgow, safe but far away, while her bonnie prince – that's me – fought to reunite her with her creation. Then, in 2014, as the cancer of ISIL spread throughout Iraq, we made one massive push to bring our diplomacy to where it was most needed – America.

The number of pages required to thank everyone who helped us would be a saga in itself. Without the British Council's sustained support, we would never have existed at all. The one and only Iraqi politician to believe in us, Dr Barham Salih, responded brilliantly. Our Iraqi team and players, facing unimaginable odds, kept their faith throughout. The German Friends of the National Youth Orchestra of Iraq and Beethovenfest lifted us onto a new plane. The Scottish Government, who had followed us from the start, put their money where their mouth was, and brought us to Edinburgh. And finally, through the Grand Theatre de Provence, who had never spent so much time and money on one single concert before, we joined a gathering of giants in Aix-en-Provence. To everyone who helped us in any way, great or small, thank you.

This book was made possible in part with support from the Friends of British Council USA, with whom we worked closely in 2014, and the British Institute for the Study of Iraq, who also helped to finance our tutors. I am also grateful for Creative Scotland's support. My deepest gratitude of all goes to Sandstone Press and my editor, Robert Davidson, who showed enormous faith in my work.

This epic journey has profoundly changed everyone.

It has profoundly changed me.

Paul MacAlindin
Music Director of the National Youth Orchestra of Iraq

ONE
Iraqi teen seeks maestro

October 2008, and my Dad had just been discharged from Dundee Royal Infirmary to recover after a minor operation. I decided now was as good a time as any to head home to Scotland and check up on the old boy. As is my ritual, after touching down in Edinburgh from my hometown of Cologne I hoofed it over to the centre of town where my favourite pub, The Barony in Broughton Street, lay waiting to serve up a pint with fish and chips.

Sunday 19th October was a decent day by Edinburgh standards, but it was also soon after Lehman Brothers filed for insolvency in New York. This confronted many artists around the world with a crippling downturn. My recent concerts in Armenia, New York and New Zealand had been well received but I needed a radical new direction if I was to weather the recession and refocus my energies.

Sitting alone at a bow window table inside the Barony, silvery Edinburgh light shone down on a used *Glasgow Herald*, lying by my fish and chips. I flipped through the newspaper, arriving at page 13 with the headline, 'Search for UK maestro to help create an orchestra in Iraq'. Thank goodness for 'Maestro'! Had it just said 'Conductor' I'd probably have turned the page. Continuing to read, I understood that something potentially big might be happening. Zuhal Sultan, a 17-year-old pianist in Baghdad, sought a conductor to help create a national youth orchestra of Iraq.

Let's get this into perspective. Barely out of war, with no discernible orchestral tradition that I knew of, what could there

1

be to work with? Who was playing music? What did it sound like? Who was teaching? What condition were the instruments in? How could I and every other Westerner have been media bombarded with bloodshed and tragedy, but still be unknowing of who Iraqis really are? What was Iraqi culture? Fixated on the article, fish trembling on the end of my fork, I simply said to myself: 'I know how to do this'.

In that single moment I imagined Zuhal and her mates applying for the first ever course of this orchestra, the British Council making good on finance and logistics, as it might just, possibly, maybe, be persuaded to do. I also sensed that if I didn't seize this opportunity, I'd never get another chance to found a national youth orchestra, and what an enormous honour that would be. Hitting 40, I still had the energy. Alone in the Barony, I consumed lunch and consummated my future.

Torn-out article in hand, I headed up the road to St James Bus Station. I'd be damned if I let my German mobile fall victim to extortionate roaming charges, so I found a payphone instead and contacted an old chum at the British Council in London. 'Have you heard about this?' I asked Paul Parkinson, a former composer of monk-like demeanour, now tasked with shipping hip-hop and other trends around the world. We not only shared a love of classical music, but also quickly agreed that the UK's participation in the Iraq war made this project highly relevant. Paul listened quietly and said he would 'look into it'.

Later that day, in the old fishing village of Anstruther, in the East Neuk of Fife, I found that Dad was on the mend and in good spirits. Dad was his own kind of warrior. A journalist and sub-editor on various Scottish newspapers in his working life, he had always found a way to lead others in the local community. He had been a classic tub-thumping Thatcherite until one day, working as a pensioner stocking shelves in a Tesco supermarket in St Andrews, his faith in Maggie's free market was shattered. It was a Saturday, an hour before closing, and time to mark down the price of perishables with a labelling gun. A line of other pensioners formed behind him, clawing for each item as it was repriced.

He finally saw the mark Thatcher's neo-liberalism had left on society and with that, he and I, who loved each other enormously in spite our different views on life, came a step closer, and I felt that my earlier student self was vindicated. And yet, as one of Thatcher's Children, I was about to embark upon the ultimate neo-liberal odyssey. To paraphrase Norman Tebbit, former Chairman of the Conservative Party, I was about to get on my bike, and look for work. I flew back home to Cologne.

The press release about Zuhal had been issued from the London office of Raw TV's Jo Woolf, producer of reality show Battlefront for Channel 4. Released nationwide, only the *Glasgow Herald* had picked it up. Jo wasn't difficult to connect with. Battlefront coached British teenagers to campaign for social change, following their progress on national TV. One had determined to stamp out cyber-bullying. A couple were rallying against homophobia. Another, whose cocky assuredness and disarming unkemptness had won him a huge following, was trying to get a law passed to ban smoking in cars. As a kid, he'd endured second-hand smoke in his parents' car and ended up with asthma.

Jo discovered Zuhal through British Council Iraq, and brought her on board as Battlefront's international teen. She didn't really understand what she was letting herself in for though, as Zuhal was marooned in Baghdad, and the complications of creating a youth orchestra in a middle-eastern conflict zone were beyond anyone's experience. Jo took responsibility for Zuhal's mission, but unreliable mobile and Internet connections frustrated her. As Iraq came out of war, telephony was mainly wireless, haphazard, and satellite Internet expensive. She had to stay cool, build faith in Zuhal and keep going. Trust, which would be built on experience, would come in its own time.

At the beginning of November, Jo set up my first meeting with Zuhal on Skype. Back home in Cologne, laptop poised in Brownies, a local coffee shop with Wi-Fi, I waited for her call from Baghdad. Brownies was an overpriced yuppie haunt for people who sat in front of laptops and needed to feel part of society without actually having to pull themselves offline. Being one of these people it became my regular haunt for the project's cyber phase. On that first contact with Zuhal, what came out of my mouth felt like an hour's worth of verbal diarrhoea. Zuhal, obviously smart and self-assured, could convince anyone they were talking to a 17-year-old at a posh boarding school. Sometimes though, I had the feeling that she was the 40-year-old and I was the teenage girl.

Later that day, I summarised our meeting to London in an email:

'Hi Jo.

Zuhal and I have just had an hour of Skyping.

'Here are the main points from my perspective:

'- There is already substantial support from Zuhal's contacts around the world, particularly Allegra Klein in the US.

- In Iraq, there is also a lot of positive support for Zuhal and the idea of the Iraqi National Youth Orchestra. The two main steps are to set up a fundraising account and attain charitable status for the orchestra in a country other than Iraq, and to have the account taken care of by a trusted organisation

- Zuhal has important administrative support from the librarian of the Iraqi National Symphony Orchestra

- We discussed how responsiveness from Battlefront was not as much as she might expect. In my opinion, Battlefront may not be the right medium for communication to stakeholders in the UK Classical Music market, simply because most aren't Generation Y. They're based in Britain and don't know how to help someone in Iraq, and the classical music business has an insular, past-oriented culture that doesn't connect via the web as well as the entertainment business

- The electricity cut out during our Skype call. This is why classical music is such a good art form for Iraq. You don't need to plug in a cello!

- We discussed El Sistema. We both agreed that this has something for Iraq to look at.

- We discussed parental support, which is critical to effective youth orchestra logistics, and support for players of poorer families

- The first strategic goal should be a concert next summer with c. 18 players
- The first step to that goal is to identify the potential players (already largely done) and for me to use my youth orchestra contacts in the UK and Germany to identify online teachers. I promised to get back to Zuhal about this with initial feedback in about a week.
- Administrative effectiveness is really important if the players are to work together and online in a secure environment. To that end, I'm sending Zuhal a link to the openlearn website, which gives free online mini-courses in management and other topics. We also talked about delegation.
- Leadership effectiveness is also very important. So far, the positive feedback to Zuhal has been due to the idea itself, and also to the way Zuhal sells it. We cannot underestimate the way in which this orchestra's success or failure will depend on how people in Iraq perceive its leadership.
- Therefore, I believe that Zuhal is the ideal person to make the initial decisions about leadership, and should continue to be the public face of the orchestra
- Fundraising can be about setting up an NYOI website with a Paypal donation facility in the same country as the NYOI charity. It can also be about offshoots to the Battlefront programmes, such as a book on the project. If the most lucrative market segments are identified, then the book, with accompanying DVD, can be a continual fundraiser, with sequels as the orchestra develops. Off the top of my head, and without knowing much about selling books, I think market segments include: motivational and personal growth, music industry generally, Gen Y leadership, families connected with kids making music, business case studies
- We should wait for the first concert before approaching classical music promoters with a concrete touring proposal, though Classic FM et al would be great to get in on the game now from a PR fundraising perspective.
Best
Paul'

Looking back on this now, it was all there, though the spectre of who to delegate to already mocked me.

Zuhal got back to Jo. Jo got back to me. I was the chosen one, but I still knew very little about her. Who was Zuhal Sultan? Her interview with the girls' magazine, *New Moon*, gave me some idea.

When she was six years old, Zuhal's mother noticed her listening to music and mimicking it on the toy piano in her Baghdad home. She signed Zuhal up for private lessons straight away. Zuhal was highly complimented by her first teacher, likening her ivory hands to the softness of pitta bread. By the time she was nine, she received a scholarship to the Music and Ballet School of Baghdad, the first music school in the Middle East. Before 2003, the school was staffed by post-Soviet teachers, working to a very high standard, who maintained something of a Western tradition in Baghdad.

Things changed when the invasion and war began in 2003. Zuhal was 12 when her beloved music school was on the brink of collapse as most of the teachers had fled the country. Just being seen on the streets of Baghdad with an instrument case was dangerous; it was viewed as a sign of wealth and Western cultural values. During the worst of the violence, she and the other students tried to continue her classes despite the risk of travelling to and from school, peaking in civil war by 2006. This went on for a long time, so just sitting back and saying, 'Oh, I can't go out; I can't go to school' was absolutely ridiculous to her. They knew they had to go on, so they managed to keep the school open and teach themselves.

Zuhal came from a very scientific family with no particular musical background. Her parents were scientists who had studied and met in London; one of her brothers was a doctor and the other an engineer. She loved science and mathematics. Nevertheless, music was her main passion. During the Iraq war, her mother had died of illness in hospital and her father had been killed during an armed bank robbery he was unlucky enough to be caught in. While neither was a direct casualty of war, both parents, along with countless thousands of Iraqis, had perished as a result of crumbling public services and a society descending into anarchy. One brother became her guardian.

Zuhal's music training continued through video Skype with a piano teacher in New York. She performed at UNESCO in Paris aged 15 and played a Mozart piano concerto with the Iraqi National Symphony Orchestra. The British Council also signed her for their 'Global Changemakers' programme, which was how she connected with Battlefront.

She joined the Iraqi National Symphony when she was 15; that group of 70 musicians of varying ages and religions felt like a big family to her. In the midst of all the violence in her country, the orchestra had a precious feeling of unity. She became driven to ensure that more young musicians experienced this and wanted the world to see it. Life had been difficult in Iraq since the war began, but was improving day by day. That's why she felt it was time to look at the deeper aspects of rebuilding, through the culture and the arts. One night, lying awake, the idea came to her and, at 17, she set out to create her country's first ever youth orchestra: The National Youth Orchestra of Iraq (NYOI).

I spent the following weeks sitting alone in Cologne's coffee shops, staring into the abyss. Helping a 17-year-old Iraqi set up an orchestra was bound to change the course of my life. I still didn't know what was to be done or how to do it, working with young Iraqi musicians after a war in the most countercultural project imaginable. There was no apparent fit between them and Iraq, them and me, or us together and the music business. An inspired British Council was my lifeline, and to some extent we stared into the abyss together.

Reassurance was also required, preferably from those close to me. Come the end of October, the first person I told was my old friend and ex, Sir Peter Maxwell Davies, who was enjoying his role as Master of the Queen's Music. Within his world back in 1990s Scotland, I'd experienced the foibles and failings of the music biz, its lack of transparency and wilful blindness, priceless experiences that would mould my perspective of the Iraq project. Some years after our relationship came to an end and turned to friendship Max's world fell apart when his business manager was jailed in 2006 for false accounting. I looked on from my new home in Cologne, quietly concerned although quite apart.

During my phone call with Max in his Orkney home, I managed to declare myself the 'Musical Director of the National Youth Orchestra of Iraq,' barely able to speak the words without choking. 'All my love goes out to you!' came his immediate response and then he blurted out, 'And I will be your Honorary Composer-in-Residence!'

In a moment of inspirational brilliance, he'd nailed it. 'Honorary' was useful to us both, as it not only meant he would never really have to be 'in-residence' in Iraq, but also that he owed me a free piece of music. As a few minutes of Max's music would put a hole in anyone's bank account, this was a neat offer. Max had also marched in London, along with so many other British people, against the Blair government's war. He was genuinely passionate about what had happened, and became our first genuine big-name supporter. For my fledgling team, his public acceptance alone boosted morale. Moreover, his approval told me that what I was doing was right.

My first visit to London came in mid-November 2008, to discuss with Paul Parkinson at the British Council what we might do next. I gave him good news about reconnecting with my old friends at the organisation, Making Music, who were so taken with Zuhal's mission they'd decided to work with Battlefront to set up the orchestra's UK charity. I was clear that Iraq's shattered financial system couldn't be trusted to handle such a project, being warped by corruption at the best of times. So, a transparent, permanent bank account and fundraising solution outside Iraq seemed the obvious solution. The quality of people galvanised by our quest lifted my spirits, but big names alone meant very little. Only shared passion would bring the mountain to Mohammed.

My first visit to Battlefront's office reminded me of the newsroom journalists Dad took me to see when I was a kid. The open plan office, Spartan and edgy with casual young media types wired into PCs (in Dad's day there were typewriters), felt like a reality TV set in its own right. Unpretentious and realistic about making programmes by teens about teens, Jo took responsibility for protecting them. That is, from people who might want to work with a 17-year-old on a project like this for exploitative reasons and who might resemble people like me.

Jo kept me engaged in her world. Sharp, sparrowy and intuitive, she wanted me on board as Zuhal's mentor. Online, we had to somehow guide her over the hurdles without really understanding her day-to-day reality in Baghdad. By the time I'd returned to Cologne, I decided that Jo and Battlefront were brilliant. After clearing me to work with young people, she had put my mentoring page online and asked for some campaign advice:

'When Disney Corporation develops a new idea, it gets put through three different teams of people, each in separate rooms. In room 1, you'll find the positive energy people, the 'Dreamers' who think up the vision for the future film or attraction, just like your campaign dream, and pass it onto room 2. There, the 'Realists' who manage, take the dream and work out how, step by step, it's going to happen, then pass it onto room 3. In this room, the 'Critics' analyse and bring up all the doubts and problems and possible risks. If they pass it back saying, grudgingly, 'not bad,' they're very impressed! There is a fourth campaign role, the 'Observer,' who takes in all the feedback and rotates it round the different rooms till everyone is satisfied with the result. In your campaign you can play all 4 roles yourself, looking at the problem from different angles, or bring in team members who are naturally good at one role. According to Disney, you need all four roles for a new idea to become realistic. Sounds like hard work? Welcome to the reality of dreams.'

I now found myself advising British teens on how to build a campaign. I hadn't felt this useful in ages but, more to the point, who were our 'critics,' who were our 'observers'? My self-confidence got me through each step, but ahead lay a high-risk trail. I felt both thrilled and drained.

We reached January 2009 with much on the go. Allegra Klein, of whom I had learned in my first correspondence with Zuhal, was a secretary in a New York law firm and director of the US charity 'Musicians for Harmony'. Allegra already had a track record of engaging in the Middle East, as well as good connections in Manhattan. Zuhal and Allegra knew each other from 'American Voices', a US State Department-funded charity which ran performance workshops in the Kurdistan region of Iraq.

The first Skype conference between Zuhal, Allegra and myself initiated us as the triumvirate who would actually meet in Iraq and set up the first course. Over the months, we grew to appreciate the enormity of our task and it both scared and exhilarated me. Having urgent need of audition videos to select the best players, choose suitable repertoire for their level of ability and put together a viable orchestra for performance in a two-week course, I asked Zuhal to persuade her friends across Iraq to apply.

Young Iraqis had already heard many promises that evaporated as millions of dollars slipped down official back pockets. Their belief in Zuhal no doubt sprang partly from blind faith and desperation, but also because she was one of them. She and her friends across Iraq, notably the young pianist Boran Zaza in the Kurdish region, sat for hours at laptops or Internet cafes uploading or burning a wide range of musical talent for me on video. In 2009, five minutes of video could take up to ten hours to upload, as long as the power didn't cut and set them back to square one.

Zuhal's own contacts from the Iraqi National Symphony Orchestra, where she was orchestral pianist, provided us with a backbone of young talent in need of help. Another of her networks was American Voices' summer courses in the Kurdistan Region, which had brought young Iraqi musicians from all backgrounds together since 2006. Through their cultural diplomacy, some good teaching practice was becoming available to Iraqis for the first time since the war. As the videos came in, my heart broke. Hungry souls reaching for music, trying to feel it in the darkness, left me in no doubt that everyone needed help: technique, good instruments, proper teaching, most of all people who loved music and would treat them with respect. They needed us.

I wanted so much to show them compassionate and collaborative leadership, as unlike the botched masculine dictatorship they were getting as I could make it. I couldn't fathom that a country trying to rebuild itself after war wanted to crush its young talent, especially as the young make up the vast majority of its population. While fundraising dominated our agenda every week, fairness and principle were essential to build trust in these shattered young musicians, already divided and demoralised. I had no desire to inflict the same duplicitous games on them that I knew from my own career.

Allegra's insight into cultural diplomacy often guided me through difficult decisions. In particular, who would be the concertmaster to sit on the front desk of the violins and lead the orchestra? As the audition videos would clearly show, the Arab violinists topped the Kurds in ability, but Allegra pointed out that an Arab leader performing in the Kurdish town of Suleymaniyah, our proposed base, would create tensions. My gut churned over the dilemma.

After walking purposefully around that small part of Cologne that is my own little world, I found an Internet cafe and wrote the e-mail that allowed a Kurdish violinist to lead one half of the concert, and an Arab violinist to lead the other. Splitting the leadership in our very first course felt sickeningly wrong. Nevertheless, with one final gut-wrenching pang I emailed my decision to the team. It was done; another risk added to the rising mountain of unanswered questions.

TWO
The $50,000 tweet

At the beginning of March 2009, I returned to London for a first meeting with Tony Reilly, Director of British Council Iraq. An affable chap with handsome grey hair and a warm English accent, he listened keenly as I powered through our progress. The way had already been smoothed for me, and he agreed without much ado to support the orchestra's first summer course in Iraq. Tony was a bit of a chancer, definitely the right man for war-scarred Iraq. For this I was truly grateful because by the same token I was being one hell of a chancer. We both sensed the excitement and scale of this opportunity: a true way to bring divided young people together and nourish them with real training. It didn't have to be perfect, and given the state of post-war Iraq, I'd hung that idea up on a peg already. We just had to make it happen.

British Council London caught the imagination of *The Times*, who ran a large article on Zuhal's quest and a picture of the 17-year-old, looking into the camera with a deeply dazzling Arab soul pouring out of her dark eyes, framed by a roundish face and with a grand piano in the background. As the paper went to print, she was already en-route to London via Amman, courtesy of the British Council, her fame assured. Amid the daily e-mails and weekly Skypecons, I saw that the omens were good.

We hit the end of March with many outstanding questions still to answer, but a growing sense of hope in the team. Jo finally caught Zuhal on camera, triumphantly arriving at Heathrow. After months of her evading Battlefront's requests for video reports of life and auditions in Baghdad, Jo badly needed to lift Battlefront's reporting onto another level. That Zuhal hadn't really bought into Battlefront spoke intuitively of a decision I came more and more to understand. Despite her golden media persona, she also sensed herself gradually forming into an adult, and was not yet prepared to buy wholeheartedly into the responsibility and cost of fame. Living in Baghdad also carried a certain risk to women who attracted the wrong kind of media attention.

At the first stop of her itinerary, an e-campaigning forum at Oxford University, she wowed them. Zuhal really could get on stage and deliver. Meanwhile, I flew back to London for our first ever face-to-face meeting after months of skyping. So many issues had not really been talked about on a deeper emotional level. Video or voice Skype usually didn't work well between Zuhal in Baghdad, me in Cologne and Allegra in New York. Instead, we resorted to hours of text chat. We were doing everything 'right' and it felt exciting, but we were also three very different people with no way to read our underlying emotions. We still needed to get to know each other.

The project reached a huge milestone on 2nd April, our first big step into the limelight. Battlefront had booked the afternoon at the Wigmore Hall, London's premiere chamber music venue. Jo kept everything under control. This event was set to platform our extraordinary campaign while also creating great TV for them. Zuhal and I were allowed to meet briefly backstage in the morning before she was whisked off to be filmed practising for her piano recital in two hours time. Jo stayed behind to manage me.

The artists' dressing room, wall to wall with black and white framed photos of classical music stars dating back decades, launched her film team into another world. Picked for their experience as embedded journalists with American troops in Iraq, they surveyed the austere expressions of sopranos, conductors, and pianists, trying to grasp the context.

Jo's film team were solid guys with great stories, but quite what they had to do with a classical recital wasn't clear to me.

I guessed they were being primed to cover us in Iraq. Jo, abuzz with excitement, could finally do her job and produce reality TV. I, on the other hand, sensed a possible lack of sensitivity on their part, and began to harbour doubts. Jo asked me to sit down at a piano and talk on camera about NYOI. We did two takes: my story of how it all began in take one, and then the version Jo asked me to adapt, which painted Zuhal as a fairy-tale heroine who singlehandedly created the orchestra. This, I felt, rather confirmed my doubts.

Once that was in the can, I tried to find Zuhal, because now I was really concerned about her and how this would all turn out. Andy Staples, a rising tenor star who was donating his performance to the recital, found her first, and I caught up with them rehearsing from a book of Schubert songs he'd brought along. This was absurd. Zuhal was sight-reading Schubert two hours before performing it in the Wigmore Hall. As she and Andy valiantly tried to support each other, the cameraman bore down on top of her hands, quite unaware of how unnerving he was. Zuhal still had Rachmaninov's Prelude in C sharp minor to practice. I left them to it, and went straight to Jo to voice my concern

'It's her choice.'

What? Was it really? How much choice did a 17-year-old Iraqi pianist from Baghdad really have? She was being led straight off a plane from Baghdad onto a media bandwagon and given one of the top venues in London to platform her cause, but obliged to play while being filmed with virtually no rehearsal. These sounded like unreasonable demands to me. Zuhal had an apparent maturity that sometimes fooled even her. She had little experience of the West. I sensed she'd lost control, but had no choice but to step back and watch.

Jo had done a great job on the audience. The event, attended by journalists from across London, kicked off after lunch. Zuhal cried backstage, then wiped away the tears and went on to perform the Rachmaninov nicely, but clearly under duress. Andy came on, gracefully warmed the audience up and got Zuhal through the Schubert, which she managed competently albeit hesitantly. James Barralet, another rising British star, donated a performance of Bach on his cello, and sat in front of the microphone that the crew had placed onstage, presumably thinking it was for filming. It turned out to be a live feed into the speaker on stage, and so he played amplified into a hall already possessing one of the finest natural acoustics in the world. I sat, frozen in disbelief. All I could feel from the stage was one artist after another being compromised in the most important recital hall in Britain.

With some sense of relief, the musical offering ended, and Elisabeth Palmer of CBS News came on to interview Zuhal, who finally relaxed and spoke with great conviction in beautiful English, taking tough questions from the audience. Why, for example, should anyone support a national youth orchestra in Iraq when there were still so many basic services to rebuild? With the right mix of humility and confidence, she pointed out that those matters had to be left to the government, and she was concentrating on what she could achieve to improve the lives of people in Iraq. One of many answers that nailed it on the head. Zuhal proved just how remarkable she was. I sat at the back listening thoughtfully, sensing that behind this toughness lay years of growing up during a war, and how fragile this young person's sense of self still was.

After the applause had died down and the after-show reception had dissipated, Zuhal and I found an empty room so we could talk in peace about the orchestra. 'Oh boy...' she uttered, as if expecting a scolding. In the short time we had alone, we talked about the auditions and funding difficulties but, all through our chat, I saw a courageous teenager doing the same as me: grasping at straws to fill in the gaps of a very shaky venture. She should have had a childhood and lived like a normal teenager. But war had robbed her of both these things, leaving her to fend emotionally for herself. Her strength and vulnerability, hallmarks of any decent artist, helped her cope brilliantly, but still she kept dancing from tightrope to tightrope, navigating around us all.

Finally she was free of the bandwagon, and with the first genuine smile I'd seen on her face all day, she told me she was going to the Barbican that evening to hear Dvorak's Symphony No 9 (From the New World). We parted company outside the Wigmore Hall, a little more certain that our first summer course was on track, but still dizzied by the bizarre route we were inventing to get there.

At the beginning of May, the World Federation of Amateur Orchestras invited me to their annual meeting in Antwerp. The title alone made me smart a bit. What could such an organisation achieve globally for amateur musicians? On my arrival, the impressive guest list of national and transnational musical NGOs had bottomed out to a cosy 21. In a narrow, monastic meeting room, the delegates assembled with an uneasy piety.

I spent 40 minutes fulfilling their challenging remit of presenting the orchestra's launch and the global implications on today's younger generation. The PowerPoint alone had taken a week to prepare, and when I finished, triumphant that I'd won them over, the members sat in deafening silence. Here I was reaching out for feedback, enquiry, intelligent criticism, and all I got was a room full of middle-aged people, neither shaken nor stirred.

Out of this, however, two important musical allies arose from the midst. Renate Bock, President of the European Federation of National Youth Orchestras, listened deeply and compassion-ately while Olive Khan, Director of the Singapore National Youth Orchestra, gave out the warmth and wisdom I had desperately sought. Like Zuhal, I too was tired of feeling alone and at sea with this project. Though we now had plenty of good people on board, finding those who could relate to me as a conductor for a project as bizarre as this proved impossible. Allegra had important input to give but Zuhal and I sensed, when it came to knowing this unborn orchestra's already pained heart, we only really had each other. In a sense, we were the mum and dad.

At the end of May, Tony Reilly, Director of British Council Iraq, arrived in Suleymaniyah, the second largest city in the Kurdish region. He set about trying to secure the Kurdish String Orchestra's rehearsal building for us and quickly ran up against their brick wall. Indeed, the Kurdish String Orchestra had been invited to the Konzerthaus in Vienna in 2007 to perform in a competition, and played with finesse. A National Youth Orchestra of Iraq was a threat, using auditioned Kurdish players but daring to call itself Iraqi. Suleymaniyah, a modern city of some 715,000 people, had carved out its reputation as an arts capital of Iraq, and the Kurdish String Orchestra sat on top of their mountain. After a difficult meeting, Tony at least achieved a tacit verbal agreement. Allegra, Zuhal and I had to be grateful for this for now, and hope the agreement would hold.

We also wanted Suleymaniyah because the Kurdistan Region of Iraq remained somewhat unscathed by the Iraq war, their security situation preventing most of the daily terrorism that inflicted Baghdad. They had a unique advantage: racial profiling. Individual Arabs blew themselves up, but individual Kurds did not. Being an Indo-European race, like the Persians and Armenians, they were genetically different enough for most Arabs on the streets to be obvious to locals. The Kurds often appeared more delicate and many shared the genetic trait of relatively flattish backs to their heads. So, the deeply embedded Kurdish secret police, kept informed by a populace of only 4.5 million and regular roadside checks, could easily monitor anyone.

Rumours also abounded that former Mossad agents had advised the Kurds on their airport security. This quasi-secret relationship between Kurdistan and Israel, dating back to the 60s, proved vital to the Kurds, as breaking free of Iraq would only happen if Kurdish regional security was effective, but financed by oil instead of America. The Kurdistan Region had one trump card. It was floating on the sixth largest oil reserve in the world.

Against this politically loaded background, bringing Kurdish and Arab compositions into the programme was surprisingly easy. Dr Mohammed Zaza provided us with an orchestration of his guitar piece, *Kurdish Dances*. Majid Al Azzawi, our Director of Operations in Baghdad, supplied us with Ali Khassaf's *Iraqi Melodies*. These weren't great works, but a step in the right direction of rebuilding Iraqi culture. I decided we should also perform Beethoven's *Prometheus* Overture, a fitting start to as bold an act of creation as ourselves, and finish with Haydn's Symphony No 99. These two works lay at the heart of my pedagogy, as the musicians couldn't help but learn about their various roles as orchestral players, melodically, harmonically and rhythmically.

I peppered the programme with two shorter works: Iain Whyte's orchestration of the 1910 Glasgow cabaret song *Deoch and Doris*, and Martin Dalby's orchestration of *Cradle Song*, in case we had time to look at them.

Deep into the wee small hours of 26th May, another hot night in Baghdad, Zuhal lay awake in bed, wondering how to fill our $50,000 funding gap. The next morning, she emailed Allegra and me about her stroke of insight:

'Hello both,

I was on Twitter last night and I spotted Barham Salih (the government official we talked about – did we talk about him?) on twitter tweeting, I followed him and was amazed by his tweets. I wrote to him this:

@BarhamSalih As a young Iraqi living in Baghdad I am extremely happy to know that someone from our government tweets – kudos to you!

And then it hit me, I didn't know he's going to response or not but I thought it didn't hurt to try:

@BarhamSalih have you ever had a chance to read this? would you be interested in supporting this initiative?

http://tinyurl.com/ragfu2 (this link contains my article in the Times)

Now, I've spotted this message from him:

BarhamSalih@ZuhalSultan Thanks! You make us all proud. I definitely want to help with this amazing project send me your phone number to get in touch

I've sent him my phone number and e-mail... FINGERS CROSSED!

Zuhal.'

Two days later, Tony Reilly and Zuhal Sultan sat in Dr Barham Salih's office in Baghdad and accepted $50,000 for the first summer school of the National Youth Orchestra of Iraq. Zuhal left triumphant. Allegra and I were dizzy with joy. That evening by Skype, Tony gave us a green light to go ahead and run the course.

By tweeting the Deputy Prime Minister of Iraq, the brilliant Zuhal had pulled off the most extraordinary funding coup I'd ever come across; a $50,000 tweet. If only it were always that easy! Now, Battlefront could push hard to get a commission from Channel 4 to go out and film the first summer course in Iraq, though time was fast running out.

I had been appalled by Zuhal's stories of young musicians in the Iraqi National Symphony Orchestra who had taken over the empty seats of players who fled in 2003, with precious little coaching or support. Those senior musicians who remained may have simply not been good as teachers, but the radically depleted work opportunities had closed round young and old like a Venus flytrap. Nobody wanted to help a young musician who could threaten their job. Meanwhile, those studying in the Institutes of Fine Arts across Iraq faced similar neglect and crippling corruption. Miraculously, a few youngsters had learnt to teach themselves in spite of politicians and Imams wielding their religion as a scimitar on Iraq's previously secular society.

In some interpretations of Islam, God created the human voice to sing His word. All else was *haram* – sinful. Western music especially stood for decadence and sexual immorality. Women who played music could be ostracised as emotionally expressive in defiance of their humble duties at home. This backdrop rattled round my head as Allegra and I started hunting down course tutors.

We hit the first of June and released the results of the video auditions across Iraq. From the 53 applicants, I accepted 33 players who I believed could get from the beginning to the end of the concert without falling apart. But the orchestra still had gaps. Without a second oboe or bassoon, I needed to find tutors to cover these seats in rehearsal and performance. I also wanted young tutors who could relate, peer to peer, to the players, and fit into a youth orchestra on stage. I had no interest in playing to cultural sensitivities around the inferior position of women in Iraq, and readily looked at talented female as well as male tutors. What we would certainly sacrifice in experience, would create the extreme countercultural message that older does not mean better, and male does not mean superior. Iraqi players had to understand that classical music was about hard work and results, not being sabotaged by players past their sell-by date. I also sought givers, not takers, who, though young, already had a top grade orchestral track record.

Back in 2007, the National Youth Orchestra of Scotland had booked me to conduct a concert in Glasgow. Mike O'Donnell, whose Mum happened to work for the Scottish Government, had played oboe in my concert. A fresh, outspoken guy who was still learning when to keep his mouth shut in a conformist business, I thought he was perfect. When I found him again, he was happily freelancing with major London orchestras. Mike had a cockiness that I felt gave energy to others, especially when dished up by his sweet nature. This guy could get away with murder, which could be useful in an unpredictable project.

Mike loved the idea and got on board immediately. With him came our first bassoon tutor, his brother, Larry. We agreed they could arrive in Iraq a day later than everyone else after a wedding in Scotland, a decision that would lead to shattering consequences for us all. Naturally, these young tutors had to let their parents know they were going to Iraq, which led to some serious familial panic attacks. However, Mike seemed perfectly happy to tell his Mum that he and Larry were 'going on a Jolly to Iraq'. And that was that.

Jonathan Thomson, a trumpeter from the National Youth Orchestra of Scotland who I had recently booked in Montepulciano to play in the opera there, came on board immediately as our lead wind tutor, and with him his girlfriend, violinist Lucy Wannell. Jonny was living near London with Lucy, where business was tough to come by, but the market and connections were considerably more fluid than up North. Jonny always cheered a rehearsal up, being not quite bolshie enough to tip over into the more obnoxious stereotypical behaviour of brass players, while loving a bit of banter. His good looks and solid teacher training made me feel I could trust him to lead the winds. Jonny and I shared common ground: older Scots in unfathomable positions of responsibility who seemed hell-bent on dragging us down to below their mediocre level so they could kick the hell out of our self-confidence. Hence, we found ourselves as refugees from Scotland, with some understanding of the plight of the young Iraqis we were about to meet.

Allegra sussed out a few string tutors in New York, including Angelia Cho. A Juilliard graduate, well-known chamber musician and teacher at the Weill Institute, Carnegie Hall, this sassy young violinist eventually bought into Allegra's experienced sales pitch. Angelia had the pioneering verve to grab this opportunity and enter into our adventure.

Another of Allegra's finds, Sheila Browne, a viola professor at New York University and the University of North Carolina, definitely looked younger than her 40 years. I'd told Allegra that I really wanted tutors under 30, but Sheila's experience as a violamaniac had already taken her several times round the world, her passion becoming her fountain of youth. She'd also served on the board of the American Viola Society and championed living composers as a soloist and ensemble musician. Come mid-July, Sheila prepared to say au revoir to her pet pig, Cosmo, and set off for South Africa to premiere a viola concerto before boarding a flight straight to the course in Iraq.

For a cello tutor, I really wanted James Barallet, who had so generously played at Zuhal's Wigmore Hall appearance. He was definitely up for it until his agent, probably out of fear, started stalling. With a tight timeframe to book people, I had to let James go. I turned instead to the Young Concert Artists' Trust in London who gave me the number of a young cellist, Dave Edmonds. Our first conversation went something like this:

Dave: 'Hello?'

Paul: 'Hi. This is Paul MacAlindin from the National Youth Orchestra of Iraq. YCAT gave me your number about coming to teach in Iraq. Are you still interested?'

Dave: 'Er yeah. I'm on a bus to Manchester right now.'

Paul: 'OK. Is there a better time to talk to you?'

Dave, a graduate of the Royal Northern College of Music, was all of 22. He'd already accomplished international recognition with the Rhodes Piano Trio, who took some of their bookings from the Young Concert Artists' Trust. As I finally got to speak to him properly, his laddish warmth felt right for the team I was trying to build. I loved the unquestioning fearlessness. Iraq wasn't an issue. Of course the musicians needed our help. I had no room for precious, arrogant mummy's boys whose education was an extension of baby-sitting paid for by their rich parents. The Iraqis needed people of steel and guts to bring the course home. Dave's relatively humble background had imbued him with both.

As I bagged one tutor after another, we were all facing the same recession, and would do anything to keep the money coming in. Though threat to life was obviously less important than paying bills, these ridiculously talented young professionals really did have one distinctive thing in common, lots of heart. Their readiness to go while the security situation was still hot gave some indication that we had the right people, and I could be proud of our little US-British team.

At the beginning of July, British Council Iraq issued the tutors their contracts, flight details and local information. I had to inform Battlefront that we still didn't know for sure where we were rehearsing or who'd provide security. They were battling to get a commission at very short notice from Channel 4 and, as time ran out, they had to give up. On 21st July, I implemented Plan B with Mike Newman, a former BBC cameraman and colleague I'd worked with on previous projects. He had 25 years' experience of filming orchestras, so for a meagre production fee, he agreed to come and document our course.

Post-war Iraq was an open book with opportunities waiting to write themselves into its history. With gung-ho bravura, Iraqis, Americans and Brits set themselves on a course of unknown reverberations, hoping against hope that this would be the beginning of something new and better. From our various corners of the globe we intended to descend upon Suleymaniyah on 1st August, and somehow realise an orchestral performance two weeks later.

Deep uncertainties remained over our rehearsal venue, cashflow and security, and so the team took a deep breath and prepared for our next enormous leap of faith, the flight to Iraq.

THREE
Kick off in Suleymaniyah

In the waiting room at Vienna International Airport, I spied a young Korean lady with a violin case. This had to be Angelia Cho, directly in from New York. I introduced myself, and we boarded the flight to Erbil together. Lasting about four hours, this had been a regular route of Austrian Airlines for some years, and was well occupied by internationals doing business in Kurdistan, and Iraqis returning from family abroad.

As we launched into the air bound on our quest, I became lulled by European comfort, and Angie, a few rows behind, looked sound asleep. The lush Austrian fields and European landscapes below slowly transformed into endless desert. Approaching Iraq, I looked down at the famous 4000-year-old citadel of Erbil, a lunar crater of stone surrounding city, surrounded by city. For the first time in the project, I felt fear. We were going to land and set up the National Youth Orchestra of Iraq, whether anyone there wanted it or not.

With just one foot out of the plane, hot desert wind blasted my face – the Breath of Allah. More fear. I stepped down onto the tarmac and walked over to the humble arrival building. No going back. There in the doorway stood an earnest lady in white medical garb, mask and headscarf, holding a thermometer. Did I have bird flu? She pressed the instrument against my forehead and cast her sterile gaze at the result. I stood there, frozen, waiting. Was I now feeling a bit ill? With an impartial wave of the hand, I was allowed to proceed. At the border, a friendly officer checked my passport, and the ten-day visa was stamped in. 'Welcome to

Iraq', he beamed. The absurdity of being welcomed to a war zone hit home, but so far so good.

Angie and I left the terminal back into the desert wind. Two burly, smartly dressed men approached us, neither of whom spoke English. They smiled and handed Angie a phone. It was Nishtiman, Assistant Director of the British Council, Erbil. We were to get into their Land Rover and be taken to Suleymaniyah, across the desert. On loading up, we sat in the back and began to survey the ground level of the airport, like children on some bizarre adventure. No sooner had the Range Rover left than it pulled up in front of a faceless building, the airport police station. Our guys went in briefly, and returned with their checked-in semi-automatic rifle and pistols. Angie later told me this was the single moment of doubt when she wanted to get out and go back to the States.

We drove through the desert, past ostentatious houses and rugged huts, chancing upon black shaggy goats by the road. As wonder overtook fear, we both stared wide-eyed at these winter-coated tramps, indifferent to the killer heat. Our driver noticed Angie flashing her iPhone at the creatures to take photos, and slowed down every time we came across any sign of life that was remotely active. We could see that our companions thought this was cute. The desert, intense, jaw dropping, vast and brutal, conjured up twisters of sand as the raw sun burnt through the tinted windows and onto our virgin skins. Checkpoints came and went, guards peered through the window and waved us on. The liveried compartment between the two front seats, a refrigerator full of bottled water, became an internal oasis where we helped ourselves. After one and a half hours, we crossed a river, returning slowly to settlements and sparse greenery. The sun had burnt my pale Scottish arm. Suleymaniyah was in the distance. Angie and I nodded off, blotting out our sensory overload.

Our arrival day was Sunday the second of August, and Allegra was waiting for us at the Mirako Hotel. In the foyer, a hubbub of young musicians arriving from Baghdad and across the Kurdistan Region of Iraq stood around beaming wordlessly at each other. We hand-shook our introductions and Allegra updated me that the rehearsal space of the Kurdish String Orchestra was not going to be given to us without an ever-increasing rent.

We didn't have the budget to handle that nonsense. Also, not every one of their rooms had air conditioning, and this was unacceptable for musicians trying to keep their instruments from expanding and warping themselves out of tune in the killer heat. I explained the situation to Mohammed Qaradaghi, our government contact, who immediately granted us free access to Telary Huner, or Palace of Arts in Kurdish, for the whole two weeks. This was exactly the gold we needed to make our course work.

Mohammed, quiet and gentle, preferred to work behind the scenes. As Barham Salih's right-hand man in Suleymaniyah, his facilitation of the $50,000 donated by Salih, our visa extensions, and immediate access to Telary Huner, were local government in action, and it was impressive. Two weeks there, Allegra warned, would generate envy among local musicians, but since we had been outpriced by the other venue, I couldn't have cared less. That Telary Huner stood empty and available for our immediate use also said a lot. With no event manager or budget for performances in place, it was hosting only two or three events a year.

Telary Huner, only three years old, was Suleymaniyah's most prestigious building, an imposing arts and conference centre with a seminar room and 1300-seat auditorium designed by Turkish architects. Bringing them in wasn't just about neighbourhood convenience. The Kurds, ever vulnerable to geopolitical tensions, needed to strengthen business with countries where Kurdistan had historical and on-going difficulties. Salih, as the new Prime Minister of the Region, was playing a kind of European Union game in the Middle East, where mutual trade could mitigate against conflict.

The brothers, Mike and Larry O'Donnell, were still en route to Iraq after their Scottish wedding as the orchestra began our first evening together. The other tutors, Sheila, Lucy, Angie, Jonny,

Dave and I had all made it to Suleymaniyah. We all piled into a couple of buses, rather like ramshackle camper vans squeezing in about 15, more if possible. Good fun, but not for a long haul. We arrived at an amusement park, our restaurant waiting to feed us. As we queued up at the buffet, observing each other, the food, and each other again, some of the team players became clearer: photographer Mike Luongo from New York, Director of Operations Majid Al Azzawi from the Iraqi National Symphony Orchestra, Allegra as orchestra manager, Mike Newman as videographer, Zuhal as Artistic Director and assistant everything and 17-year-old Sanar as British Council liaison in Suleymaniyah. Sanar had perfect English and clearly came from a wealthy family. Sounding and looking like a Western teenager, she appeared enthusiastic about our wacky venture.

My schedule for that evening said, 'Distribute accompaniments to pianists. Announce chamber music groups and their tutors'. We hit reality and the fat chance I'd get that sorted tonight. Far more pragmatically, Allegra gave out nametags with the very first NYOI logo made by Zuhal, and told everyone outside the restaurant to stay in sight. Mariwan, our first clarinettist, piped up that they were giving their free time to this project and didn't want to be kept on a leash like children. Most were over 18 and he had a point. A few of the players and I exchanged wry smiles as we slipped the tags round our necks. Sheepishly, I began 'leading by example'.

The buffet dinner was insufficient for our numbers and Allegra had already begun complaining about the fish. I looked on from afar, wondering where this would go. We'd only just got here. As we dispersed through the surrounding gardens, locals strolled alongside us through the balmy evening. Rusty fairground rides from the 60s, or maybe earlier, became frozen iron spiders under the gardens' tungsten lighting. Health and safety appeared not to be top priorities in Iraq. As Angie and I wandered around, we were discovering a menagerie of canaries just as the locals were discovering the menagerie of us. A peely-wally Scot and a polished Korean American gave by far the better spectacle. They stared eagerly, keeping a bemused and safe distance. We returned uneasy smiles, though being such foreign bodies in an Iraqi park felt alienating. And aliens we were.

Filing slowly back through the hot evening pathways, we all rendezvoused back at the buses and returned to our first night in the Mirako Hotel. All thrown together in this bizarre adventure, Kurds, Arabs, Americans and Brits sidled along through the first baby steps of the National Youth Orchestra of Iraq. We regarded each other with some caution, but also a degree of faith.

It was Monday 3rd August at the Mirako Hotel. Our rooms proved western enough and the tutors quickly procured the lounge in my suite as our bar. As the air conditioning in Dave's room wouldn't work, he slept in 45 degrees Celsius while our hotel staff, delicate young men of Etruscan elegance, seemed not to be rushing to fix anything. The orchestra settled down to its first night together all under one roof. Little did we know that Allegra had instructed reception to give us all a 7.00 am wake-up call, and that no amount of protest at the phone, or Allegra, would shut it down.

Next morning, breakfast in the top floor offered people a chance to observe each other surreptitiously and huddle with pals around tables. I tried breaking the ice with some informal introductions. Other Middle Eastern guests, families from Baghdad on holiday, kept to themselves. I sensed their wariness. They sensed mine. The breakfast buffet proved a culture shockette of granulated coffee, yoghurt, honey, fruit and tea: continental without context.

When we had all assembled downstairs in the foyer, Majid undertook his first leadership action of the day, announcing 'To the Bus!' as he shepherded us from the foyer to the basic transport waiting outside. These buses, very common throughout Iraq, took 20 people at a push. Plastic upholstered seats, baking in the sun, took protection from more transparent plastic covers. I reckoned it might be easier to fake the age of the vehicle for resale if the milometer were reset and the seats appeared as good as new. We piled in 15 to a vehicle with double basses, violins and flutes bursting out of every automotive orifice, every available inch covered by musicians, and off we trundled down the streets of Suleymaniyah passing shops, cafes, showrooms and juice bars selling everything from Mercedes Benz cars to beer. Suleymaniyah's vibe left us awestruck. Mike Newman tried to engage me in conversation, but I really couldn't get a word out. In truth, I was already burnt out from managing the preparation.

The two buses we had hired to shuttle us round town were equipped with bizarre LED screens hooked onto the sun–shade of the front passenger seat. Kurdish techno and pop videos of thickly moustached megastar Azizi Wayse clattering through the built-in speakers, soon got us bopping up and down. Competitive hilarity ensued between us to see whose bus would wobble up and down along the streets to the gyrating passengers the most. An axle packing in seemed only a matter of time.

My garb of T-shirt and jeans was uncommon for Iraqi conductors, who preferred instead to emulate the Karajan archetype in slick business suits. Tutors and players alike shared my casual dress code to focus us on the quality of work, and deliberately away from the image. We came together to sabotage expectations, just as some Iraqi music teachers were already sabotaging these young players. I had to challenge this nonsense right from the start; an act of revenge for daring to damage the youth of Iraq right after a war. So, as we finally pulled up at the side entrance of Telary Huner, little distinguished the ramshackle bunch of young tutors and younger players that poured out of the buses.

Modern Middle Eastern architecture is, in a word, monolithic. The arching geometric forms have a stark power unlike anything Western, a macho, towering strength of will imposed on desert wilderness and naked sky. Telary Huner's glass visor facade, polished marble floors and lush red auditorium with super-sized VIP chairs, made it seem like a Rolls Royce venue. Suleymaniyah, a haven for artists, had created a palace for the arts as its most important building. And we had come to fill it.

Armed soldiers, young and thick-set, raised the car park barrier and waved us into the compound. We carried on into the building. Telary Huner's interior opened into spacious grandeur, beautifully maintained, sparse and shiny, just like the shell. In the office suite we met the accommodating staff, who showed us the seminar room where full rehearsals would happen. In the foyer, a convex wall of tinted glass revealed the modern city panorama and an adjacent mosque. Here our translators, Saman and Shwan, taped flipchart paper on the wall, and got straight to work triplicating our daily schedule into Kurdish, Arabic and English. Along the hallways, more soldiers armed with Kalashnikovs walked slowly up and down, observing our goings on out of bewilderment or boredom. I cast them a friendly smile, which one or two almost managed to return.

Inside Telary Huner's seminar room, the kick off meeting began with Zuhal introducing everyone to the course team in Arabic, and then again through our translators in Kurdish. 'My name is Paul MacAlindin, and if you have any musical questions, ask me.' Right from the start, no way was I about to do anyone else's job for them. With two unpredictable weeks ahead of us, the music alone was more than enough. I'd raided the Scottish Music Information Centre for some quaint bits and bobs: Iain Whyte's arrangement of the 1910 Scottish vaudeville number *Deoch and Doris*, a dram of whisky to anyone else; and Martin Dalby's *Cradle Song*. Majid brought Ali Khassaf's *Iraqi Melodies* from Baghdad and Boran brought her dad's *Kurdish Dances*, so the Arab and Kurdish contributions were sorted. At our programme's core lay Beethoven's *Prometheus* Overture and Haydn's Symphony No 99. No other music would teach us so thoroughly how to become an orchestra. As all the introductions ran through, we felt we were doing well, but air conditioning wasn't much in evidence. It was apparently on.

We set up the music stands for our first bash through. My sole objective for week one was to get everyone once through the programme from beginning to end, and in one piece. At least then we'd know for week two what was feasible or not. The plan was every morning and from 4.00-5.00 pm to do full orchestral rehearsal, covering a movement of Haydn each day, and slipping the smaller programme items in as much as I dared.

We began that first rehearsal with the grandiose opening of the Haydn Symphony. The translators, Shwan and Samen stood on either side of me to relay my English in Kurdish and Arabic. Trusting that the orchestra would intuitively work out how to react to my downbeat, I began, and our first ever chord, painfully out of tune but nevertheless together, trembled around the room. Within a few beats, I stopped, already clocking up multiple issues and trying to work out which ones would sort themselves out in time, and which needed immediate coaching. I decided; everything needed coaching.

So, what to tell them? I couldn't say much, because every sentence took three times longer in translation and wasted rehearsal time. So, we started by building that very first chord from the bottom up, and learning to listen to ourselves as a group; the first simple but profound step in reconciliation through music.

Larry and Mike O'Donnell arrived at the hotel the evening of that first day's rehearsal while we were still at the restaurant, checked themselves in, and found a local kebab shop. Someone had managed to advise them never, under any circumstances, to eat an Iraqi kebab which, being freelance Scottish musicians, they duly ignored. Thus began the toilet wars. Those two guys' guts, utterly wrecked, spent the rest of the course in a state of meltdown. Mike, particularly hard hit, had to take the day off to stay in his room and connect 67 times to his toilet. The kebab became, literally, a bad running joke.

While I'd given Jonny the job of leading the whole wind section, Mike and Larry became the backbone for Majid's daughter, Du'aa on oboe, and Murad, our bassoonist. As there was no second oboist or bassoonist from Iraq, they found themselves playing next to their students. With the two brothers holding the woodwinds together, their students had a sturdy reference point for playing in tune. The question was, what did they understand by 'in tune'?

Murad Saffar, at twenty one, the only young bassoonist in Iraq good enough play with us, was studying journalism in Baghdad, had a great eye for graphic design and spoke fluent

English that he'd picked up from American films. I could tell because, while his spoken English didn't betray any origin, his written English looked like a phonetic impression of LA gangland action movies. Somewhat stocky, with a handsome face and lots of charm, his passion for bassoon and the Iraqi National Symphony Orchestra had kept him busy in Baghdad. The handful of other young bassoonists in Iraq at this time also had nobody to teach them, but none were able to take themselves as far as he had. He was a natural. When Larry, who was about the same age, turned up to play next to him, they hit it off like a bassoon on fire. After years of isolation, Murad finally had a real bassoon buddy who could teach him breathing, playing in tune and hunker down with him to play Haydn, man to man. That which he couldn't learn from Larry in two weeks was largely down to the state of his instrument.

Murad's bassoon was something to behold. Larry didn't know how he managed get a sound out of it. The crook, a metal pipe connecting mouthpiece to instrument, was dented, the pads on the keys had dehydrated with no chance for replacements and some notes had decided not to happen at all. It sounded like an elephant in pain. Matchwood would be too kind a word for it. Larry dialled his iPhone, already on roaming through Iraq's extensive wireless network, and spoke to the London instrument shop, Howarth, to try and buy a bassoon and have it flown out by DHL. We had enough budget for this, some $7,000, but Allegra insisted she block purchase in case it created envy amongst the other players.

Meanwhile, Howarth felt apprehensive about being paid by an Iraqi youth orchestra, and stalled for three days, bassoon packed and ready, before letting us know this. As soon as we found out, Tony Reilly at British Council Baghdad immediately reassured them by phone that he would pay by the fastest bank transfer possible, but by the time they had agreed to go ahead with the purchase, DHL would have taken a week to deliver it, and the concert would be over. No bassoon for this year, but Murad's matchwood became a burning theme for the following year.

Jonny, as lead wind tutor, rehearsed the players every afternoon. Hugely popular with the students, he was also a solid pedagogue and played second trumpet sitting next to our 15-year-old first trumpet, Frand. This plucky kid was studying at the Baghdad School of Music and Ballet under Majid, and had been invited to Jordan's 'Queen Ranya Therapy Through Music Orchestra' in 2007. He had also made it up to the Kurdistan Region, to play in the 'American Voices' project, just to be close to other young musicians and competent teachers. Frand, whose English was top notch, found himself in trumpet Elysium sitting side by side with Jonny in rehearsals and getting private lessons. Although most of NYOI's players were between 18 and 25, Frand's fresh confidence and enthusiasm made up for his inexperience, and Sheila quickly christened him 'That cheeky little monkey'.

From Ali and Frand's sister Ranya, the two horns, I could sense their deep disappointment at having no horn tutor. To be honest, in order to control costs, I'd only brought a skeleton tutor team for this first time round, to test the water. I'd stretched our membership as far as I dared, bringing in Hassan Hassun, our 28-year-old first flautist from Baghdad with his 14-year-old Assyrian student, Fadi, playing second. We fixed the rules for age limit, 14 to 29, precisely to get those two into the orchestra, as no other flautists in the auditions could cope with the music.

Our poor percussionist, Mohammed S'tar, found himself teacherless behind the two kettledrums Majid had brought from Baghdad. Together, we all tried to carry him forward, but as a totally self-taught musician, much like the rest, his reading skills were not great. Though I guessed he was a nice guy, he was also painfully shy and didn't understand a word of English.

During a run-through of Haydn's gentle second movement, I began to sense our players starting to create new connections between each other, noticing out of the corner of their eyes where they fitted with whom and how. A stroke of the bow here, a little nod of the head there, a flick of the eyelids away from the note stands to see what was happening. It all added up to a growing collective consciousness of the orchestra through Haydn's exquisite music. Much rehearsal, being wordless, needed simple play through and observation. Going academic or technical on them would be lost, no matter how well Saman and Shwan translated. I tried to convey body and language as emotively as possible, hoping the players who didn't understand would at least feel my intention. As we played away, our ensemble began to take on a comfortable hue, a sound that the orchestra rarely achieved and then, BAM!!!

Mohammed S'tar whacked at his kettledrum, shooting through the bones of everyone in the room, and our unearthly calm splintered into despair and hilarity. I raised my hand to my face and muttered 'Oh my God,' as Dave Edmonds, our cello tutor, who was playing behind the first desk of the cellos, dissolved into laughter. I could hide my anguish no longer. Mohammed S'tar looked on, nonplussed at our reactions. For him, it was a matter of counting and playing what was in front of him. That he was reading the wrong movement was unfortunate. This moment, more than any other, convinced me that every player in the orchestra needed a specialist tutor to guide students through the course.

As the first week got underway, relationships grew between players and tutors unlike any I'd seen in youth orchestras before. Angie told *School Band and Orchestra:* 'I thought it was important to give my time freely while I was over there, and they were so enthusiastic about learning anything they could. They were like sponges. They really absorbed as much as they could. Working with them was really touching for me. Some of the Iraqi musicians would stay up all night long downloading videos related to the music we were playing – they hardly went to bed. We would give them a hard time about it, being strict with them and telling them that if they didn't sleep, they wouldn't be able to concentrate.

'There was a French horn player named Ranya, who was the most outgoing person in the group. She also spoke very good English. When I asked her why she and her colleagues were staying up all night, she said, 'You guys don't understand what a gift this is for us. Your presence here means so much that we want to absorb every moment, and that's more valuable than sleeping. There's no way we'll know what happens tomorrow.'

'This a girl who grew up in Baghdad, and still lives there,' Ranya told me, 'You don't know what we see every day. My friend was just killed last week.' That put it into perspective for us.

'Seeing the way that these kids worked together, I realised that wherever you are, whatever your means or resources, it doesn't take much to make the most of any situation. Especially in music, where people have a common goal and interest, it doesn't matter what happened in the past. There was a lot of conflict between the Arabs and the Kurds and the Arabs outnumbered the Kurds. By the end of the session, they were not only working together, but laughing and helping each other, and really learning, trying to pull off something that may have been beyond their scope. Learning from them really was a gift for me. I realised a lot about how necessary it is to reach out to people through what we do. It gave more meaning to my own life as a performer and as an educator. I could be playing in concert venues, but what really gives meaning to what I do as a musician is helping, and feeling useful, needed, and relevant. They made that happen for me. They helped me realize the importance of what I do and why I do it, which is to teach, to pass on what I know to people who are eager to absorb it, and to people who need it. And that place really needs it, more than any other place that I've ever been to.'

Slowly, one by one, the war-riven personalities of the orchestra moulded the ensemble; a collection of lost young musicians with their idealistic young teachers embarking together on a ludicrous venture, with no idea where it would lead, or how it would change our lives. Although change our lives it did.

FOUR
Soothing tensions

Day by day, tutors coached their various instrumental groups, while Telary Huner's air conditioning was switched off between 2.00 and 4.00 pm. Why? Because the Turkish architects had installed a building-wide system that overloaded when trying to compensate for the intense 40s and 50s of the Iraqi summer. Show was obviously bigger than substance and the unpredictable temperatures played havoc with instrument tuning. So, we put instrumental sectionals in the office suite where wall-mounted air-conditioning units could maintain bearable temperatures and keep the instruments somewhat stable. One could understand why Iraqis simply didn't bother tuning their instruments at all, if they were unlikely to ever maintain their pitch throughout a rehearsal or performance.

During these afternoons, I gave a piano workshop to Zuhal, Boran and Zardasht. Zuhal played Rachmaninov's Prelude in C sharp minor, the same piece she'd performed in the Wigmore Hall. Zardasht, a delicate young man with exquisite sensibilities, who earned money every day at 5.00 pm playing in a restaurant, brought along some Chopin waltzes. Boran played Debussy's *Clair de Lune*. Together, observing each other around the Yamaha Clavinova, we experimented with different tone colours and imitating orchestral sounds, as far as the instrument would allow.

Boran studiously recorded all the nuggets of insight we gained into a notebook. Zuhal and I worked together on line and timing, getting everyone to count Rachmaninov's ponderous beginning out loud and clap the chords. This simple, but at the same time tricky exercise broke down their misconceptions to reveal what Rachmaninov had actually written.

By parroting online interpretations without really understanding the music, learning off YouTube often did more harm than good. In our cramped little room, I taught them how to waltz: pointless to play without learning the dance as well. I did feel uncomfortable touching Zuhal and Boran, although they dressed and sounded like Western teens. I was surely breaking a thousand rules of Islam, but they assured me it was OK. These beautiful little sessions gave me such a sense of connection with how far they had come alone, and how much further their talent could take them if only they were freed from the cultural wilderness outside the hall.

The women of the orchestra all clearly worked and lived on a level way beyond their male counterparts. In this culture where 75% dropped out of school and 86% were unemployed, they really had to punch above their weight in order to flourish. Ranya, our second horn, dressed as a Westerner and spoke fluent English picked up from American movies, just like her brother Frand. Clearly, she had somehow managed to learn a most difficult instrument, the horn, bereft of support or stability. Du'aa, our first oboe, lived in a district of Baghdad where the families of women found making music could suffer terrible consequences. She laughed this off when the neighbours complained about her practising, explaining it away as noises from the kitchen. Annie Melconian, an excellent violinist, had learnt rock-solid reliability, generosity and compassion from her family and Baghdad's Armenian community; three qualities that post-war Iraq had given up on. Perhaps it never had them.

Seventeen-year-old Boran, whose father had rearranged his guitar piece *Kurdish Dances* for us, was already hosting her own local classical music radio show in Erbil, acting as an extra trilingual translator and teaching herself piano. Tuqa, the only member of NYOI to wear a hijab, or headscarf, won over our cello tutor, Dave Edmonds, to the extent that he put her on the lead cello seat, much to her male counterpart, Hussam's disapproval.

Tuqa was extraordinary. Utterly in love with her cello, she and I communicated through music, her face furrowed with determination. We 'talked' through patience, learning, and love of music. At any time, in or out of rehearsal, she could burst into the most exquisite high-pitched laughter. Hers was a titter that could tip into rapturous ululation at the drop of a hat, only modesty holding her back from the brink.

Only a short while ago, I had been moved by the miserable nature of their audition videos, how hard they had tried to play, how joyless, how disconnected between sound and soul. Haydn's Symphony No 99 was not only my best guess at what they could pull off in two weeks, but also an injection of humour. Haydn revels in his false starts and finishes, witty turns of phrase, pregnant daft pauses and great tunes. He also creates a great listening and ensemble experience for the players. I would stop the first violins and ask which instrument was playing the same melody as them. So deeply absorbed in their own music, none could point to the flute, sitting three metres away. Lack of self and group awareness was painfully obvious.

I would just need to stop rehearsing and ask a simple question about what was happening to draw a roomful of blank expressions. It seemed as if nobody had ever asked them a question in their lives, and perhaps it was so. Our first clarinet, Mariwan Ismael, bluntly asked why it was important to bother about what others were doing. It was an honest question, shamelessly put. These young musicians didn't know how to count, listen, tune, play loud or soft, play beautifully, write remarks in their music, watch the conductor, or fit their notes with the rest of the ensemble. They were as raw as could be. As tutors, our job was to raise their awareness to become a living organism rather than a bunch of disjointed musical souls, and in so doing, help them heal their various divides. Beyond rehearsals, we delivered as many one-to-one lessons as we could. The translators, Saman and Shwan, worked overtime alongside us to deliver our support.

Much of the disconnect between the musicians and their music related to training. It was becoming clear that those without teachers were better off than those with. Also, Iraqi culture not being Western, isolation from a live experience of good classical music had starved them. Having chosen this medium, it was clear that if they were to grow, they had to leave Iraq and surround themselves with classical music abroad. On a deeper level, and particularly for the Baghdad musicians who had survived the brunt of war, music was their way to shut out bomb blasts, fear, a world upside down. Music created an important force field against reality, transporting them into a world of their own. Coming together with these goldfish bowls around their consciousness, some with very thick glass, and having to listen to others while they played, to connect with sensitivity and love, to follow rules like tuning and counting and then to communicate to a listening public, departed radically from their norm.

We couldn't, and didn't want to, shatter the barriers they had built to protect their sanity throughout childhood, but we had to expand their awareness beyond. As Tony Reilly observed, these people had lost their childhoods, and the National Youth Orchestra of Iraq was giving it back through a belated chance to play together in safety. Here was a power cut between soul and sound, and we were trying to re-establish the link.

Power cuts of the more usual kind were common in Telary Huner, and with the power went the light and the air conditioning in our windowless seminar room. In order to stay on schedule, I moved rehearsals out into the foyer, grilled by sunlight through the concave panoramic window, slow-roasting us as the sun rode across the Suleymaniyah sky. Staying in tune was a joke, but led by our Iraqi/British/American ability to override adverse circumstances, we soldiered on. Growing up Scots had taught me to deal with mammoth quantities of crap, and then leave it behind.

Ending each hot afternoon, the students could choose conducting lessons or chamber music. Tutors and players staggered back to the office suite to prod and poke at various ensemble pieces: a wind quintet version of Scott Joplin's *Maple Leaf Rag*, a movement from a Mozart string quartet, a trumpet duet. Having never taught conducting before, I took my first class of budding maestros, including Zuhal. Here, thousands of miles from Europe, I could experiment freely. We warmed up by bouncing tennis balls in an attempt to loosen the wrist. I distributed some fibreglass batons bought in Cologne and we went through basic conducting beat patterns. One by one, they conducted Beethoven sonatas with me at the piano, and we all studied the Haydn for try-outs with the orchestra in the following week. The miracle of learning became slowly apparent to the tutors. Our progress became visceral the further they went, because nobody had told them that classical music needs years of proper teaching and good instruments to yield results.

Though these hot days, crammed full of learning, proved to be a big enough challenge, the food very nearly became the deal breaker. During lunch and dinner, we visited an Iranian restaurant where we appeared to be the only guests. Outwardly, it was airy, clean looking and modern: a buffet of salads, chicken wings, assorted stews and meats, virulent-coloured jelly deserts, and luminous green and orange fizzy drinks fed the troops. Every day, our western stomachs took the hit. Only Jonny and I seemed to get off scot-free. Mike O'Donnell reassuringly pointed out to me, 'If you go under, it's over'. No pressure on my bowels then. Here, we came across Iraqi toilets for the first time; a ceramic basin in the floor to aim whatever you were aiming at, and a hose to expel the results. These were not in great shape, and Sheila remarked that these are the first things you check when booking a restaurant. Clean toilets meant good overall hygiene standards. It sounded like a plan.

During this first week, strife mounted in the team. Larry and Mike were fuming at Allegra for blocking them over the purchase of the new bassoon for Murad. Allegra and I were not co-ordinating well on rehearsals. She was frustrated with Sanar, our 17-year-old British Council contact, and the tutors were getting angry at seeing her and Majid taking a siesta on the couch in the office suite while the rest of us were working our butts off in the heat. In such an experimental adhocracy, passions easily flared.

One day, Allegra took the day off without letting me know, to recover from swollen feet, meaning that Zuhal and I suddenly found ourselves left to manage the course. We discussed what to do in front of Telary Huner. We needed to work closely together to get everyone through the day. We primed our translators, Saman and Shwan, to ensure that moment-to-moment communication kept flowing. Any potential conflict brewing beneath the surface was brought to us for action. All our tutors quickly adapted to what, by our standards, were adverse circumstances, and delivered consistently great coaching. I began to truly see how well brought up and responsive our young players were, completely open to new ideas and, in spite of our tutors' youthfulness, remaining utterly respectful of what we had to offer. Music suddenly stopped being a fight against one's instrument and began to reveal its true meaning to them as we scraped technical and musical obstacles out of the way, bit by bit. Flow replaced 'fight or flight'.

Still, our most powerful theatre of conflict remained the restaurant. Here, people sat with their own kind. The tutors spoke with the tutors, the Arabs with the Arabs, the Kurds with the Kurds. We were self-segregating. When I saw what was happening, I turned to Shwan and asked:

'This is pretty bad, isn't it?'
'Yes. It's really bad.'
'What can we do about it?'
'I don't know.'

As foreign tutors, we had some insight, but also a lot of duty, to try and lead by example. Mike Newman, our videographer, became the first to deliberately pick up his plate of food and walk over to a free place to join some Kurds. One by one, we followed suit, whether we shared a common language or not. The simple act of sitting, eating and exchanging first smiles together proved as binding as our rehearsals. As we rotated around the tables, attempting small talk or simply sitting calmly in each other's presence during meals, we slowly evolved into family.

The very next day, Allegra and Zuhal got their heads together and came up with an icebreaker for that evening in the hotel's breakfast room. We all turned up exhausted after another long, hot day of rehearsal, reluctant but dutiful.

The game was simple. Everyone, tutors, translators and musicians sat at breakfast tables with sheets of paper. We wrote down our names, our town of origin and a fact about us. Then we had to find a partner, preferably someone who didn't speak our language, and exchange answers, by way of introduction. The simplicity of the task allowed people to help each other understand the simple statements.

We broke into pairs to introduce our partner to everyone. Zuhal dragged various pairs up onto the floor and role-played this, helping along in English and Arabic so everyone would understand. I was introduced as Paul from Scotland, and I liked doing Olympic freestyle wrestling.

Two hours of icebreaking had melted before we wearily returned to our rooms. I could see for some that the ice had been broken through, while others were themselves simply broken. We all faced mounting stress. Our faith in each other to create a concert was being tested hard in every way imaginable, driven only by our shared sense as pioneers and the first real hope in years.

Leading this journey were not only myself but also Kawan Elias and Mohammed Adnan, our Kurdish and Arab concertmasters: Kawan delicate and boyish, the best of the Kurdish violinists, and Mohammed Adnan, a strong and confident violinist from the Iraqi National Symphony Orchestra in Baghdad. Neither spoke the other's language or English, but in spite of this, or perhaps because of it, they got on well. For the first half of the concert, I'd allocated Kawan to lead the first violins, and therefore the orchestra, while Mohammed Adnan was designated to lead the orchestra in the more challenging second half. When they were not leading the first violins, they exchanged places to lead the seconds. This proved quite complicated, but somehow they made it work.

The differences between Kurds and Arabs were never more pronounced than in the violins. The very capable Arab musicians, who were all colleagues from Baghdad, clearly provided a strong foundation for the strings, but also a source of tension for the Kurds, who had come from all over Kurdistan to play and had little experience playing with each other beforehand. So, the Kurdish violinists, who I'd put mostly in violin two, were musically weaker than their Arab counterparts in violin one. I seated one Kurd in violin one and one Arab in violin two as a yin-yang solution, to see what would happen musically and diplomatically. We all felt vulnerable, which is useful if you're an artist and need to keep open to the energies of others, but dangerous if you're dealing with too much uncertainty.

Reading up on Kurdish and Arab Iraqi history had primed me for these tensions, but one particular aspect was as insidious as it was interesting. Kurds are genetically different from Arabs. Many look almost Etruscan in their delicateness with finely drawn faces and long bony fingers. The Arabs are generally bigger and more thickly set, with a much stronger physical personality. They can spot each other's ethnicity a mile off, and this is one reason why the Kurdistan Region is to date the safest part of Iraq. Kurdish terrorists do not blow each other up, whereas Arab terrorists do, so an Arab immediately draws attention.

Although the Kurdistan Region is divided along party political and tribal lines, the 2003 invasion had brought these factions together to seize their chance for greater autonomy, and ultimately independence. Making their Arab neighbours in Iraq out to be dangerous and untrustworthy was part of a calculated security and nation-building strategy to drive a stake through the political heart of Iraq. There was little love or contact between either, especially after the Kurdish genocide led by Saddam Hussein which, peaking in the 80s, impregnated the living memory of its survivors, our players' parents. The Kurdish lack of interest in learning Arabic, a major regional language, was driven by the centuries of hatred and the closed world that Kurdistan was in danger of becoming. Of all these problems, the Kurdistan Regional Government feared isolation the most, and in stark contrast to the Arab part of Iraq, opened itself to international visitors with a free 10-day visa at the border.

During our brave little summer course, our two concertmasters, Kawan and Mohammed Adnan agreed with each other through our interpreters, Saman and Shwan, to talk to their people in the orchestra and keep any misunderstandings to a minimum. One such tension surrounded the sole Kurd I'd put in violin one, Hana Faisal. I'd placed him on the outside second desk of the firsts, where the audience could see and hear him. He was effectively surrounded by Arabs who were used to turning to each other and making comments during their rehearsals back in Baghdad. That they did this here freaked Hana out, who understood no Arabic. On top of that, Mohammed Adnan wanted him to sit on the inside, out of view, as he was the weakest player in the firsts. I allowed Mohammed to organise this, as he needed to know that he had leadership authority from me for his violins, and at the same time I posted a translator right next to Hana to relay anything the Arabs were saying, mainly musical information, in Kurdish.

I sat down afterwards with Hana, being translated through Saman, and asked him how it was working out. He smiled back. It was OK. Was he sure? Yes. Though a little convoluted, it seemed to be working out, and shone some transparency on the whole of the violin section.

Though unease between the Kurds and Arabs was sometimes palpable, everyone worked to keep it in check, and I worked with the tutors to keep us all hard focused on music. Because their primary barrier was language, sitting people down next to each other to play the same music became the primary communication between them. Since the Kurdistan Regional Government had taken over the running of the region in 1991, many young Kurds could only speak one of the six dialects, Sorani Kurdish. Though our translators, Saman and Shwan, had learnt Arabic at school, many had not, or were just pretending not to understand on principle. Of course, few of the Arabs spoke any Kurdish.

Occasionally, this communication block, in spite of the translators' best efforts, set some Kurds on edge, but Jonny and I knew how to read people and began to wonder where their discomfort was really founded. Kurdistan, not unlike parts of Scotland, suffered a huge minority and persecution complex, in this case from Arabs, Persians and Turks, and with good reason, given the living memory of these players' parents. After years of systematic genocide, it was a miracle that our Kurdish players existed at all. Some of them returned to a default setting of victimhood with no perceivable threat. Every tension had to be enquired about and understood with compassion to keep rehearsals on track, without the tutors feeling they were being played for sympathy. However, the other side of the coin could also not be ignored. The Arab players had lost their childhoods and family members to the recent war. They had adapted their survival instincts to this 'normality' and, through family and music, tried to keep a window open on another world where one day, perhaps, they might be allowed to flourish.

Through all of this, one figure worked quietly away in the background; our deputy concertmaster, Annie Melconian. A petite Iraqi Armenian from Baghdad, her quiet, determined work ethic became our pillar of strength. Her strong musicianship and perceptive team playing put Annie's insights on the orchestra and the other musicians at another level altogether. Her precision, dedication and professionalism were one thing, but she also knew how to handle the Baghdad guys and go out on a limb to argue for the orchestra as a force for education and reconciliation. Being tough and female with Iraqi men ran its risks, which I suspected her non-Arab background and outsider status permitted her to get away with, but only somewhat. Throughout the course she fed me kind advice on matters such as Iraqi punctuality – there isn't any. One day, she came to me out of the blue:

'Paul, if you're happy, we're happy.'

I was bowled over. It meant so much that after only a few days, she had identified an umbilical chord between the orchestra and myself. Unlike western orchestras, these young people, who had defended themselves against war and terror, were too naïve to defend themselves against moody maestros. Or maybe they just trusted me because I actually delivered what I promised.

Annie put my conducting into a whole new perspective. In spite of our continual challenges, I strengthened my resolve not to show disappointment, and stay upbeat.

We staggered back each afternoon to a consolidating full rehearsal, in the hope that some of the day's learning would be integrated. By the time we'd reached Thursday, after a first week of painfully slow progress, utterly exhausted, we'd played through the whole programme. On the final day of week one, I ran us through the last movement of the Haydn, and within eight bars, the power cut again. My heart sank. Conducting in pitch darkness was futile but, when I lowered my arms, they carried on playing right to the end with a new sense of resolve in the sound, so I sheepishly continued conducting, standing on ceremony. Just before the final bars, the power came back on, and I shared a knowing smile with Sheila, sitting across from me in her viola section. We understood that, at the end of a tough week, confronted with so many deep problems, the orchestra had just proven how resilient and determined it was to stay the course.

As Ranya, our second horn, explained afterwards, power cuts are so common in Iraq that musicians memorise the programme to get to the end of the concert. This had happened to the Iraqi National Symphony Orchestra in Baghdad on many occasions.

Our first Friday arrived, the beginning of the Muslim weekend. We all spent our first day off together in another amusement park, where different parts of the orchestra vied for my attention. They were clearly in competition, and I found myself tested with playful intrigue. Managing to attempt a few rusty rides with various players put us a little more at ease with each other. However, I really drew the line at the shakier contraptions they tried to coax me onto. As Mike Newman and I walked around, we both noticed that the more conservative families, whom we identified with women wearing headscarves, were utterly at ease with the more liberal families, whom we identified with women in modern western clothing. In fact, if one thing remained stable throughout the next five years, it's that I never really knew who in the orchestra was Sunni, Shia, conservative or liberal. When it came to making music together, nobody cared. We truly were a little utopia, collectively building a bubble round us against the worlds we hailed from.

That evening, our last in front of that bowel-shattering Iranian restaurant whose fare had floored every westerner except Jonny and me, we sat at tables on the lawn, munching through the dry heat and intensely lit darkness of night. Suddenly, out of the restaurant emerged Tuqa, our lead cellist, with a cake. Today, Boran turned 18, so we gathered round her to sing 'Happy Birthday'. Sherwan struck up his infectious rhythms on the daff, a Sufi hand drum, with Mariwan on clarinet whipping up a catchy Kurdish tune and, as if a magic switch had been turned on, got the whole orchestra dancing on the lawn. We linked arms, we whooped, we circled around Boran, Mike Newman filming jostling feet and crazy smiles, the atmosphere a catharsis of tiredness, frustration and joy at having gotten halfway through the course and still holding together.

Allegra rested her swollen feet quietly on the sidelines, smiling knowingly. She knew that, although our musical labours had led to this precious moment, no workshop could have replaced the breakthrough of that evening: our irrepressible relief and lack of inhibition, our knowledge that we were becoming friends, learning to become an orchestra, and permitting ourselves to party through the night.

FIVE
And the walls came tumbling down

We arrived at the start of week two, and a number of things had been achieved. We had changed restaurant to Costello's, which did a good pizza, served beer and had spotless toilets. We had played through the whole concert programme and were on the cusp of recasting ourselves from rabble to ensemble. Barham Salih, who had taken over premiership of the Kurdistan Region, popped into the restaurant to see how we were doing. The chamber music sessions at the end of each day proved our weak point, mainly through tiredness, but were still roughly on track for some kind of informal presentation at the end. Most importantly, nobody had walked out of the course.

Frand and Jonny's teacher-student relationship blossomed, while Majid, as Frand's trumpet teacher in Baghdad, sat in on lessons to observe. Tensions obviously existed between the two teachers, first because Jonny had a completely different perspective on playing to offer Frand, but also because Majid, in his mid-40s, felt some discomfort at being surrounded by so many young teachers.

Majid was integral to the course. A large, jovial figure, Baloo the Bear from *Jungle Book*, but with a moustache, he adopted the role of shepherd, gathering us up into the buses, providing logistics for the percussion instruments and players from Baghdad and organising music as our orchestral librarian. But, as I saw him sitting in the corner of rehearsals, or sometimes lying on the floor, those sad eyes becoming sadder, I realised that he was taking the brunt of my teaching strategy. By using orchestral players who'd already reached an international standard in their 20s, we offered the support that he couldn't give back home in the Baghdad School of Music and Ballet.

It took me a while to realise the sense of loss he was experiencing, in terms of face and years. What drove Majid to do all this for us was his passionate love of Iraq, of young musicians and particularly his daughter, Du'aa. Mike O'Donnell gave Du'aa a number of oboe lessons during the course, which Majid videoed to take back to Baghdad, just like a good dad should.

As Suleymaniyah offered little in terms of nightlife, the lounge of my suite became the tutors' bar. The hotel owner didn't really allow alcohol on the premises, but if we asked one of the porters, they popped over to the off-licence down the road, and brought back chilled cans of beer to put in our fridges. Iraq, at least for men, always had a back door solution for everything. One evening, Majid promised the course team a special treat in the tutors' bar – masgouf, a form of carp. This utterly delicious national Iraqi dish is seasoned and barbecued on an open fire altar.

During dinner our photographer, Mike Luongo, and I got talking about his book, *Gay Travels in The Muslim World*. We especially talked about the hugging, kissing and holding of hands between the guys on the course, in other words, normal male heterosexual behaviour in the Middle East. Without being able to touch women before marriage, they developed intense bromances instead. Walking down the street hand in hand didn't mean a homoerotic relationship. Or maybe, sometimes it did. Given the absence of a gay rights or women's movement in the Middle East, they had kept the masculine intimacy that Western culture, with its different take on puritanism, had abandoned.

We resolved to plough through each day as before with full rehearsals in the morning, sectional rehearsals in the afternoon, consolidation with full orchestra and chamber music or conducting thereafter. Having acclimatised to the quirks of Telary Huner's air conditioning and sweltering temperatures, we had decided to make the best of it. We guzzled countless packs of spring water to stay hydrated. Even the thick-set contrabass of Samir Basim, a player from the Iraqi National Symphony Orchestra, cracked in the heat during rehearsals and he took a day off to effect an emergency repair and keep it going. Instruments of all sorts were experiencing problems, first because of the dry heat, but also because they'd never before been played so intensively, were too poor in quality to hold up and had owners who didn't know how to take care of them.

Meanwhile, Mike Newman fixed up our first interviews with BBC Radio Scotland's morning news, and BBC World Service. He'd been trying to sell our story but hit barrier after barrier. Editors quite freely admitted to him that nobody wanted a positive story from Iraq. It just wasn't newsworthy. Disaster got better ratings. So for this year at least, we stayed out of the limelight.

As I became emboldened, we tried reseating the orchestra unconventionally so they would hear each other differently, deepening their sense of togetherness. We even tried out the original seating of Haydn's Symphony No 99 from the world premiere in London in 1791. My little conducting class had a go at standing in front of the orchestra to conduct the beginning of the symphony. Zuhal proved, unsurprisingly, to be among the more assertive maestros. I even walked around the orchestra, letting them play conductorless. Anything to get them listening and communicating more to each other.

A poetic ray of enlightenment shone through the daily grind when Angelia, Lucy, Sheila and Dave, our four string tutors, formed a quartet to rehearse some Beethoven for the impending chamber music concert. Gathering slowly around them on the floor of the rehearsal room like woodland creatures in a forest, the Iraqi players sat listening, watching in rapture. Classical chamber music almost never happened in Iraq. Simply by rehearsing it intimately, wordlessly, the tutors could show how inherent an activity to the students' musicianship this was. For the umpteenth time in two weeks, the walls of ignorance and misunderstanding came tumbling down.

Time was marching on, and we needed to pull briefly out of our work routine and start thinking like an organisation.

With so little time together in Iraq, we had to put every precious minute to good use. Zuhal initially disliked the idea of handing our strategy over to the players, but I insisted I knew what I was doing and we should simply trust them. On Sunday evening, I gathered everyone into the hotel's breakfast room, where pens and four different colours of A5 paper lay on the tables. We had to get through this fast, because we were all tired. A lovely colleague of Allegra's from the Iraqi Peace Foundation, who spoke both Kurdish and Arabic, began with a workshop on the meaning of values. Once she had warmed the group up, I took over and presented four questions on the flipchart:

What are your personal values?

What do you value in music?

What do you want NYOI to do in future?

If you ran your own youth orchestra, what values would you have for it?

Everyone took one sheet of coloured paper, yellow for question one, green for question two and so on, and answered in the top third of the paper in their own language, either Kurdish or Arabic. Some answered in English.

In 45 minutes, we were done. I thanked everyone and handed the papers to our translation team. They now faced the huge task of making sure every piece of paper had its contents translated into all three course languages, Kurdish, Arabic and English. A couple of days later, we posted all the results around the wall of the rehearsal room for everyone to see.

'When I perform music, I feel that I'm in a beautiful world that's endless. I joined the orchestra to develop my musical skills and learn about cultures so I can grow my talent and abilities, also my self-respect and self-confidence.'

'One thing has made Iraq more beautiful and that is music, in which we express our feelings. For this reason I can say it extends to everybody's lives.'

'Showing the spirit of collaboration, love and the feeling of unity between the members in addition to great performances and reaching a level that competes with other youth orchestras.'

'They must really love music, must not only have a high level of music but of manners as well. To be considerate, think about how others feel and respect their values. To be serious about hard work.'

'To be one of the best orchestras in the world, and definitely in Iraq. I also hope we can have annual activities in Iraq and abroad'

'Throughout my entire life, I've never learnt as much as I've been learning from the past week. That is why I think this orchestra deserves a lot of praise'

"I want to pass a message to human beings through the music I'm playing. And I want everyone to benefit from this message."

Their dreams went far beyond anything Zuhal or I could have envisaged. From a position of war, isolation and terror, they expressed eloquence, hope and vision, given anonymously and spontaneously from the heart. These multi-coloured pieces of paper around our rehearsal room told me who I was working with, and how far we were ready to go to keep playing together. They had given us not only a strategy but also hope that reconciliation through music was real. Just as we were making progress, the shadow of Baghdad cast itself over us.

This second week's most imposing intervention came from Maestro Karim Wasfi, Music Director of the Iraqi National Symphony Orchestra, and his four thick-set government bodyguards, up from the capital. They were present to prevent the recurrence of a near fatal assassination attempt he'd suffered at the beginning of the war. Many of his players were with us, so he wanted to check us out. The wide lapelled gangster suit, purple shirt and tie, and those of his four similarly clad protectors, seemed at odds with anything I'd seen so far. As I stood before the orchestra in my puny T-shirt and jeans, I felt as if Chicago's gangland had descended to wipe us out. Only the violin cases containing machine guns were missing. Or maybe not. Out of the corner of my eye I could see him sitting at a distance from our rehearsal, jet-black moustache and hair glinting like a vaguely familiar dictator, as we played through our repertoire. Allegra had already warned me to take him with a pinch of salt. Without saying very much, he left and joined us later at Costello's for dinner.

As soon as he walked into the restaurant and took a proprietary seat amid the players, their tone turned solemn. The boss was in town, and nobody could tell if he approved. The tutors and I sat at a table across from him, and let him do what he had to do. I believed the orchestra was far too evolved as an ensemble for anything to happen to us now. I had to trust that Karim would read us not as a threat, but a supplementary activity that only enhanced his players' skills in Baghdad. We had a perfunctory chat later in the changing rooms of the concert hall, and seemed to part on good enough terms.

The stress of rehearsals was beginning to take its toll. Tuqa, our lead cellist, reported she had a very sore arm and Dave, our cello tutor, knew exactly why. She had poor technique through self-teaching, had pushed herself too hard, and the arm had given up. He told me he'd give her a lesson on how to correct this, but for a day, she sat on the floor in the corner of rehearsals, resting but forlorn, as she rubbed her arm. A single lesson might be a quick fix for now, but couldn't undo the years of neglect she'd suffered.

With just a day to go before the concert, calamity struck again. Du'aa, our first oboe, reported that her instrument was broken. She was distraught, convinced that bad luck was following her around. Her tutor Mike O'Donnell tried to console her and assess the damage. Iraq didn't have oboe repair shops; whatever broke stayed broken. Her instrument was a model almost unheard of in the UK, but common elsewhere, so Mike made some emergency modifications to his own British instrument so that she could use his. We sourced another oboist in Suleymaniyah who could lend Mike his oboe to play next to Du'aa. This replacement oboe came, like many cheap imports, from China, but it was what we had to work with, so Mike took it on and prepared to do his best. This was a huge change from his freelance work with the London Symphony Orchestra. Iraq's instruments constantly suffered a vicious circle of disrepair and makeshift repairs.

Later that evening, we all gathered again in the breakfast room of the Mirako Hotel and performed our chamber music pieces to each other. *Maple Leaf Rag*, the first movement of Mozart's String Quartet No 17 in B flat major, Frand doing a trumpet solo, the string tutors in a string quartet performing Beethoven's Opus 18 No 1, and a couple of clarinet duos, all of which amounted to a first step in opening everyone up to the possibilities of making music together after we left. Moreover, chamber music sensitised them to correcting each other, reading each other's feelings and body language: in other words, group teaching. A wrong note, rhythm, or balance between parts became everyone's problem. During our little concert, group after group produced simple but sensitive vignettes, in tune, accurate and fun.

Of course, chamber music already existed in Iraq. It was cheap, underground and informal but, depending on where you lived, especially after the sectarianism that arose during the war, religious authorities could probably find a way to shut you down. More likely than not, players performed classical Iraqi music in small chamber groups for weddings, parties, family festivals, restaurants and the like. Even in liberal Iraq, music as pure listening pleasure was rare. Physically getting to other musicians and starting a rehearsal on time were also rare as some roads were still dangerous.

Once our relaxed little concert was done, we retired to our rooms. But then, across the corridors, in and out of people's rooms, a buzz started to generate. That night before the concert, everyone eagerly wanted to break through to another level. We were used to them practicing all night long, but tonight the fever intensified unabated. As we wandered around, Angie and I caught the last movement of the Haydn symphony, and as we tentatively opened a bedroom door, there sat four of the players as a string quartet working their way through it. Hussam on cello and the others smiled back at us. We were nearly in tears. They were experiencing the deepest learning before our eyes, with no tutor to guide them. We knew they'd be fine, not just for tomorrow, but thereafter too.

The day of the concert arrived. In the main auditorium of Telary Huner, Mike Newman and I were busying ourselves on stage with microphone stands, seating and the like, while Allegra took care of the lectern and the introductory speech she was to give. While we were busy, she'd managed to arrange herself an interview with Al Jazeera English. Majid sat at the back of the auditorium and watched.

Mike had already done all he could to rig the lighting for the concert, but when the hall management had shown him around, he realised the scale of the nightmare. Though the theatre had all the necessary equipment, much had been installed incorrectly, and it would take him a week to rerig it. He had been given two days.

The acoustics of the hall were meant for amplified voice and music, not acoustic, so the orchestra on stage felt, to my ears, dry and unsupported. Somebody had glued a beautiful red carpet to the stage, sucking up our sound instead of reflecting it out into the auditorium. However, the opulence and sense of occasion that Telary Huner gave us were lost on nobody. Plush VIP chairs on the front row, a capacity of 1,300, and a stage that our small band of 33 tried not to be swallowed up by. Majid had already brought the percussion and music stands along with a rather ramshackle conductor's podium, all belonging to the Iraqi National Symphony Orchestra.

Everyone stayed focussed. As we ran the final rehearsal, we all felt we had done everything we could. We had developed discipline, listening and unified action in two weeks: a considerable improvement on anything else Iraq could produce. During the break, I turned to Mike O'Donnell and said: 'We now have a fifth form high school orchestra.' 'From Basingstoke.' he added. Rediscovering our sardonic British humour masked a real sense of relief at having survived the arc of the last two weeks, bowels and integrity mostly intact.

Over the two weeks, Allegra, Sanar and Zuhal had worked up a local marketing campaign including radio slots, flyers and banners. As a result, Suleymaniyah's public started flowing into the hall, quite unsure of what lay in store for them. We had to allow free admission, simply to attract people to an evening as controversial and unusual as ours, a tactic that pulled in about 750 people, including Karim Wasfi, who was busy distributing flyers for his own music academy in Baghdad.

Standing in the male toilets of Telary Huner, I changed into my white tie and tails, a ritual act of empowerment which brought me a little closer to becoming the sort of alpha dictator that Iraq had become used to. With two weeks of good quality, compassionate teaching behind us, I didn't feel too bad about that. Mike Newman positioned his camera in the central mixing booth of the auditorium to complete his film. Allegra gave a talk introducing the concert to thank the sponsors: the British Embassy, British Council, Dr Barham Salih. We could finally get down to performing.

Cataclysmic lightning bolts of music shot out from the opening of Beethoven's *Prometheus* Overture, followed by a primordial chorale led by Du'aa on Mike's doctored oboe and Mike on the plastic counterpart. The legend of Prometheus, a spirit who enlightened humankind with art, knowledge and laws of conduct, could have been seen as timely in Iraq's miserable condition, if it weren't for the fact that Iraq, 5000 years beforehand, had already done that job for itself.

Tuning remained a painful issue. Although the overture is centred on a bright C major, two weeks of fluctuating rehearsal temperatures, years of self-teaching and a Middle Eastern music culture with several ingrained tuning systems played havoc with us. Nevertheless, our public was on side.

Ali Khassaf's 10-minute piece, *Iraqi Melodies* from 2009, based itself largely on *Chemali Wali*, a traditional melody that wove its way in many guises through Iraq's musical consciousness. Ali Khassaf, a clarinettist at the Iraqi National Symphony Orchestra, at least knew what an orchestra was, and could do a good job of setting a tune with the right instruments in mind. Iraqi composers in Iraq with the same insights proved thin on the ground.

I valiantly attempted to bring a spot of humour to the evening with the Harry Lauder hit, *Deoch and Doris* while Kawan Alias, our Kurdish concertmaster, gave his best to bring an authentic Scottish lilt to the interpretation.

In the middle of the orchestral programme, the two lovely sisters on violin and cello, Sabat and Sawen from Erbil, sang a Kurdish song, *Waku Nay Kunkuna Jargm* by Adnan Karim, accompanied by one of our pianists, Zardasht. As few in Iraq had experience of an orchestral programme, I reckoned a sung duo in the middle of the first half proved just as valid a musical experience as anything else we offered. Both had wonderful voices but, like many, were too closed in their own worlds. In rehearsal, I'd encouraged both to sing through their eyes, and reach out to the public, so they could in turn reach back. As they poured their souls into the auditorium, the fundamental tones of sadness and loss darkened the hall. Listeners recognised their yearning and we, sitting in the orchestra, felt their epiphany.

I'm thankful to the sisters for this insight, because the last work in our first half, Dr Mohammed Zaza's *Kurdish Dances* from 2008, took on a contrasting aspect of Kurdish culture – a sharp cut with the past to embrace Western modernism. Jagged and brisk, this orchestral transcription of his guitar piece gave us the upbeat finale we needed before the interval. Over the next five years, all the Arab composers, to a fault, wrote for us in a style celebrating traditional Arabic music with vigour and bombast, whereas the Kurdish composers cut themselves from the past with schooled modernism and an ever present note of mourning.

Years later, I would ask a wise friend of mine, Elisabeth von Leliwa, why she thought this was, to which she answered that the Kurds needed to mourn their genocide leading up to the 1980s, and had achieved the relative cultural calm to do this. The Arabs, particularly in Baghdad, were still in the thick of terrorism, and had no chance to process the horrors they'd recently lived through. Indeed, Baghdad's hopeless romanticism of ancient Iraq as the cradle of civilisation contained notes of bitterness and failure that couldn't possibly become the foundation for a better future.

Immediately after the first half of the concert, five young men accosted me from the local university with broken English, coming right up to the stage and ushering me down onto the floor. Feeling somewhat hierarchically challenged, their insistent, good-natured raw energy won me over, so I clambered down in white tie and tails and joined them for a photo call with their iPhones. Arms around each other, their uninhibited male physicality felt liberating, and quite a counterpoint to the standoffish Germans or Brits.

After the interval, we swapped concertmasters, and the more experienced Mohammed Adnan took over, who I needed to get us through the Haydn. We began with the very simple arrangement of *Cradle Song* by Martin Dalby. Mohammed Adnan gently played through his small solos, and the audience warmly applauded. Everyone loves a lullaby.

Then, with aplomb, we began Haydn's Symphony No 99. All the tutors had joined the orchestra to beef us up for the show, and here was where I needed them most. They were my rock in a performance that could go either way. I wanted Haydn to inject joy back into people's lives. What we received from the audience more than justified the choice, and Haydn would have loved it. Not only did they applaud after every movement, they also broke out into applause at every pause in the music, mid-flow. That Haydn loved throwing in false endings made the game between the public and us all the more gleeful.

At the end, the 750-strong audience rose in a warm standing ovation. We were now an orchestra: somewhat disciplined and schooled but most importantly, reconciled with each other. Nobody could know that without auditioned players from across the whole of Iraq, we could never have achieved this standard in two weeks. An almost impossible achievement in Iraqi terms, the audience sensed what they were witnessing and gave us their approval.

Most significantly, we showed that, in an environment such as Iraq, having a neutral leadership from the outside was enough to bring people together. In intercultural terminology, we call this the Third Space: we were neither truly Western, Kurdish or Arab, but nevertheless, we felt safe enough to concentrate on music together, make new friends, and rebuild Iraq's decimated culture one note at a time.

SIX
In darkness let me dwell

Directly after the course, I travelled to London to report to the British Council and catch up with Alan and Mark in Leyton. Two of my oldest friends, they've been together now for 20 years. I'd shared many a Christmas and New Year in their Victorian tenement, filling myself to the brim with Mark's bountiful cooking and their tender loving care. Their beautiful home not only became my base when visiting London on NYOI business, but also my sanctuary from burn-out. Filled with stories of Iraq, my avid friends tried to get their heads round my escapades. Our encounter with Karim Wasfi, he in sharp suit and tie, moustache lavished with gleaming balms, and me in T-shirt and jeans, a challenge to his supreme authority in Iraq, bewildered and amused them. At the British Council, the ever-sagacious Paul Parkinson seemed happy at the integrity of it all while Alan and Mark seemed content I was still alive. I felt they had no choice but to support a friend who had quite clearly gone off the deep end.

I also caught up with Michael White, music critic for the *Daily Telegraph*, with whom I'd been acquainted back in the 90s. Michael had a deep, gently reflective view on the classical music business. Far from being soft, he managed to cut to the heart of matters without tearing strips off people. He put me up over a couple of nights at his place during the end of the 2009 Proms season. Our 12-minute video report on the course was complete and so, laptop perched on knee, Michael and I settled down on his living room sofa to let the show commence.

We discussed classical music in the Middle East, particularly the music academy founded by the Sultan of Oman, which became the foundation of the Royal Oman Symphony Orchestra. Apparently, scouts from London had been requisitioned to scour the country for kids showing the slightest musical talent, who were then sent to a purpose-built music academy, all expenses paid, and developed into the Sultan's private orchestra. On passing their exams, these handsome male musicians were lavished with gifts of expensive cars and watches. All I could offer the Iraqis was a couple of weeks of decent lessons and a show at the end but, either way, we were both in the exhausting business of carrot-and-stick leadership.

When Michael went on to review Beethovenfest in Bonn, he told their Director, Ilona Schmiel, about us. Shortly afterwards, when I was back in Cologne, they invited me for an initial meeting with their team. This is how the long arc to Germany began. With the German ball in play, it was time to forge our strategy. I still had dozens of pieces of paper where players had written their values, dreams, desires for NYOI, and the message was clear. These inspiring young people wanted to learn how to play in an orchestra, promote their culture and become a symbol of peace and hope to the world.

The love, commitment and respect that they'd shown me in Iraq became core values for us all to live up to. That was impressive enough, but they went much further. They also showed they wanted to work hard together with discipline, good communication, transparency, better teaching, listening, and learning while bringing the whole of Iraq together. From a bunch of young adults who'd thrown themselves into this unique project on a wing and a prayer, their desires struck me as fresh, dynamic and highly articulate. Knowing a little of where they came from, they were decisively stepping away from their status quo.

Exhausted, I hung onto the energy from what we'd achieved and what they'd expressed in writing. Somehow, I hoped this would carry us, or rather me, forward, as there remained nobody else to seriously delegate to. Zuhal had moved to Scotland with her brother and was starting life anew. Allegra had left the project to focus on consulting work in Baghdad. The players had gone back to their homes in Iraq, clearly not yet ready to manage a complex, fragile organisation. I was on my own.

Zuhal began skyping me intermittently from her new home in Glasgow. We shared dark times and hope for the orchestra. Though furiously intelligent, her own coming to terms with Scotland's education system seemed stuck to say the least. I needed to take the next step to turn the orchestra's raw feedback into a winning strategy. We simply couldn't compete against other youth orchestras who were better educated, less isolated and owned better instruments than us, so we had to carve out an entirely different niche in order to survive and flourish.

Our strength lay in Iraqi diversity through Kurdish and Arab Iraqi musicians and composers. I had to eliminate the expectation that we should sound like Venezuela's Simon de Bolivar Youth Orchestra or Barenboim's West/East Divan, so our background stories had to be as vital as the music itself. We offered intercultural outreach to foreign youth orchestras and audiences. Since we worked online and transnationally for most of the year, we would emphasise the role of technology across borders. Video auditions and the like kept us in line with current youth orchestra trends at no extra cost, but survival depended on our diplomatic role.

We could triumph as grassroots representatives of the Iraqi peoples, working together with foreign governments and youth orchestras to create a better future, and signal through our YouTube channel that pride in being Iraqi was possible. Our one course a year on top of our unique background made us rare and exotic to Iraqis because we were an orchestra, as well as to the West, because we were Iraqi. My head already swimming with ideas, I determined for us to become as innovative, community oriented and accessible as possible under these ludicrous circumstances. As a stagehand at Scottish Ballet once said to me, 'How to make a silk purse out of a pig's ear.'

So, if 2009 was the year we became operational, 2010 would be the year we began our strategy. If we were lucky, 2011 could begin our role as cultural diplomats with Beethovenfest, but what

I wanted more than anything was to bring them to Scotland, to bring them home. So I started pressing buttons.

'Dear Paul,

Good to chat this morning and look forward to meeting up with you and Zuhal next Friday, 6th November at 2pm, at the Grosvenor Hotel near Haymarket Station.

Am keen that the Edinburgh Youth Orchestra takes part in this project, mid August 2010, and have already spoken to Julian Lloyd Webber who is happy to do a workshop in Edinburgh when you are here.

All best

Marjory'

Thus began the mission to bring the National Youth Orchestra of Iraq to Britain.

Marjory Dougal, the General Manager of the Edinburgh Youth Orchestra, was a power-house of ideas and connections that had put her and her orchestra on the map for the past 30 years. Beneath her genteel guise amongst the bourgeoisie of Morningside, she had amassed a formidable amount of local and international experience. I needed her players to sit next to mine, and her experience of Edinburgh, but most of all I needed her belief in our visit. I also saw that Zuhal needed to get connected to other young musicians in Scotland, and hoped that gateway would be through Marjory.

I flew to Scotland to meet Marjory and Zuhal, forge an alliance and bring us to the Edinburgh Festival. With current pledges of about £50,000 from sponsors so far, we had only about a third of what I reckoned we needed to get the orchestra to Britain. I tried reaching out to the Cabinet Minister for Culture and International Affairs, Fiona Hyslop, which also led to nothing at this time, though a motion passed by the Scottish Government in support of the orchestra (much thanks to the mother of the O'Donnell brothers, herself a Member of the Scottish Parliament) remained fresh in my mind. I was not to be beaten!

During our meeting, Zuhal remained quiet, while Marjory and I jammed away at the possibilities. I tried to bring her into the discussion, but something was wrong. The Zuhal sitting next to me was a fish out of water, not the young woman with such a tremendous resilience, and a furiously intelligent voice, that I knew. Still only three months into her relocation to Glasgow, I wasn't surprised. To Glaswegians and immigrants alike, Edinburgh, which calls itself a city, looks like a town and behaves like a village, can seem impenetrable.

However, Marjory, with her defiant positivity, stayed open to the idea, and gave me her blessing and partnership. It was still basically down to me, alone, to see how much I could achieve. Underlying this discussion, I had two wishes: to nurture these young Iraqi musicians amid the throng of the Edinburgh International Festival, the most fertile paradise they could wish for, and for me, some sort of reconciliation with my homeland.

On 13th December, I came home to my tiny flat in the middle of Cologne, to discover the power had been cut off. It was simply impossible to do enough teaching to keep NYOI and myself afloat at the same time. Crunching the orchestra's considerable problems was eating up to four hours a day in Internet cafes across town, and my obsessive drive was fully focussed on keeping NYOI alive, rather than myself. This first truly dark phase of NYOI's history set a pattern for future years: winter became a time of tension during our YouTube auditions, major financial insecurity for the project and myself, and crunching problems seemingly without solutions. I lived in a state of pure blind slog, having faith that my emotional drive, forged by the strategy, would keep everyone focussed on the next course.

So, who else to turn to? British Council Iraq still wanted to help, while expecting financial independence for the orchestra as soon as possible. We would probably not see more than two years of seed-funding from them, as they knew such initiatives had to root themselves in their home cultures to become at all sustainable.

I soldiered on. Ironically, I found myself suffering the same power shortages that had become routine in Baghdad. As the coldest winter in recent German history closed in, I stayed in internet cafes working on NYOI, charging my laptop and mobile phone on their electricity, shaving every morning with water boiled on a small camping stove and showering in my local budget fitness studio before teaching. Various heating experiments from camping stores such as glowing mini coals or hand held chemical bags provided little succour, the best solution being an old-fashioned hot water bottle and sleeping with my hand in front of my mouth to warm the air I breathed at night. I was about as low as I could go.

Come the New Year, I started seeking sponsorship. Cold calling those who advertised and worked in the Middle East required me to set up a spreadsheet of some 150 key firms, mostly in the UK and Iraq, but also Norway, America, UAE, Austria and Ireland. Here, I recorded telephone numbers, emails, the names of CEOs and their PAs. Oil firms, but also downstream support services, banks, construction firms, architects, hotel chains, mobile telephony and security firms became targets. I researched many through ads and articles in books on the oil business, analysing their responses to my approaches for follow-up and scouring their websites for corporate social responsibility priorities. One oil company had funded the replacement of a local school's windows and doors; surely the job of local government, and surely they could have afforded to rebuild the entire school? Other examples showed more generosity and ambition. With only a mobile phone in my pocket, I used public call shops to phone cheaply abroad. Thus the city of Cologne became my office, jumping from internet cafe to call shop, updating my admin late at night in my lightless apartment with my laptop previously charged up in town.

Meanwhile, Zuhal was battling to get a place to do her English A-Levels at a Scottish school, a non-starter as most teach the Scottish equivalent Highers. Her ambition was to get into Oxbridge, and she was convinced that A-levels were the only possible way. Eventually, she enrolled herself in a distance learning college in London. This plunged her into an isolated world of self-study, a familiar state of affairs for ambitious Iraqis, all while looking after her brother's new baby in their small Glasgow flat. That she could walk straight down the grid system of Glasgow's city centre without checkpoints or fear of suicide bombers, taking the cool rain onto her face, and sit in the piano booths of the Mitchell Library to practice, already felt like progress. But mostly, she was alone.

By February, with online auditions already underway, and no sign of new funding, British Council Iraq's Tony Reilly and I took stock of the situation. I knew that by cold calling potential sponsors, however polite they appeared on the phone, we were wasting each other's time. These very industries and cultures relied on insider influence, skilled manipulation of relationships and more often than not, corruption. As one CEO of a Scottish oil firm said to me, 'I would never support an organisation with the word Iraq in the title. Iraq is a time bomb, just waiting to go off.'

Oil politics between Baghdad and Erbil were indeed an ongoing high-end poker game, with oil fields around the disputed territories, like Taq Taq and Baba Goorgoor near Kirkuk, as military and terrorist flashpoints. Anyone sponsoring an Iraqi youth orchestra would offend the Kurds, because of the word 'Iraq' in our title. Anyone funding an orchestra operating in Kurdistan, containing many Kurdish musicians, would offend the Federal Government in Baghdad. Tony Reilly tried to help as much as he could, but I had just made the second year more expensive by increasing the tutors from seven to twelve and the orchestra from 33 to 42, in my eyes essential to increase reach and quality.

In this dark mid-point of the project, the orchestra and I were nearing breakdown, because our fates felt fused one and the same. After I'd shown Tony the evidence of my fundraising efforts, he made the life-saving decision to inject $50,000 into the 2010 summer course, and gave his staff in Erbil, Nishtiman and Karda the green light to support me further. I took another breath, and dived into setting up the next round of meetings. I jumped back on a plane to London.

My first port of call at the Kurdistan Regional Government in London took place with Bayan, their High Representative.

Fluent in English, Kurdish, Arabic and Japanese, she came across as an elegant, relaxed lady in a class of her own. Something else about her spoke of the earthiness of Kurdistan, her sense of rootedness there. Because they were not a country *per se*, she couldn't take ambassadorial or consular status, but was one of many such representatives around the world working for the Kurdistan Regional Government's political and business interests. She quite rightly quizzed me on why I was creating this orchestra. It was obvious to me; her musicians badly needed teaching and I was honoured to be asked to set up a national youth orchestra. At that time, her government's strategy was to support the whole of Iraq, and she did so by landing me with a pile of books on the oil business in Kurdistan. Maybe I could find some sponsors through it, she suggested. She did her job, and we kept each other in the loop, as it were.

Far more key to the orchestra's role in Britain was the following brief communiqué:

'The Chairman, Dr Salah Al Shaikhly and the Vice Chairman, Sir Terence Clark of the British Iraqi Friendship Society would be delighted to meet with you on Monday 15th February at 11.30am at The Goring Hotel, Beeston Place, London SW1 (near Victoria Station). I will also be joining them.'

Thus ran my invitation from Laura Curtis, Secretary of the British Iraqi Friendship Society.

This exclusive hotel lay tucked away in a London back street. Empire was the theme, with plush yellow sofas, blossoming summer décor and sparsely populated lounges with austere leather armchairs, I did my best in shirt, jeans and sneakers to blend in, which meant I didn't. Having discreetly tucked myself away in one corner of the empty summer lounge, I set up my laptop to review some research on the Society. Within a couple of minutes, a politely anguished waiter descended to gently point out that laptops were not permitted. How could I have possibly brought the tone down with this shoddy piece of 21st century junk? As a lone guest, damage to everyone's credibility was thankfully minimised. On removing the aforesaid item from view, I hastily ordered a coffee, in the hope that face could be saved and a generous tip would restore the status quo. We were as ghosts, interacting with fragile apparitions of each other across time and class.

Dr Shaikhly, Sir Terence and Laura duly arrived, and I felt we could get down to business. As we discussed the orchestra, I sensed slight apprehension. Being an unknown quantity, dressed somewhat out of turn with the hotel, it was Laura's emotional skills that bridged the interest between these two very senior former diplomats and this strange young man. Sir Terence remained open and jovial throughout, while Dr Shaikhly observed me as if from afar. His parting advice, to include an Arab instrument in the concert, stuck with me as I left.

I have to admit, I'm not great with diplomats: too much well trained façade, too little transparency. However, I was to learn over time that the most powerful weapon of diplomats and politicians is gut feeling, an intuitive understanding of the person in front of you. Most have neither the time nor the inclination to look into anything else. So that is what I had to learn to speak to.

By March, the northern hemisphere slowly tilted towards the sun and increased daylight hours and warmth in my flat in Cologne. I lay awake feeling my heart, a hare's foot thumping in alarm against frosted turf. Lying in bed, I worked the stress out of my body with muscle tensing exercises and modified yoga poses. My hands clasped across my chest to calm me to sleep and await the next morning, my whole body and psyche engaged in a blind battle to keep us going. After playing international youth orchestra director in front of everybody and facing a collapsing existence in Cologne, I had reached the end of my tether. Running NYOI felt like driving a car off a cliff once a week to see how softly I could land. Eventually, by no longer feeling the pain, I had worked out how.

Against this anguished backdrop, I prepared to return to London for the next networking event:

'The British Iraqi Friendship Society (BIFS) is delighted to announce a forthcoming lecture on the Oil & Gas sector in Iraq. The lecture titled Iraq's Oil and Gas Sector – Current Reality and Future Prospects, will be given by Mr Majid Jafar. This event will be held on Monday 22nd March 2010 at 17.30 at the Jumeirah Carlton Tower, Cadogan Place, London SW1X 9PY.'

The invitation arrived with my £10 entrance fee waived. Nevertheless, I still had to cancel teaching in Cologne and fly to London. My personal finances still stayed on the back burner compared to the chance of making new contacts for the orchestra. With any luck, I might awake the interest of a potential sponsor. The modern classicism of the hotel was sufficiently banal to confirm it made its money from business clientele who, upon arriving, I had every intention of imitating. Clad in suit and tie, I sat alone in a cafe downstairs at reception, musing through a window at the absurdity of a conductor attending a talk called 'Iraq's Oil and Gas Sector'.

Upstairs in the featureless conference suite, I arrived ahead of time to fan out DVDs of our film from the 2009 course next to canapés, various trade books and pamphlets from the energy sector. As people started arriving, I began my well-practiced role as an unknown quantity in a closed circuit. Sharply dressed career women mingled with the Old School in various states of rumpled-suitedness. Occasionally, a welcome diversion arrived in the shape of a crisp young chap with broad rugby shoulders, fresh out of public school and a regional name quaintly at odds with his accent. Nevertheless, I focussed on the larger goal of working a room full of trade attachés, academics, journalists, Middle Eastern analysts, oil people and risk data crunchers, trying to get a foothold as the atmosphere warmed. Slowly, folk permitted me to enter their space and chat with them. Laura Curtis, calm and controlled, came over and gave me a friendly once-over. 'You look different' she said, incredulously. I hoped this meant my one ally was still onside. The doors swung open to the beige seminar room, replete with large screen and lectern, holding 150. About half that capacity, in we all went.

Majid Al Jafar, a handsome young businessman and Board Member of the British Iraqi Friendship Society, gave his hour-long lecture and took questions. As Executive Director of the Crescent Petroleum Group and a board member of several other energy companies, he definitely knew his stuff. To my discomfort, I understood a great deal. How much more should I have to learn to keep this orchestra alive? As he showed graphs of Iraq's oil output over the 20th century, I began to get a sense of how hard Iraqis had worked to extract their sole resource from the ground, how they had improvised and innovated on next to nothing, and how thoroughly they had been thwarted as the graph's output plummeted at the onset of yet another war. Theirs was a story of triumph and tragedy, cycling from one conflict to the next. Iraq's modern history and curse was its oil, a curse that may soon end. Majid Al Jafar paraphrased another oil magnate; 'The stone age didn't end due to lack of stone'. That would be one to remember for my next orchestral conference.

Here, I was way out of my depth as various analysts commented from the floor. The Director of Transparency International challenged him on the Iraqi Federal Government's contracts with oil firms. Each stage of production had to be signed off by a government official, ergo, that official had to be bribed. In the previous year, Transparency International had rated Iraq as the fifth most corrupt country in the world, with Afghanistan one place better than them. Floating on the world's third largest oil reserve, the people of this country didn't matter to anyone. No wonder so many young Iraqis had sunk in despair into the thick black sea beneath their feet. At the end, I went over to Mr Al Jafar and thanked him. With grace, he gave me his card and took one of my DVDs.

Back in Cologne, my hunt for 12 suitable tutors began. It was a little like putting together a jury. Angelia Cho on violin and Dave Edmonds on cello were indispensable. Many new people came on board – Joanne Quigley, a highly experienced teacher and freelance violinist from Dublin, and Dobbs Hartshorne, a maverick bass from New Hampshire with years of experience performing in the Middle East and Afghanistan. Our viola tutor from Poland, Ilona Bondar, had recently graduated from the Royal Academy of Music in London and sounded as if she had a bright, clear-headed disposition. Daniel Agi came on board as a highly experienced flautist from Cologne and though German, his Syrian heritage meant he could teach in Arabic. Helge Harding came as clarinet tutor from Berlin, Gwenllian non Davies as oboe tutor from Cardiff and Nic Macorison as bassoon tutor from London. Turning again to alumni of the National Youth Orchestras of Scotland, Adam Clifford joined as percussion tutor while Sarah Maxwell became our horn tutor. Andy, recently graduated from the Royal Conservatoire of Scotland, replaced Jonathan as our trumpet tutor.

This was a more broadly experienced team than last year, but I still kept the accent on youthfulness. My feeling for the right tutor for NYOI still lacked finesse but with the pressure I'd put myself under, I just needed people who could do their job.

The ongoing meetings with Beethovenfest in Bonn, just 29 minutes in the train from Cologne, fuelled my hope that we could fly to Germany in 2011, and must unquestionably survive 2010. While outwardly calm, I hungered for their professional support, their eagerness and resources to make it work. Clearly, offering a couple of weeks' stellar teaching a year in Iraq then casting students back out into the wilderness was somewhat sadistic. These young musicians had sole responsibility for creating Iraq's cultural future, so they needed to broaden their minds, end their isolation and learn how music education in other countries worked.

The year became still warmer, and I could feel the spring climate enter my bones. British Council Iraq was fully on board again and the Martyr Saad Palace in Erbil had been donated to us for free by the Kurdistan Regional Government as rehearsal and concert venue, though there was still much for us to do financially and logistically. I'd signed the orchestra up to membership of the European Federation of National Youth Orchestras and the League of American Orchestras. Our

Facebook, YouTube and Twitter feeds came online, but attempts to set up a British charity to support the orchestra were leading nowhere. We desperately needed one to help us build a sustainable future.

It was on a cold, dry January day back in 2009 that Georg Witteler, a business coach, first contacted me out of the blue:

'Dear Mr MacAlindin

By chance, I came across an article in the UK's *Sunday Mail* 'Composer's Classical Peace Mission from Scotland to Iraqi War Zone' (21.12.2008), about your collaboration with Sir Peter Maxwell Davies. Through my love of Scotland, I have come across the music of Max and collected pretty much every CD of his music.

I can't read music, and so my love of music has grown as a result, for over the years, I have collected about six thousand CDs, including much contemporary music. Max has a special place in my collection, as his music reminds me of my deep connectedness to Scotland. Next summer, I will visit Hoy with my partner – Max's first home in Orkney.

You're probably asking what this guy wants with me. You are a Scottish conductor who has worked intensively with Max, produced many interesting concerts, and now live in Cologne.

Many grounds indeed to wake my curiosity and get to know you. That you're also a coach is something we have in common. Would you care to meet up? I'd be delighted to hear from you!

Yours sincerely,

Georg Witteler'

Oh, fantastic! Max had done an interview about the orchestra for the *Sunday Mail*, which they'd spun as if he were going out to Iraq, and now I had a groupie knocking on the door in Cologne. Typical. I could run, but I couldn't hide. Georg and I agreed to meet up in Café Rico, Rudolfplatz, my favourite haunt for catastrophising about Iraq over coffee and, I swear, I could not have been warier. In fact, he turned out to be genial. Round-faced and bespectacled, his enthusiasm and warmth still failed to put me at ease, though it had a certain naive charm. The chuckle in his voice as he recounted his passion for Max's music set me on edge as many fans had done before.

Nevertheless, through Georg Witteler's efforts and substantial network, the German Friends of NYOI officially founded themselves in May 2010, as a Cologne-based charity to support the orchestra's visit to Beethovenfest the following year. I settled on this local solution with relief and, as the trees of Cologne budded their vibrant greens, our infant infrastructure sprung to life. By June, I managed to get my electricity back on. Slowly returning to civilisation, I set out on my next diplomatic mission, to the US of A.

Orchestral conferences are morbid affairs, not uncommonly leading to suicidal tendencies in those raring to get things done, and so it was with little hope that I departed for Atlanta and the 2010 League of American Orchestras conference. As a new member of the League, I needed to put us on the map. Painfully isolated, and with the Iraqi team grounded by visa, financial and flight barriers, I alone had to keep pushing to bring us out of the shadows.

This huge conference brought together orchestral managements from across the US and abroad to discuss how to innovate fast enough to survive radical social and technological change. Or not. American orchestras have a particular scene, being hard up against market forces and relying greatly on donations and sponsorship. Over the week, I keenly sensed differences between Britain and America over the subject of Iraq. Many Brits still felt guilty about the war, with much popular opposition to it. American delegates didn't give me that feeling at all though, partly because their media had shielded them from the brutality of war, partly because of loyalty to their armed forces and misinformation about what the war was really for.

I saw no light go on in anybody's eyes at having trillions of their taxes invested in a pointless war that had decimated countless Iraqi lives. America still feels itself to be a self-sufficient superpower, with no pressing need to get too close to others as others usually come to them. Importantly, many Americans also harbour deep distrust of federal government, keeping Washington at arm's length from their regional and local business. So the very concept of a centralised National Youth Orchestra appeared un-American. It was inevitable I should try and bring NYOI to the States, but this was going to take time.

Melody Welsh, Chair of the Youth Orchestra Division, welcomed me warmly to her fold, a relatively under-represented constituency, as many youth orchestras had less motivation or cash to turn up to Atlanta than I evidently did. I rode rough on my learning curve as professional outsider, deeply frustrated at the slowness, trying, failing to hold back on my opinions, making the same old mistake of breaking out in passionate analysis amid a crowd who were just trying to get to the end of the financial year in one piece. Melody and her colleague Bob, a bold and generous Texan, were at the sharp end of the youth orchestra spectrum. We could talk turkey.

Elsewhere in the conference, dynamic sessions such as marketing Gyorgy Ligeti at the New York Philharmonic, social media and fundraising kept me awake, and to be honest, what did my lot really have in common with a youth orchestra in the midwest? Their problems were light years away from mine, and trying to build bridges between us felt contrived. If NYOI ever started tackling their kinds of problems, we would know we'd reached normality.

I inevitably came across some individuals who identified themselves to me as supporters of the State of Israel, and were scanning my reaction to see if my leadership of NYOI would put me at odds with them. Since the beginning of the project, I'd slowly grown fed up with people testing me for anti-Semitism, triggered by the word 'Iraq'. That Arabs and Jews both stem from the same lineage, and are therefore both Semitic, while Kurds have nothing to do with either, is irrelevant to almost everyone. I had no interest in pointless discussions about toxic geopolitics, preferring to talk instead about how to turn 42 young musicians into an orchestra. My little Middle Eastern peace process took me as far as I could personally go. While others were content to 'like' articles posted on Facebook, I was happy enough actually doing reconciliation.

One free half-hour consultation set up by the League with a visa lawyer told me everything I needed to know about the genuine challenges of bringing NYOI to America in future. Leaving Atlanta, I felt I had broken the ice in some places, and frosted over others.

Back home in Cologne, I continued working throughout June and July as one third of our little production team, along with Karda and Nishtiman in the British Council offices in Erbil. Their main *raison d'etre* was to run English lessons and exams, which exacerbated the difficulties we already faced in creating another national youth orchestra course in a country with no context. Majid also came up from Baghdad to scout out and book the hotel and restaurants. To mitigate costs, accommodation was split between a hotel for the tutors and female players, and university accommodation for the male players. Nishtiman had already secured the Martyr Saad Palace as our venue, a huge plus for us, and asked me if I thought student accommodation would be appropriate. Of course, I said. After all, it was the same place used by American Voices when they came to Erbil for their music workshops.

What I failed to understand was the difference between how Western and Iraqi students are accommodated.

SEVEN
The wounded orchestra

I was in a good mood as everyone converged for our 2010 course at the Sunhills Hotel in Erbil, a pleasant, modern building situated next to the Erbil Civilisation Museum. The owners were in the process of installing a fire escape, as though especially for us. Sophia 'Just call me Phia' Welz, the gun-toting former police officer and youth orchestra manager would rescue us all from everything. Phia brought with her a sunny and indomitable disposition. She also brought years of no-nonsense leadership from the South African National Youth Orchestra, where young people from all backgrounds came together in a spirit of success and reconciliation. I needed to pick her brains on how they did things there, auditions, tutors, repertoire; and I also needed someone who knew how to make an orchestra flourish in a rapidly changing, non-western country. The huge difference between them and us was their years of experience in a country that loved music. I also wanted Zuhal to learn from her, and become stronger for us.

The hotel restaurant, '007', had an excellent menu and the kind of broad, black leather armchairs that a Bond villain would likely sprawl out in, plotting the downfall of some regime. Phia, Zuhal and I discussed the execution of our course over dinner. I couldn't wait to hand over the mountainous project management. Phia was a tough nut with a sassy, gum-chewing South African accent. I needed to use the little energy I had left to concentrate on the music. Yet again, months of firefighting had resulted in my utter burnout before the course had even begun. I could always fake an upbeat mood to hide my exhaustion. Yes, I should be delegating, but to whom? Who else was mad enough to do all of this?

Communication between the British Council in Erbil and the tutors over flights to Iraq had not been great. Although Angelia had refused to go from New York via Amman as a single travelling woman, she hadn't felt comfortable enough to spell the reason out, so I had to jump in and help smooth out the vicious cycle of email exchanges. As this was the first year where a complete tutor team, one for each instrument of the orchestra, was being invited from abroad, logistics and financing became a huge headache. I'd trapped myself in the middle of my creation. The Iraqi team, particularly Majid, still didn't really grasp the full scale of things, or the need to set up an organisation in Iraq to look after it.

What scared me most was the $20,000 hole in our budget. Phia arrived straight from her own youth orchestra course in South Africa. Having landed herself in the midst of this, she had to try and solve our financial shortfall while managing the orchestra. We brainstormed donations at the concert – not culturally appropriate; tickets – no box office facility and nobody would come if they had to pay to get in; busking on the street – not possible in 50 degrees Celsius and culturally unacceptable; handing out flyers in the malls – again total culture shock, and so on. I was beginning to understand why culture didn't seem to happen round here. Phia resolved to target the plentiful supply of non–governmental organisations in Erbil.

Our trump card was Tony Reilly's determination to get as much publicity for the British Council and the orchestra as possible. The Iraqi camera crews, journalists, and radio interviews were all lined up to report on us in the Martyr Saad Palace. We badly needed this coverage, as so many Iraqis either didn't know about us, or simply refused to believe we could or even should exist. Even Hugh Sykes, the BBC's Baghdad correspondent, planned to come up to Erbil to file a report for BBC World. He had already made Ranya and Frand Nashat's acquaintance, the horn and trumpet siblings, and had previously interviewed them in Baghdad.

In 2010 we kicked off our strategy, and publicity had to be the backbone if it was going to work.

The course began to creak immediately. The guys from Baghdad, numbering about sixteen and mainly violinists, turned up to the dorms that had been set aside for them, while the women and tutors checked into the hotel. They swiftly appeared at the hotel foyer, angry and let down. Murad, our first bassoon, had filmed the filthy state of the dorms on his iPhone, and was showing everyone. Toilets were broken. The place stank because excrement was smeared on the walls. Air conditioning in the 50-degree heat was haphazard or non-existent, so they would have to sleep on the roof anyway. Why hadn't we checked them out before we started? Phia talked with the British Council on the phone. It wasn't going well. 'It may not be your fault, but it's your responsibility' I overheard Phia saying.

Comparing their situation to the Mirako Hotel in Suleymaniyah last year, the Arab guys felt downtrodden, and rightly offended. Karda, from British Council office in Erbil, discussed with me what to do. Our British Council liaison, he came across as a quiet but jovial chap, tall, clean-shaven and eager to learn from our eccentric project. Standing with him in the hotel entrance, we summed it up; either they fall ill and leave the course, or they leave the course.

Karda went into overdrive, getting the dorms cleaned and repaired as much as possible overnight, installed with TVs, fridges and fans. Meanwhile, the guys spent their first evening with us in the hotel, paid for by a quick cash pool of $900 dollars from Majid and me. I felt a failure at bringing excellent and experienced violin tutors to Iraq, only to have their contribution put at risk over a question of accommodation. In the absence of any decent violin teaching, just how hungry were these musicians really to learn? After all I'd suffered to get us this far, who did they think they were? Many European national youth orchestras would be happy to live with student dorms just for the chance to play, learn and go on tour together. A young artist's lot is not glamorous, no matter where one lives, but without any experience outside Iraq, how were they to know this? And with no knowledge of the appalling state of these dorms, I didn't see what was coming.

The whole two-week residency was set to take place in the Martyr Saad Palace, a luxurious conference venue just outside the airport. The rehearsal facilities were better than most youth orchestras could ever dream of. We had ample state-of-the-art rehearsal space, air-conditioning, full security and Spectrum, a western firm, to manage the venue well. The auditorium capacity, 1300, also gave us the huge task of filling it.

Now a larger ensemble of 42 players, with many new faces, Zuhal took us through her icebreaker session for the orchestra, forcefully upbeat. We gathered together in the auditorium, players strewn across plush blue seats, somewhat wary. I presented four donated violas to the players, imported by me, Zuhal from Glasgow and Adam from London. Murad was given a good-as-new bassoon, brought over by Phia from South Africa. Herself a bassoonist, she'd sourced it through a colleague at the Kwazulu-Natal Philharmonic in Durban, who had shipped it to her in Johannesburg just in time to take with her on the plane. Last year's problem bassoon crisis had, for the time being, been laid to rest.

Fluttisimo, a flute supplier near Cologne, donated electronic metronomes for each player in the orchestra. Mike O'Donnell, Du'aa's oboe tutor from 2009, had sold me a reed-cutting machine, intended to improve her playing. I presented all of this with aplomb, hopefully to sweeten everyone up.

However, the guys from Baghdad were still unhappy with the renovated accommodation. Even after the clean-up, we still fell beneath their expectations. Some were also wounded by their new positions in the orchestra. Mohammed Salam, who had led the violas in 2009, hadn't prepared the music, and I sensed that this was a symptom of underlying discontent in Baghdad. Ilona, our new viola tutor, asked my permission to appoint a young Kurdish woman, Rezhwan, as leader, as she'd actually prepared her part. I had to agree. If the music weren't paramount, we'd lose hold of the reason for being here.

The orchestra's spirits began to slowly fall apart throughout the day. During lunch in our designated restaurant, disaffectionately christened 'Chicken Shack' by our new oboe tutor, Gwenllian, the Baghdad guys surrounded Zuhal on the baking hot pavement as she begged through her weeping for them to stay. She even agreed to move into the dorm with them. Ranya, our plucky Baghdad horn player, also confronted them through her tears. She needed teaching badly, and this course was her one oasis in a year of drought, which they now threatened to destroy.

Majid came to me before the first afternoon's full orchestra rehearsal to say he'd done everything he could, but eight of the 14 male players from Baghdad, all violinists, wanted to go home afterwards. I conducted the rehearsal coolly, without incident, slowly preparing a speech in the back of my head as we worked through Beethoven's 1st Symphony and, ironically, Iraqi composer Lance Conway's *Heartbeat of Baghdad*.

When we reached our scheduled stop at 5.30 pm, I lay down my baton and worked with our translators, Saman and Shwan, to make my last stand. This orchestra had nothing to do with Zuhal or me. NYOI was their orchestra. Its future lay in their hands. If they left now, NYOI would stop, and be near impossible to start up again. I simply wouldn't have the life force in me to keep it going after such a hiatus and the Baghdad team didn't yet have the expertise to take over. I hoped my serious concern for the bigger picture, not only for the orchestra, but also for its role in Iraq, somehow came across, especially to those who didn't directly understand me. Meanwhile, Mohammed Adnan, last year's concertmaster from Baghdad, who I'd asked to play the Mendelssohn Violin Concerto with us, remained unseen in Erbil, waiting to hear the outcome from his colleagues.

I walked off to the back of the auditorium to join the other tutors as Majid took over the stage to try one last negotiation. Helge, standing behind his clarinet students, emphatically stated that leaving the course now was totally unacceptable, as the tutors had come here during their holidays to support everyone. The discussion between Majid and the Arab players grew heated, with Murad on bassoon particularly laying in. Arguments in Arabic shot across the orchestra too fast and furious for the translators to interpret.

The Kurdish players sat bemused on stage in the middle of this maelstrom along with Burju, our second bassoonist from the National Youth Orchestra of Turkey and Stefano, our second oboist from the National Youth Orchestra of Italy. Though we remained clueless amid this barrage, we did certainly feel the rage being unleashed, the heartfelt emotion behind the voices, and we knew it was bad. Dobbs, our bass tutor from New Hampshire, looked upon the debacle. Deep from his chest he uttered: 'This is a very teachable moment.'

Indeed it was.

These were the same players who, last year, agreed that our values were love, commitment and respect, but by accepting a cost-saving solution that they should be accommodated in a dorm, I had thwarted their expectations. The orchestra faced extinction, the British Council faced a disaster and I faced a wasted year of preparation. Their press officer from Baghdad (whose name I omit for security reasons) talked quietly into his mobile, reporting the crisis blow by blow. The fun-oriented bubble of culture that I had hoped to instil in these desperately unhappy musicians had already burst. We were facing a real crisis of survival and, in so doing, were becoming Iraqi.

That evening, I poured myself an ample bath and lay in it, trying to make sense of my inner turmoil. Helge, our clarinet tutor, knocked and spoke through the hotel door:

'I've got some good news for you. The Baghdad players have decided to stay.'

'OK. That's good. Thanks,' I replied with pseudo-professional calm. I waited a few moments, up to my neck in water, then burst into tears.

The morning of day two, as we got into the taxi for Martyr Saad Palace, Phia reported that the eight violinists had indeed left the hotel for Baghdad. More significantly, the Arab guys who remained, Murad on bassoon, Samir on lead bass, Hussam on cello, Frand and Almujtaba on trumpets, were in crucial positions that simply could not be replaced in an emergency, and they, mercifully, had chosen to stay. I went into overdrive to rescue the orchestra while driving along a main road in Erbil to a rehearsal that could no longer happen. How to continue? The key lay in the Kurdish string players and Boran, our pianist who had been such a Kurdish tigress for us in 2009. Together, they had a network that could fill the eight empty seats. But how quickly, and with whom?

As soon as we arrived at Martyr Saad Palace, I met up with Boran, Zana, a violinist from Suleymaniyah, and Firman, a viola player from Ranya. With staggering level-headedness, they agreed to contact friends who could fill the seats immediately. My teeth ground themselves to dust. To blindly accept players I had to defile the sanctity of my own audition process, but I had no other option than to trust them to do things Iraqi-style. That morning, we followed our planned routine of group rehearsals, and by mid-afternoon, new faces began to appear from across the Kurdistan region, filling our empty violin seats. By the end of the third day, the violins were back up to full strength. They may not have been the star pick, but they could play, and appreciated the support given by our violin tutors, Angie and Joanne.

In front of the hotel, I held an emergency meeting with Angie about the Mendelssohn Violin Concerto. Our soloist, Mohammed Adnan, had left with the other eight violinists. We looked at the three options: to coach Zana Jalal, our concertmaster, to play it; to replace the Mendelssohn with Beethoven's ballet music from *Creatures of Prometheus*, whose overture we had performed last year; or for her to relearn the Mendelssohn from her Juilliard days and perform it with us. She went for the last option before I even finished saying it. I felt relief we were going for the safest and best decision. I knew her for her supreme confidence, generosity and talent. Nobody earned their fee when things went well, but rather when things went wrong. This tight situation was why she was here.

This whole experience irrevocably defined us; confronted with unforeseen values and expectations, we had stared into the abyss together, and the orchestra had healed itself from within. More profoundly, the fury of Zuhal after we'd recovered from shock, shared by Majid, led to the banning of these same eight players from future NYOI courses. We couldn't work with people who walked out when they didn't like what they found. Planned visits abroad were way too important and expensive to carry such a liability with us. This early tipping point also gave the Kurds a significant foothold in the orchestra that the Arabs would never regain.

In the evening of our third day, Zuhal, Phia and I went shopping in the massive basement supermarket of the Majidi Mall in Erbil. As we walked through the check-out, who should we see coming in but the eight violinists who'd left the course. Zuhal, her home county English now a gleaming scimitar of wrath, sliced through their moment of recognition: 'I hope you're enjoying Baghdad, guys'. Without a further glance of acknowledgement, she marched with Phia and me out of the mall. We never saw them again.

Finally, we had settled down to a daily routine of group and full orchestra rehearsals, individual lessons, chamber music and conducting classes. The players had never in their whole lives had so many qualified or motivated teachers empowering them with so much talent and compassion.

This year, a number of important observers were present. Karl-Walter, the Chair of the new German Friends of NYOI in Cologne, had flown in under his own steam to find out about us first hand. For someone who had just adopted this role, his commitment far exceeded my expectations. I had learnt that lunch and dinner at 'Chicken Shack' across the road was my theatre of politics. As I moved from table to table with Saman or Shwan in tow to translate for me, we could head off future crises, check the morale and help everyone settle down. Compared to last year, most players were much less suspicious, trusting we were only here for the music, and so we relaxed more quickly into a routine. As Karl-Walter watched me working, the word 'Herculean' came to him, and a key turned in his mind to engage much more deeply with us in future.

Our second observer, the British Council media liaison, told me his story. In order to work for the British in Baghdad's International Green Zone, he had to leave at five every morning, take a taxi to a certain point, change into another taxi to reduce the risk of being followed and queue for three hours to get through the three security checkpoints at the gates. He arrived at the office at ten o'clock. His apartment overlooked a railroad track where the local militia regularly executed people with a bullet to the head, and left the bodies to be run over. Anyone caught moving the corpses was executed too. Baghdad had descended into 1920s gangland Chicago: Mafioso, violent, paranoid. I slowly realised that Baghdad's residents engaged in a daily battle to maintain even the slightest level of dignity. This was the home our Baghdad violinists had returned to.

Our third observer, Gill Parry from Edinburgh, came to film. She'd produced both music and Iraq documentaries before, and seemed perfect for us. To my relief, she arrived in Erbil just after the blowout with the Baghdad players. Gill went straight to work, filming me with our singer, Tara Jaff, who had just flown in from London. Tara, a living Kurdish legend and self-taught harpist, clearly felt nervous at never having worked with an orchestra before, so we sat down with each other in her room, Gill's camera ready to roll, and talked through the two songs I'd orchestrated for her, *Qaflechi* and *Chang*. It was so important for me to have an Iraqi language sung on stage, to help define who we were. Though reassuring this legend felt rather odd, Tara herself had what I sorely needed: a sense of wisdom and wonder, a feeling for the players, for her country, to help me bridge the gaps of my understanding. However, she wasn't the only wise old soul.

As rehearsals built up a head of steam, Dobbs, our bass tutor, became utterly worshipped by his two students, Chia from Ranya and Samir from Baghdad. Equally enthused by them, Dobbs used the ample rehearsal time to give each one intensive individual lessons. When we met outside his rehearsal room, he quietly declared Chia to be the most physically gifted student he'd ever met, picking up in 30 minutes what his American students could take six months to learn.

In the background, Chia beavered away at his bass, dark eyes on fire. Even without a common language, their understanding bordered on love. Dobbs summed it up beautifully: 'Paul, the most important thing for music students is not what I thought;

a nice school and regular lessons. It's a driving will to learn and become better.'

Within the first few days of the course, Samir came knocking at my door, asking to come in for meditation advice. Though I'd brought along my meditation cushion and a little rug, I hardly thought the wacko ride I'd given myself with NYOI qualified me to help someone find inner peace, but was happy to help him adopt a seated pose. He delighted in even that. In these intimate moments, I found it hard to reconcile my relatively humble status in the West with that of lifestyle leader to young Iraqis who had more resilience than I had at their age.

Samir was a comfortable, stocky 27-year-old with a gentle nature. In his day job, he was a medical service engineer, but once a month, he played bass with the Iraqi National Symphony Orchestra in Baghdad, a generously paid position from the Ministry of Culture. Some prodigiously talented young adults wouldn't stand for being told how to improve, but Samir opened his soul up to Dobbs as disciple to guru, and took on board the culture and insights of a great bassist. He discovered a new relationship with his instrument, and I could only describe his presence during rehearsals as 'live'. At my conducting classes, he instantly delivered a rich, Mahlerian sound with a natural musicianship oozing out of him. Samir epitomised a young Iraqi who, with very little support, had fostered his innate musicality in an environment that was out to kill it, and even him.

In one quiet moment between rehearsals, I collected myself next to our supply of bottled water. Presently, a Kurdish member of the hall's staff, an elderly gentleman, sat down next to me. In a gesture of genuine warmth, he told me how proud he was of what we were doing. The music was, however, so foreign to Kurds, he found it hard to relate to our world of sound. I knew we existed in a rarefied bubble, and our players had entered into a love of classical music with precious little support or context at home. It didn't get more pioneering, or exhausting, than this.

After our traumatic first week, my brain, already fried from a year of unpaid preparation, could barely stagger on. The new tutors, coming fresh out of their Western careers, showed little grasp of this, largely as I chose not to waste my energy complaining. The pot boiled over when Helge pushily suggested the orchestra should experience another style of conductor, namely himself, to see how that would work out. He had not understood that many players, particularly strings, could not yet read basic conducting patterns, thus my need to keep advanced issues such as conducting styles out of their way and open their ears and eyes to each other. I mustered all my strength to diplomatically fend him off while holding back the desire to throttle him.

Our free Friday arrived as an oasis to recharge and de-escalate course tensions. Karda at the British Council office in Erbil arranged a bus to take us to the town of Shaklawa in the mountains. We could finally be tourists. Well, most of us. What he'd billed as a stroll up a hill to see a famous Christian hermit's cave, became a hilarious exercise in humiliating unfit Brits. We all set off from the car park at the base of the trail, quickly realising we had the wrong shoes, the wrong impression of a hill in Kurdistan and the wrong time of day to handle the heat. We certainly demonstrated our resilience with varying degrees of success, stopping at rock outcrops along the way to 'sit down' and 'take a selfie'. Our youthful gaze followed a diminishing blob of white hair steaming upwards along the winding mountain path. This was Dobbs who, in his seventies, was still running marathons, and taking this ascent in his stride.

Once we'd reached the hermit's cave, a little disappointed the hermit was gone, we rolled exhausted back down for an evening out on the town. Like much of Iraq, Shaklawa only came alive at night when the temperature dropped enough to go out. Walking through streets electrified by people and noise, we felt like salmon swimming upstream. Neon competed with bling assailing us from all sides. Clothes racks lined the pavements, hanging brilliant pinks, sequined greens and vile yellows spilling over into cafes with sizzling kebabs and fruit cocktails. Electronics and grocery shops vied for the attention of shisha shoppers.

Three of the tutors, Dave, Andy and Nick, found a rooftop shisha garden and planted themselves for the evening, drawing on last year's ritual in Suleymaniyah's Amsterdam Café of ordering apple and pineapple flavoured water pipes. Ordering one-apple got you green, ordering two-apple got you red; or was it the other way round? Phia, Angie and I spied an Iraqi sweet shop, wall to wall with thickly packed nougat in cellophane. Turkish Delights appeared in various guises: pink, green, white all competing vividly for our child-like attentions. Much of the ware, however, lay in multi-coloured ropes of soft sugar on the counter, purporting various flavours. Like barbecued snakes in a rodeo, these were lifted over a chopping board and sliced into bite-sized chunks with scissors and packed to order. Phia wielded her pack of dried figs triumphantly at my video camera, and we returned to Erbil, having somehow survived week one.

EIGHT
Turning the key to Germany

We entered the second week of rehearsals with a surreal sense of achievement. Throughout the course, Dobbs had been gently pestering me to help him get a Kurdish translation of a short story he'd written for his solo bass act, and wanted to test it in front of the orchestra. This would be paired with a story in Arabic he'd already performed in rural concerts throughout Afghanistan, illustrated by various plucking and sawing sounds from his instrument. Saman and Boran eventually obliged, though they still had to use the Arabic for "beaver" – qunfuz – as the animal didn't exist in Kurdish, and recorded the story for him to learn for his show.

As we filled the multi-coloured seats in the Martyr Saad Palace's smaller auditorium, Dobbs mounted the stage with his bass, specially retuned for the event, and performed a Bach cello suite. Silence: we fell transfixed, transported by this intimate sphere of sound glowing around him, expanding within each of us. After the last note, he paused, and casually asked, 'Did you feel something?' Then followed his Arabic story, obviously hilarious to those Arab speakers present, ending with a huge cheer from them. Samir particularly raised the roof, his heart clearly singing the joy of having Dobbs in his life. Finally, the Kurdish story lit up the Kurdish players' faces as much because a foreigner had performed in their dialect, Sorani, as anything else. He earned another massive cheer. So Dobbs, this Father Christmas figure from New Hampshire, bound us under his spell and opened up a pathway of possibilities to the players.

The orchestra's spirits were now high, and the playing strong. Around 10.00 pm that same evening, our cello tutor, Dave Edmonds, received a knock on his bedroom door. Hussam, our lead cellist, beckoned him out, promising a surprise. He led Dave across the hallway into another room where, set up in a line, all six cellos smiled back, awaiting an impromptu group rehearsal. What could Dave do in the face of such motivation, other than to oblige?

Nurtured by our tutors under better conditions, the chamber music workshops developed much more strongly than in 2009, with a Mozart divertimento and a Haydn wind trio among the works now under our belt. Phia sourced a local school with a decent theatre where I could bundle the various ensembles into Iraq's first ever kids' concert. We wanted this so incredibly badly, not just for the local schools, but to show the players what a little local initiative and hard work could achieve after the course had ended.

After our morning run-through in the theatre, we hit a situation. One school had arrived on time, the other would arrive about an hour late. With an auditorium half full of restless 10-year-old boys needing to be entertained until we could officially begin, I ushered Adam, our percussion tutor, on stage to start some clapping games with them. In slow, clear English, he introduced the first game, and immediately got cheeky answers back in English from the kids. They were great, so responsive and alive. Once he'd run dry, I sprang up to do African singing games, followed by three of the Kurdish players striking up some folk music on a daff, violin and clarinet. Gill stood in one corner with her camera on a tripod, soaking it all up for the documentary, while Majid sat on the floor in another, desolate. Again, I felt his sense of loss that we weren't doing this in Baghdad. He told me in hoarse tones how he wished for these concerts to happen all over Iraq. Again, he found himself in pain at the lost years of Iraqi culture.

When the second school of boys finally piled in and seated themselves, Boran moderated our programme in Kurdish, taking the kids through Mozart, Haydn and Bizet, but also Tara Jaff's two songs, *Qaflechi* and *Chang*, with our strings backing her. Of course, the kids delighted in Dobbs' Kurdish fairy-tale. Ilona, our viola tutor, performed a solo viola piece by a female Polish composer, responded to by our first cello, Awder, performing a traditional Kurdish song on her instrument.

The power of two women performing to a theatre full of 10-year-old boys in Iraq felt quite extraordinary. Our biggest leap of faith came from Sarah, our horn tutor, with Ranya, our first horn, who played a duet together. Ranya's first solo exposure in public, supported by Sarah, gave her the confidence to know she could take bolder steps in future if she wanted. Afterwards, she told Sarah she wanted to found an army of female horn players in Baghdad. Throughout our concert, Boran's moderation shone with cool from start to finish, talking to the kids as though they did this together every week, even though Zuhal pointed out that we more likely appeared to come from another planet.

Although Ranya dressed like an American teenager, she could only look this way in public with her younger brother Frand's permission. Under many societal restrictions, quite how she picked up the most difficult instrument in the orchestra, the horn, and worked out how to play it herself, remains a mystery to us, in part due to her famously nebulous answers. As a woman in the Iraqi National Symphony Orchestra, she certainly wasn't getting much help from her older male colleagues. Nevertheless, she had a decent compensator, an older, lighter predecessor of the modern horn, and had hit it off with Sarah, who I knew would empower her. At the beginning of the course, her prejudices towards Kurds were clear; she considered them just plain stupid. By the end of the course however, she was completely won over, as they had effectively rescued her only chance to get real teaching. The truth remained inescapable to all. Without competent players from the whole of Iraq, this youth orchestra simply could not exist.

The women of NYOI held us together in many ways. Adam, our percussion tutor, had decided with me to choose Boran as Iraq's first female timpanist. Though a pianist in our 2009 course, her musicianship and perfect English made her an impressive student. Meanwhile, Zuhal worked alongside Phia to run the course and receive mentoring, but I sensed her disappointment at not being able to play piano with the orchestra this year, as none of the compositions required it. I determined to fix this for 2011. Annie Melconian, whose letters of reference Angie and I would soon write for her scholarship to the University of Wisconsin Madison, took over leading the orchestra as the Baghdad representative at the front of the violins. This singular act of courage would likely lead to harassment from her male colleagues back in the Iraqi National Symphony Orchestra in Baghdad. Without complaining, she shared this role with Kurdish violinist Zana, though nobody else in NYOI could remotely compare to her strength and discipline.

She talked movingly to BBC's Hugh Sykes about the composition, *Heartbeat of Baghdad*: 'In the beginning, the *Heartbeat of Baghdad* reminds us of the past, a bitter-sweet thing. And then you find all the instruments getting louder, just like the torment and the troubles in Iraq. All these things that Iraq went through, it's all in it. But there is still peace, there is still hope. Yea.'

Since last year, we had got to know Annie better, and she shone out: a principled, tough, well-schooled Iraqi Armenian with perfect English, she was born to lead us. In contrast to her mutinous colleagues from the Iraqi National Symphony Orchestra, she still hungered for new insights from our two violin tutors, Joanne and Angie. The women in the cello section, Tuqa from Baghdad, Awder from Suleymaniyah and Sabat from Erbil proved endlessly positive and attentive. Sabat's sister, Saween, a modest violinist, transfixed everyone with her incredible voice. Incanting deep Kurdish sorrow without a trace of Western vibrato, the filigree butterflies emanating from her glottal twists and turns fluttered straight onto our stomachs. Our new viola leader, Rezhwan, had turned up fully prepared and very able to keep the lads in the violas under her thumb, while Ilona tutored them. They were a sound double act. Our first oboe, Du'aa, Majid's daughter, explained her life in Baghdad during an interview with the Royal Overseas League magazine, *Overseas:*

'I'm a girl and I play music, and some people think it's not really appropriate for our culture. There was a time when I couldn't tell people I'm a musician. I still have to talk to the person and find how open-minded he or she is, so I can say 'I play music, I play in an orchestra'.

With NYOI, she found herself in heaven, not only with Gwenllian as her exclusive teacher, but also sitting right next to Stefano from the National Youth Orchestra of Italy. A completely schooled young professional, he'd been working with Riccardo Muti in Milan a week before arriving in Iraq. The European Federation of National Youth Orchestras had sourced him for us along with Burju from Turkey. We flew her in from Istanbul to play second bassoon alongside Murad from Baghdad, and it slowly became apparent why Murad was not rebelling with his colleagues: as well as now owning a decent bassoon, he and Burju were falling in love.

Emboldened by the kids' concert, we embarked on another adventure through Majid, who had connected with the Institute of Scientific Research outside Ankawa, Erbil's Christian quarter. The day before our concert in Martyr Saad Palace, we all arrived around 5.00 pm, to meet the tech support and set up for rehearsal and performance in their substantial garden.

The lighting engineer had come and gone, leaving a bunch of floods hanging around the circular iron frame of the concrete bandstand, upon which we would play. It took a few seconds to work out there wasn't enough light, but Phia had come prepared with a box load of LED bike lamps to attach to the music stands so everyone could read their music.

The sound engineer stood at his mixing desk so that Tara's voice and harp could be amplified. He set up the desk firmly to one side of the orchestra, which would have worked had there been enough microphone cable to reach Tara. As there wasn't, we politely suggested he move the desk nearer to her. This he did grudgingly and disappeared into the evening, not to be seen again. I told Tara to pack her harp back up and relax for the rest of the event. Occasionally, the floodlights surrounding us burst into desolate fireworks, one right over my head, as we rehearsed. Clearly, no one had worked out the circuit load. LED bike lamps clung valiantly to the music stands as the evening closed in on our rehearsal.

Around seven, the audience, about 350 invited guests, assembled on plastic garden seats on the grass. Among them sat Katharina von Hodenberg from Beethovenfest in anticipation, fresh from Germany, our future in her hands. Karl-Walter stayed close to her, to keep the opportunity on track. Gwenllian, hard-wired to be helpful, suggested that she use Gill's spare camera night light to point at me so the players could see the beat. Perched at my side for the whole evening, she held that lamp true and fast while Gill had a great time capturing our antics on film.

We began the concert properly around eight, NYOI totally unfazed by the makeshift set up, increasing gusts of wind and unabated heat. After all, they'd done outdoor concerts in Iraq before, and this was comparatively well organised by their standards. Pages of music started wrestling themselves free from clothes pegs clinging tenuously to music stands. The band played on. Angelia Cho mustered all her considerable class to pull off the Mendelssohn Violin Concerto in dry 47-degree Celsius heat. We battled through the Beethoven, triumphantly nailing the tricky opening to the last movement, before rounding off in a rapturous finale.

To the Iraqi listeners, we were wonderful, to the tutors, a bit of a disaster. And Phia? Phia was missing. No matter. Tired but exhilarated, the orchestra assembled in the institute car park and, in the absence of any transport onwards, celebrated. Through the pitch-black night, flashing iPhones, drums and clarinets wailing though the night, a fantastical orgy of dance, whooping and raw guttural joy ripped through us all. One player pointed the headlights of his Range Rover at our birling dervish. The unearthly tungsten glare set our laughter and shadows on fire. Place an Iraqi on the edge of hell and he'll still throw a party.

Katharina von Hodenberg looked on, still and thoughtful, outwardly unmoved by the frenzy which I, as resident alpha, had thrown myself into. 'Pol Pol Pol Pol!' they chanted into the circle, guys dancing with guys in unadulterated macho revelry, Tuqa ululating in ultra-soprano. Katharina caught my eye, and I went over to assure her that this evening was a trial by fire, and we had passed it. Diplomatically, she agreed.

From nowhere, buses arrived and we all clambered precariously in. Phia was working behind the scenes. Our ramshackle spontaneity flowed onwards and we ended up, 15 minutes later, in a restaurant for dinner, sponsored by the Institute, and sat down to eat. But when the tutors were allowed beer and the players not, the orchestra staged a walkout, with Katharina, Karl-Walter and I swiftly following in sympathy. Some other players had gone on to the water park for another restaurant, so I asked for some dinners to be packed up in bags to take with me.

The Institute director and restaurant owner politely petitioned me to understand that this was not their fault. By this time, I'd lost track of who was saving whose face, so I charmingly agreed with them, and left. With just 24 hours before the final concert, we were on the verge of falling apart again. Crammed into the buses, I caught most of the tutors and asked them to start pumping up the orchestra's morale. After considerable debate, off the buses went to the water park which, on arrival, was shut.

We arrived at the car park at midnight. There sat the group who had arrived ahead, forlorn and hungry. They sat down on the grass with the bags of food I'd picked up in the restaurant and began to eat. Thankfully, the car park was floodlit, but now the whole orchestra, tutors, and Katharina von Hodenberg were stranded in the middle of the night in Erbil, with no Phia in sight and no exit plan. She'd spent the whole two weeks trying to manage the orchestra and raise $25,000 to close the budget, a challenge that no-one could realistically take on cold. We stood around in clusters and tempers began to flare.

As my mobile phone had no reception, I borrowed Ranya's and phoned Phia to order buses to take us back to the hotel and dorm. She got straight on the case. Joanne twice demanded to know if we were just going to stand here in the car park, and I reassured her, twice, that buses were on the way. Dave and

Ilona started chasing each other around the car park for fun, their notion of boosting morale. Katharina stood apart. 'Eckelhaft,' she said. Disgusting. As the buses finally arrived to take us back, Joanne's husband cornered me: 'I know it's not your fault. But it doesn't have to be like this, you know. It doesn't have to be like this.' I stood there in front of him, dazed and beaten as the large frame of Majid stomped towards one of the arriving buses in utter malcontent.

Given what we were trying to do and where we were doing it, how else could this be? In our second year, we had a brilliant tutor team, stellar rehearsal facilities, an excellent concert venue and strong musical contributions from Lance Conway, Tara Jaff and Angie Cho. We had already taken a huge step from 2009. Phia and I put ourselves under immense stress to keep everything in place, though neither of us could make particularly good decisions at the end of two exhausting weeks in Erbil. I felt it vital that we protect ourselves from burnout in future.

Back in the hotel foyer, as everyone settled down to the night before the concert, Zuhal, Phia and I huddled in the corner, their slender forms swallowed by the luxury leather armchairs. I reached out and held the arm of each. 'We just have to get through the next 24 hours,' I calmly uttered, holding back a soul reduced to rubble inside. We were so close to claiming a second year of survival, but patterns were already emerging. Just as Allegra had become the butt of the team's anger in 2009, so had Phia this year. Neither knew the territory, both had arrived cold into a very unpredictable situation, and both were charged with delivering a national youth orchestra for which Iraq had neither the infrastructure, nor the context. No matter how well prepared, it just didn't work.

My feedback from the tutors as conductor and musical director was always very good, which is to be expected from people one has hired, and may hire again. Sometimes, the frustration that is meant for the boss ends up aimed at the subordinate, who becomes a scapegoat. In the worst case, she unconsciously senses this, and starts playing the role out. Standing under someone's shadow does indeed distort how one is viewed, ending up as a magnet for anyone's frustrations. Carl Jung called this the Shadow, where in this case the subordinate risks becoming the shadow of the boss. It can readily be seen in the partners of famous people. But in NYOI, high levels of stress and unrealistic expectations led to mistakes from all of us. In every sense, Phia's nerves were as frayed as mine. But the tutors had to vent, and she was the target.

I rallied the tutors and asked them to do whatever it took to get us through tomorrow. We'd survived mutiny, near collapse and a garden concert in 47-degree heat. The main concert in the Martyr Saad Palace was finally upon us.

Majid and I met at breakfast, and I knelt down at the table, arms folded on the edge, chin on my hands in supplication. 'I'm sorry,' I uttered. 'I'm sorry too,' he replied. We were tired and fed up. I didn't feel his words but honestly, I don't think either of us felt anything. I got up off my knees and went to another table. The rotund figure of Majid, his role, his very person, was something I found hard to relate to. We were bound by one nebulous ideal: the importance of this orchestra to young Iraqi musicians. For his daughter, Du'aa, who loved her oboe lessons, and many others who had been struggling with music for years, it was essential that NYOI hold together.

Over the worst, the orchestra now arrived in an orderly fashion at the entrance of the Martyr Saad Palace. We'd got used to the daily routine of guards frisking and scanning us. One was obviously so amused by my weary compliance he burst out laughing as I stood in the metal detector and guffawed 'MICHAEL JACKSON!' While doing nothing to lift my spirits, it was at least cute. Onwards to the auditorium, two plain-clothes minders sat in the back row today as on every day, ready to shoot potential attackers.

Gill Parry had hired a local firm to record and amplify the orchestra for her documentary. They were clearly more familiar with rock concerts. Though only Tara Jaff, our Kurdish singer, needed amplification for her voice and harp, it took me a while to persuade the two sound technicians that the orchestra was playing acoustically in the auditorium, and didn't need their help.

I couldn't for the life of me work out how they were planning to mix anybody live from the position of their sound desk backstage.

The orchestra felt settled as our general rehearsal passed without incident, and when we prepared backstage, I could taste the familiar excitement shared by all youth orchestras before a concert. The guys looked great in their black bow ties and dinner jackets, the young ladies elegant in concert black. Trial by fire, great coaching and willpower had fused us again into an orchestra of improbable musicians, led by this unlikely Scot.

Introduced by Tony Reilly, Director of British Council Iraq, and Dr Barham Salih, Prime Minister of the Kurdistan Region, who had plugged our $25,000 shortfall at the last minute, the concert began with Lance Conway's *Heartbeat of Baghdad*, Majid with us on stage playing a Raq. This looked and sounded like a big tambourine to me, to which Adam later retorted, 'I would never dream of calling a viola a violin'. That was me put in my place.

Then, Tara Jaff entered with her Celtic harp to sing *Qaflechi* and *Chang*, using a simple string arrangement I'd written to help them create the warm sound they so lacked. She kept Sherwan behind her, in the violas, playing his daff throughout to keep her rooted in the ensemble. Tara's pure, mellow voice rang out in Hawrami Kurdish, as though her sense of spirit were soaring above her people's suffering.

To close the first half, Angie came on in a striking blue dress to play the Mendelssohn Violin Concerto. A very tough piece for the orchestra, they mastered the balance and style after two solid weeks rehearsing with us both. Her eye caught Dr Barham's jaw dropping on the front row as her poised performance unfolded. Nothing like this had ever happened in Erbil before.

Next, the fiendish opening of Beethoven's First Symphony that had laid many a professional band flat, launched our second half. Like the course itself, Beethoven was forcing us to walk a musical tightrope. Zuhal, sitting in the auditorium, likened us to 'little balls of energy' as we tore through his music. After two weeks of steady coaching, I finally felt I could let rip with my conducting and bring us to a new level.

Afterwards, I numbly sat through the British Council reception, letting the event speak for itself. The British Ambassador and Consul General appeared delighted at the evening's political and cultural result. Allegra Klein, now based in Baghdad, made a brief appearance backstage, sheepishly uttering one single word: 'Congratulations'.

The Prime Minister's office arranged that everyone could stay one evening longer in Erbil, so we could all come to his residence for a garden party the evening after the concert. Finally beginning to rest, the orchestra and tutors spent an easy day together in the August heat, as Katharina von Hodenberg from Beethovenfest returned to Germany to report.

That evening, piled up like Keystone Cops in our trusty minibuses, we trundled off down the road towards Dr Barham Salih's private residence outside Erbil. Darkness had already descended when our escorting cars pulled us over onto the side of the road to await the go-ahead to arrive. Some 15 minutes later, we were issued onwards, and pulled into a car park at the head of the entrance to his official residence, a villa with a splendid garden and swimming pool. There to meet us was Mohammed Qaradaghi, our government contact from last year. Through the garden archway we filed, shaking hands and wishing a good evening in Kurdish, 'Ewrat bash', to the line of welcoming officials.

The perfect buffet dinner of meats and salads, Transylvanian wine and white garden loungers felt like just reward for a remarkable two weeks, and yet another unlikely concert of young musicians from across Iraq. Dr Barham switched jovially from English to Arabic to Kurdish with the players and tutors, but I started to notice, as the key to the orchestra and an unknown quantity, he was avoiding me. We soon found ourselves in each other's proximity, and as if the Red Sea were parting, the players standing between us stepped out of the way to ensure we made eye contact. He faltered for a split second then asked: 'Tell me, how do you like Kurdistan?'

A fair question to ask a visitor, I froze as the past two years flashed in front of my eyes. All the misery, hardship and running around Europe, and then head down through the course, floored

me for a decent answer. I hadn't exactly taken in the sights as
a tourist would, but being in a country as homophobic as Iraq
left me reticent about doing so. I blurted out something about
the black shaggy goats Angie and I had encountered on the road
through the desert back in 2009, and saw he was hoping for
something better. We juggled with each other for a few more
sentences, rescuing each other a little, trying to unlock a better
dialogue, but it was too late. The brain was fried, and I could
do no more. I managed to say one intelligible thing, our plans
to visit Germany next year, and the colour drained from his face.
I knew at that moment, our sole supporter in Iraq was gone.
We smiled at each other politely and the Red Sea of guests closed
back in and swallowed the conversation, and the remains of my
ego, up with it.

Later that night, in front of the hotel, the orchestra partied
one last time. Frand looped his favourite riffs on his trumpet,
which he called 'My Lady,' while Kurdish percussion rattled
through the night. As he jived on the hotel steps, streetlights
flashing across the brass tubing briefly mirrored his own name's
ancient Arabic meaning: Frand – a star-shaped glint of the sun
in the blade of a sword. This was the right instrument for him.
Dave, our cello tutor, spun round and round with Frand and
Waleed on the pavement before being accosted by several players
who tossed him into the air several times. These extraordinary
young musicians had done something that nobody else in Iraq
had ever come close to, and they knew it.

Annie Melconian summed it all up in an interview: 'To the
people of Iraq, to the politicians of Iraq, I want them to think
like musicians. On the stage, there are some Kurdish, Arab,
Armenian, Assyrian, who all come from different backgrounds,
different languages. Maybe some people have disputes between
them; maybe. But even if there is something, on stage we all
have the same goal, making beautiful music, making people love
music or to forget everything about anything outside of the
concert hall, and just concentrate and feel the music.'

If we stayed in Iraq, we could symbolise Annie's idealism until
our luck ran out, which was soon. However, the moment we

went abroad we would become a maverick diplomat, one that may decide not to come home, as many had done before. More significantly, the Kurdistan Regional Government had already changed its strategy from supporting the whole of post-war Iraq to focusing only on the Kurdistan Region, a response to the intransigent federal government in Baghdad. Our symbolism did not, in any shape or form, fit this change. Still, knowing the sorry state the players were in, I made a promise to them in the Martyr Saad Palace: 'I've got to get you out of Iraq.'

Next year we would set ourselves to become the best cultural diplomats Iraq had seen for 5000 years.

NINE
That's what friends are for

Katharina von Hodenberg had indeed green-lighted our 2011 visit to Beethovenfest. We faced a mountain of challenges. Back from Iraq, Karl-Walter and I reassembled with the recently formed German Friends of NYOI, a Verein.

A Verein is basically a club with charitable status to raise its own money, tax free, for a non-religious or non-political cause and possibly also to implement projects. That the orchestra remained a nebulous adhocracy was no problem. A Verein could simply support the idea of something. There are countless thousands of Vereins across Germany: tennis clubs, choirs, social causes, local projects, which legally require a minimum of seven members including a Chair. Ours was retired school teacher Karl-Walter Keppler, alongside our Vice-Chair, retired lawyer Will Frank and a treasurer, the founder Georg Witteler. Vereins are the lifeblood of Germany: nowhere else can you find more legal actions between individuals and organisations. This is part of the fun, a paradise for ego-tripping, petty politics and playing out neuroses in the name of the greater good.

Our little Verein wasn't quite as bad as that, yet. It felt at home in Georg Witteler's cosy living room. The meetings always began jovially, surrounded by Georg's own highly colourful digital collages printed on glass at great expense. We frequently began with brunch or offerings of homemade soup and bread at the dinner table, where we chatted casually about the Cologne Mafia and such. Duly sated, we adjourned to the lounge. I took the path of minimum interference: there was too much else to do. Sitting in on these meetings around coffee and cake, observing the team spirit being forged through deep discussions then unravelled by personal frictions made me wonder where this was all going to end. In truth, both Beethovenfest and the German Friends found themselves in uncharted waters. We knew basically what had to be done, it was just that it had never been done before: to raise money, about €350,000 of it, and get European Schengen visas for an entire orchestra from Iraq, one goal being intimately bound to the other.

Karl-Walter, the one member of the Verein sitting around coffee and cake who had actually been to Iraq, acted differently from the others. Although the oldest in the room, he was clearly the most driven. A white-haired walrus of a man and retired high school teacher of History and English, he'd mounted many exchange visits for students to America. While he stayed with us in Erbil, the challenges we faced lit him up from within. Everyone fell in love with our players, at best so outrageously open, passionate and happy to be together, but their experience as musicians in the midst of conflict moved Karl-Walter the most. And from this place, his imperious chairmanship navigated the others through their doubts and fears.

Two things were clear to us all. The Iraqis were still not ready to produce a course like the ones I had built, and the financial onus for 2011 lay on Germany. However, the German Friends had started well with a cash injection from the Goethe Institut of €15,000, some of which went towards paying for my work over the next eight months: a pittance but better than nothing. I managed to conjure up donations from the British Institute for the Study of Iraq and Gulfsands Petroleum.

Now, I had two bowling balls to juggle, Beethovenfest in 2011 and the UK visit, which I aimed for 2012. I felt sure that the British Iraqi Friendship Society would play a key role in the UK visit, so The German Friends booked my flight to London and sent me off to their Annual Christmas Dinner in the Royal Garden Hotel, Kensington, to dig for gold.

It was 17th December 2010, the afternoon before the dinner. The cold air and distant sun set me up for eager gains. I decided it was a good time to gatecrash the offices of the Iraqi British Business Council, chaired by Baroness Nicholson of Winterbourne. I'd sent e-mails to no effect, which left them with no choice but to receive an unannounced visit from me. They had an office suite in Whitehall, along from the Palace of Westminster, where earthy streets hark back to 19th century London and civil servants pep up their impatient careers with yuppie panache.

Their street entrance, a modern glass door with pin code access, stood between them and me. Just as someone was popping out for lunch, I slipped in with a smile. Entering the Iraqi British Business Council, all was stillness: austere classical décor, clean and void like a showroom. There I found a young Irishman, Mark Duffy, holding the fort. My unannounced visit surprised him, and the direct address, 'Hi. My name's Paul MacAlindin, Musical Director of the National Youth Orchestra of Iraq' created the required shock and awe to tailspin my way further down the corridor.

He ushered me into a beautiful meeting room and left me alone to study a collection of old maps of Iraq, Kurdistan and Mesopotamia. I slowly walked round these imperial parchments, rooted in some ongoing historical struggle to make sense of terrain, sometimes detailed, sometimes uncharted. The scale and proportions were bizarre, perhaps a mixture of ignorance and pragmatism to suit the needs of the reader. I also sensed passionate enquiry, a stylish intent to precisely reveal the mysteries not only of Iraqi landscapes, but the souls that identified with them. These misshapen metaphors mapped my own inner landscape, forming but uninformed. I felt like a naïve, gung-ho 19th century Brit, interceding in a foreign land that still reeked of war. Mark came back in. We sat down.

I told our story as he took notes, glancing from notepad to table top and back again with studied intensity. As my tale unfolded, I tried to glean what he was thinking. When we had finished, he leaned back in his chair and said he would report our meeting. He was very impressed, he told me. I thanked him, and we parted company.

That evening, the British Iraqi Friendship Society Annual Christmas Dinner took place at the Royal Garden Hotel, Kensington Gardens. The most successful, influential Iraqis in London attended this function and I found myself at a table with other artists and foundations connected with Iraq. Most people were friendly and open, willing to swap business cards and chat. Some came directly up and asked who I was. I knew this definitely wasn't an orchestra conference.

The famous author, Lord Jeffrey Archer showed up, looking rather old and worn, a handsome young assistant circling him. The British Iraqi MP Nadhim Zahawi made a clear, dynamic address. A solitary Middle Eastern man dressed in his long white thawb and headdress sat alone at his own table for 12 in the corner. Security firm reps, energy companies with their trade fair displays, diplomats from the Kurdistan Regional Government and board members of the British Iraqi Friendship Society were rubbing shoulders in the ballroom of over 200 people. After dinner, a red-faced, red-clad Master of Ceremonies got us to our feet as we thrice toasted 'God Save the Queen!' I sat with one of the directors, Eric Le Blan from Merchant Bridge Investments, and we talked about the orchestra coming to Britain. The Society had to play a key role. I could see no other way.

We also needed a solution for our visas. In 2010, an Iraqi applying for a visa had to fly to Amman, stay in a hotel for about a week, wait to be called for a screening interview, hand in his visa application, wait another 21 days, and receive an answer. Applying alone cost thousands. Royal Jordanian had monopolised the Baghdad to Amman flight. If you were in the Kurdistan region, you used to have the choice to throw your money at a visit to the Consulate in Damascus. The Foreign and Commonwealth Office explained that Amman was a regional visa hub, streamlining processes to save money. Iraqis believed it was set up to keep them out of the UK, screening out the poor and preventing them from staying illegally or engaging in terrorism against an aggressor.

Back in Cologne, the German Friends wanted results. I didn't happen to have a sponsor in my pocket, and building reputation with this network would take a while. Of course, I could only lobby while the real decisions happened behind closed doors. We had to be patient.

Soon, I received an e-mail from the Iraqi British Business Council. 'Baroness Nicholson of Winterbourne requests the pleasure of the company of Paul MacAlindin to a reception on Wednesday 19th January, 2011, at the House of Lords.'

They had taken note.

The New Year turned and we faced the familiar uncertainty of our coming summer course. I faced a huge amount of administration alone while the German Friends worked at the money issue. Armed with a fresh range of burgundy ties and shirts, the German Friends organised my flight to London. Naturally, I stayed over at Alan and Mark's in Leyton who, over the ironing board in their Victorian flat, told me emphatically which combination I was to wear.

On 19th January, I arrived at the Palace of Westminster with my invitation to the Iraqi British Business Council's winter reception. Student demonstrations against education funding cuts were mounting outside the Palace, and the perimeter was thick with bobbies. I asked the way in, and got a brusque reply from a constable with darker things on his mind. Inside, the House of Lords was in late night session. Aged Lords taking a break from debate cast shadows along ancient corridors of power. Baroness Nicholson personally greeted everyone, clocked my reason for being there and said they would help as much as they could. She was quite a Dame, smallish and intense, her sunny face amplified by an auburn bouffant. With another pocket full of our 2009 documentary DVDs, I entered the fray to publicly relate, mercilessly, obliquely, Britishly.

Their reception took place in one of the covered terraces overlooking the Thames. As people chatted away merrily over wine and seafood canapés, including an absurdly bijou fish 'n' chips in hand-held plant pots, I exchanged away all the business cards the German Friends had printed with our new blue logo. Lord Lawson, Chancellor of the Exchequer during Margaret Thatcher's time in government, wandered in with unconvincing waves of henna hair to grab a glass of wine and listen in. Baroness Nicholson, with her trademark warmth and plum tones, announced that a large plot of land in Baghdad's green zone had been donated for IBBC's operations there. The Baroness herself is one sharp cookie. She had supported the Iraqi people in the 1990s when they had very few friends, and held them close to her heart. Twenty years later, she was spearheading UK trade there. I couldn't argue exploitation from someone who had genuinely held out for Iraq's people for so long.

There in the corner, standing tall and alone, surveying the terrain, was Andy Edwards, the burly ex-British marine who had built up Consilium Risk Strategies into a contender on the Iraqi security market. Dusty-blond, handsome, a self-declared Christian in his first breath, he was one of the few British business people to have kept up a dialogue with me from the start. Consilium already supported the reconciliation work of Reverend Andrew White, the Anglican Bishop of Baghdad, so they understood Iraq's wider needs.

One thing struck me about the evening. Those caricatures of politicians which one sees in the London press are frighteningly realistic. I shook hands with a charming young man from the Iraqi Embassy, and told him why I was here. He stared down, trying to find a diplomatic response that came out unconvincingly as yes, a good thing to have. At that moment, a couple of old men swooped in, grey suits shrouding their hunched, eager bodies, and started to make fun of the guy. They had sensed weakness, teasing him by assuming he didn't know what an orchestra was, not having a briefed response at hand, reducing his self-esteem to dust. I walked away, unsure of what to say or do, the situation suddenly embarrassing.

Mark Duffy, my first contact at the Iraqi British Business Council, was also working the room. By the time we met, my sales pitch was in full swing, handing DVDs of the orchestra out willy nilly, making him slightly wince, while my merrily lubricated 'prospects' happily played along. In spite of this, I was back among a group of people who would only budge if all the right buttons were pressed peer-to-peer at board level.

As the party faded, two delicately liveried stewards delighted in relating to me the quirks of running a smooth House of Lords. This would have passed as genteel stand-up drag comedy. Westminster was indeed run by the Stately Homos of England. Out of DVDs, out of smiles, I returned to my own stately homos, Alan and Mark in Leyton, and spent the rest of the evening telling them all about it. Back in Baghdad, my players were stealing their way through the streets, instruments concealed in carrier bags, terrorists were murdering decent Iraqis on a daily basis, and gay men like me were being kidnapped by militia, tortured to death and left on the side of the road to be eaten by dogs.

And Zuhal had shut down. The little contact I could get with her told me how miserable she'd become. Though Glasgow provided incomparably more safety than Baghdad, with it came terrible loneliness through a ridiculous workload of five advanced level exam subjects. Feeling totally disconnected to the Scottish school system, she had become a recluse. I tried to keep connecting Zuhal with friends in Scotland, and through this effort, my old friend Carol Main became the accidental catalyst for our British strategy.

It was a grey January lunchtime in Glasgow. I wasn't there, but I just knew. Carol was waiting for Zuhal in the foyer of the Royal Scottish Academy of Music and Drama in Renfrew Street. She picked up a copy of *The Scotsman* and came across a story. Within minutes, she was on the phone to me in Cologne.

The Weir Group, a Scottish construction firm had been, according to the BBC, fined three million pounds for sanctions breaches, and also had £13.9 million of illegal profits confiscated by the High Court in Edinburgh. The 'Cash Back to the Community' programme would administer the fine for the benefit of the Scottish people. However, the real victims of this crime were the Iraqi people and so, minutes after hearing from Carol, I got onto the Scottish Government. About five different departments passed me on till I finally ended up with Trevor, who got blasted by my opening line: 'What are you doing for the people of Iraq with that money?'

He chuckled and mentioned that the news had only just been released, and they were still working out what to do. I'd written to Fiona Hyslop, the Cabinet Secretary for Culture and International Affairs, begging for money back in 2010. She'd said no, but the Scottish Government had passed a motion in favour of Zuhal and the orchestra in 2009. Now that the money and the motive were potentially in place, Trevor and I began a thorough review of the orchestra's proposed visit. That Beethovenfest plans were underway only added assurance to our Scottish trajectory.

Trevor and I must have had four or five calls and much information exchange over six weeks before a final decision was announced. Fiona Hyslop agreed to include us as beneficiaries of the Weir Group fine, to the tune of £100,000. After two desolate years of fighting, we had taken one big step on the way to Scotland.

Since the end of the 2010 course, we had also been running the 2011 auditions. Throughout December, the players' videos flooded in. I asked for help from Lena Pappagianis, a young music graduate of Oberlin University who had contacted me back in 2009. Along with our tutors, our translators, Shwan and Saman, and our new network of regional representatives in Iraq, we pulled together to help move the enormous bureaucracy needed to finish the auditions on time. Speed and accuracy were tactically essential. I had to finalise our list of accepted players fast and buy Beethovenfest as much time as possible to sort out the political hornet's nest of visas.

This year's auditions now attracted 150 applicants submitting 250 videos, coming in via YouTube, e-mail and special delivery DVDs from all over Iraq to Cologne. Their quality had vastly improved since the dark days of 2009, with sharper images, better sound, and more accurate playing. Most importantly, the players sounded happier and more musical. This alone proved our efforts across Iraq were worth it. Players wanted to compete, and they trusted in our fairness. Successful players would join our four-week summer course in Erbil and Beethovenfest at no cost, free of the daily misery of terrorism, prejudice and corruption. Auditions not only tested musicianship, but also provided the taster of a fairer Iraq.

The driver behind our participation in Beethovenfest was the festival's Director, Ilona Schmiel. She had turned it into an international magnet for the most exciting names of the day. More importantly for us, she had developed the *Orchestercampus*, an annual residency in Bonn by an exotic youth orchestra, usually of very high standard. NYOI was by far her most ambitious and risky project yet, with players who I knew weren't ready for this exposure, but never would be unless somebody believed in them and got them into a better place.

Ilona knew Bonn extremely well, and could negotiate its horribly petit-bourgeois self-importance with a grounded attitude that also attracted people from across the world to her festival. Especially for NYOI, she also needed consummate political skill and relentless positivity. Even though I could sit in her office with Karl-Walter and work with them on multiple angles of the project, I personally needed her nurturing spirit and her team's vibrant professionalism to keep me going. More often than not, the German Friends' dogfighting round coffee and cake kept sucking my energy dry.

Come mid-January, Ilona Schmiel phoned me with an urgent request for the list of players and their hometowns. I sent the Excel file through to her office. The German Foreign Ministry wanted hard evidence in the next 24 hours that the orchestra contained players from the rest of Iraq and not just the Kurdistan Region, if they were to align politically with the project, and grant visas. Although Ilona had obtained the personal support of the German Foreign Minister, Guido Westerwelle, some of his minions were fighting Beethovenfest to stop the orchestra from coming.

Beethovenfest also had a media partner, Deutsche Welle. I had to somehow present them with possible Arab and Kurdish composers to commission for our concert. *Orchestercampus* usually invited a youth orchestra for one week, performing one new work in one orchestral concert. This year, they wanted NYOI in residence for two weeks, performing in Berlin and Beethovenhalle in Bonn, with both Kurdish and Arab Iraqi world premieres. Our symbolic unity was underscored by the date of the concert, 1st October, just before German Reunification Day.

My laptop was already clogged up by a large array of Iraqi compositions, few of which were worth presenting anywhere. Together, we settled on a Kurdish Iraqi composer based in Holland, Ali Authman, and the new conductor of the Iraqi National Symphony Orchestra, Mohammed Amin Ezzat in Baghdad. More importantly for Deutsche Welle, Ali Authman could walk the tightrope between an ethnic Kurdish sound and a modernist idiom that fitted their concept of our residency. I insisted on Mohammed Amin's composition because, as kitsch as I knew this would sound to sophisticated German ears, his music rang entirely true in Iraq.

I also had to suggest suitable Iraqi soloists for the concert, and present videos to Beethovenfest, among them Janaid, the concertmaster of the Iraqi National Symphony Orchestra. Unsurprisingly, Ilona Schmiel passed on all of them, and sought an international artist to work with us instead. This sent Majid up in arms. How could no Iraqi soloist be good enough for them? Indeed, they weren't. First, Ilona came back with the name of Michael Barenboim, Daniel Barenboim's son, and was immediately vetoed by Majid. If the Iraqi media found out NYOI was working with a Jewish soloist, the lives of the players would be put in danger on their return. This looked like tit-for-tat, but from what I knew of Iraq, I believed him. We already had enough work reconciling musicians from within Iraq, without adding an unnecessary layer of regional complexity to the project. As we worked through various other soloists, many of whom just didn't want to play with an Iraqi youth orchestra, Beethovenfest landed Arabella Steinbacher, a 28-year-old protégé of Anne-Sophie Mutter. She jumped at the opportunity to perform the spiritually and musically taxing Beethoven concerto with us. I added Haydn's Symphony No 104 to the programme, our 'joy' fix, and we were set.

On the 1st March, Karl-Walter and I turned up to the Cologne Chamber of Commerce's daylong seminar on doing business in

Iraq, to learn what we could. From chemical manufacture to security and construction, the delegates' overall feeling accounted for Germany's lousy competitive position there. Germans were just too risk averse, as Beethovenfest was also finding out with sponsors and visas. However, a vast number of people were still willing to rally round the orchestra's visit.

By mid-March, our Honorary Composer in Residence, Sir Peter Maxwell Davies, had donated a new piece, *Reel of Spindrift, Sky*. This seven minute long Orkney inspired work fitted our small forces perfectly. Without him even knowing the players, he'd precisely pitched to their abilities and given everyone something of challenge and interest.

Meanwhile, Dave Edmonds, our cello tutor, ran a half marathon in Cheltenham and raised £750, while the Ludwig van B. Foundation in Bonn organised a town-wide busking event amid pouring rain that raised €750 alongside a huge amount of buzz. Karl-Walter managed, after much politicking, to get €5000 out of the Rotary Club. Meanwhile, friends of mine created a Kickstarter project that, though it failed to raise any money, gave us a terrific promotional video.

Our first international recognition came on the 13th April from UNESCO, who decided to honour twenty young people with the title 'Young Artist for Intercultural Dialogue between Western and Arab Worlds'. One of these was Zuhal. Though she had a permit to stay in the UK, she couldn't get a Schengen visa in time. UNESCO called me, and I stepped in as her representative for the ceremony in Paris.

The top floor of their headquarters brimmed with a good hundred young people from across the Middle East and Europe, performing music, presenting films, networking. After nearly three years of slog, we had reached the top of someone's list. Steeped in the buzz of these young talents, I stepped up to claim the award for Zuhal. Director General Irina Bokova and the Spanish Ambassador to France seemed somewhat taken aback to see a white middle class conductor in a suit. Ironically, it was I who had written Zuhal's nomination, although somebody else had composed the citation:

Zuhal Sultan at Dr Barham Salih's garden party, 2010 (KRG)

Me in the Barony Bar, Edinburgh, where my adventure began (Markus Naegele)

Our honorary Composer-in-Residence, Sir Peter Maxwell Davies (Gunni Moberg)

The mountains of Suleymaniyah during winter

The first group photo of the National Youth Orchestra of Iraq,
August 2009 (Mike Luongo)

Me rehearsing the orchestra in Telary Hunar's seminar room, Suleymaniyah 2009
(Mike Luongo)

Sheila Browne teaching Firman Saeed viola, Suleymaniyah 2009
(Mike Luongo)

Dave Edmonds working with Hussam Ezzat, Suleymaniyah 2009
(Mike Luongo)

Partying on the bus between our hotel and the Talary Hunar Concert Hall, Suleymanyiah 2009 (Mike Luongo)

ABOVE: Mike O'Donnell, me and Mohammed Salam celebrating Boran Zaza's 18th birthday, Suleymaniyah 2009 (Mike Luongo)

RIGHT: Boran Zaza's 18th birthday party, Suleymaniyah 2009 (Mike Luongo)

The Erbil Citadel

Annie Melconian leading the orchestra, Erbil 2010 (Tariq Hassoon)

Johnny Thompson teaching Frand Nashat and Murtada Aziz, Erbil 2011
(Tariq Hassoon)

ABOVE: Duaa Azzawi performing in our children's concert, Erbil 2011 (Tariq Hassoon)

RIGHT: Duaa Azzawi and Mike O'Donnell consulting in Telary Huner, Suleymaniyah 2009 (Mike Luongo)

Our garden concert in 47 Celsius heat, Erbil 2010 (Tariq Hassoon)

LEFT: Dr Barham Salih, Prime Minister of the Kurdistan Region of Iraq, introducing 2010 concert with Zuhal (KRG)

ABOVE: Bashdar Ahmad, Sherwan Mohammed, Dr Barham Salih, Tara Jaff and Daroon Rasheed at the garden party, Erbil 2010

Dr Barham Salih, Prime Minister of the Kurdistan Region of Iraq, introducing 2010 concert with Zuhal (KRG)

Angelia Cho teaching the first violins, Erbil 2011 (Tariq Hassoon)

Daniel Agi teaching Waleed Assi, Erbil 2011 (Tariq Hassoon)

Sarah Maxwell and Ali Mahdi rehearsing, Erbil 2011 (Tariq Hassoon)

Murad Saffar and Burju Gedik together in Erbil 2010 (Tariq Hassoon)

Dougie Mitchell coaching the winds, Ministry of Culture, Erbil 2011
(Tariq Hassoon)

Our audience for the Kids Concert, Erbil, 2011 (Tariq Hassoon)

The Institute of Fine Arts, former home to Saddam Hussein's torture chamber,
Ranya 2013 (Paul MacAlindin)

Majid Azzawi and players filling in visa applications in the orchestra office,
Baghdad 2011 (Tariq Hassoon)

Zana Jalal playing Beethoven's violin concerto in rehearsal, Erbil 2011
(Tariq Hassoon)

Me and Zana Jalal, playing Beethoven's Violin Concerto in Saad Palace, 2011

Majid Azzawi, Erbil 2011 (Tariq Hassoon)

Hussam Ezzat doing the Bedouin eyes in rehearsal, Erbil 2010 (Tariq Hassoon)

Left: Chia Sultan playing bass, Erbil 2011 (Tariq Hassoon)

Above: Ali Mahdi having a break from horn, Erbil 2011 (Tariq Hassoon)

Tuqa Alwaeli, Erbil 2011 (Tariq Hassoon)

'Zuhal Sultan founded the National Youth Orchestra of Iraq at the age of 17 and has organized its activities ever since. Among these activities have been several collaborations with the Western world. Her usage of social media in founding and organizing the orchestra have been remarkable. The International Music Council had nominated Zuhal on behalf of the European Federation of National Youth Orchestras, member of the International Music Council.'

In truth, the hyperbole surrounding Zuhal was wearing thin on me and the British Council. Our sacrifice and risk-taking counted for little when the media wanted a heroine.

Meanwhile, the real work was happening elsewhere. One of our players, Hellgurd Sultan, flagged a huge problem for the Kurds. The two-week course in Beethovenfest overlapped the first two weeks of their employment as civil servants, teaching in schools throughout Kurdistan. If they were not to lose their jobs, they required special permission to fly to Germany.

I didn't really notice Hellgurd when I first met him in 2010. A viola player from the small town of Ranya, he appeared slight and rather timid. When he stood in front of the orchestra to practice conducting, his whole presence lacked self-confidence, and dare I say it, masculinity. But beneath that, an aesthetic intelligence was brewing. He could look tellingly into events and find creative solutions where others found cynical despair. With solidly self-taught English, he chatted to me over Facebook as one of our newly appointed Regional Representatives, a voluntary position to help with auditions, visas and sheet music. Out of everyone in NYOI, there were very few like Zuhal or Hellgurd I could turn to about our complex problems. Especially now, I was overjoyed to find someone in Iraq who could think further ahead than 12 hours and analyse a potential crisis before it happened.

Hellgurd and I worked to give information about our players to the Kurdistan Regional Government in Berlin, to pass onto the Ministry of Education in Erbil, but we heard nothing back. Would they be allowed to keep their jobs and go to Germany? Berlin assured us they had gone to the highest level on this matter, but it remained open. Given the last minute nature of

Iraqi business, I wasn't worried just yet, but the Kurdistan Regional Government now had a useful weapon; they had suspended the Sword of Damocles over our heads by a horse-hair and if it fell, so would this year's course. The Kurdish players, amid growing nervousness, trusted us to find a solution.

Meanwhile, the fight to finance not only the German visit, but also the two-week summer course in Iraq prior to it, proved relentless. The relationship between Beethovenfest and the German Friends grew tense as it became clear that no financial support was forthcoming from Iraq. I declared Scottish neutrality and focussed instead on Iraq logistics and course preparation with the tutors. Karl-Walter was particularly scathing of Beethovenfest's ability to get money from sponsors before he could.

Nevertheless, Ilona Schmiel still had a *coup de theatre* up her sleeve. The German President, Christian Wulff, had made an issue of securing Islam as a religion that had a home in Germany. He, like many others, saw the divisions between Muslims and other Germans as a deepening wound in society that required urgent political attention. NYOI's visit presented him with a gift, a youth orchestra from a largely Muslim country that had been destroyed not only by war, but also by bloodthirsty news reporting, and which loved playing German music, especially Beethoven. The Office of the President of Germany confirmed that Christian Wulff agreed to become Patron of the visit, and attend our performance on the 1st October.

Touché again.

As the final pieces of this vastly complex jigsaw shuddered into place, we had built a massive PR strategy, a two week summer course in Erbil, a concert in the Martyr Saad Palace, a workshop concert in Berlin, a two week residency in Bonn and a final concert in Beethovenhalle, mostly paid for through Beethovenfest, with courageous support from the German Friends. Meanwhile, the Iraqi Ambassador and Kurdistan Regional Government representation in Berlin both grudgingly acknowledged what was going on.

But, as we prepared to fly out to Erbil, the issue of the Kurds' leave of employment still burned in the back of our heads.

TEN
Mission Improbable

Katharina von Hodenberg, my partner in crime at Beethovenfest, met me at 7.00 am in front of a throbbing information desk at Cologne Central Station. It was Thursday 1st September. The colourful mélange of passengers, young and old, weird and dull, buzzed hither and thither. Cologne was going to work.

Through her bleary eyes, she handed me my contract. I checked it through, perched it on top of my luggage and scrawled my signature. Katharina escorted me to the platform and we hauled my bag into the carriage. Over the months, we'd come a long way together. While most people were off to work, I was off to Iraq, to get into the groove ahead of the orchestra's arrival. Another day, another downbeat.

Landing at Erbil airport was now routine, the border guard moving from booth to booth to find a terminal that worked. I herded myself around in tow until he could log on and do his job. He noticed my new passport on his system and welcomed me to Iraq. When I got to the hotel, the staff welcomed me warmly and took me up to my room. As the door opened: Boom; pink walls, pink curtains, pink bedding and rose scented 'air freshener' made heady by the heat knocked me, wide eyed, out of kilter. I caught my breath. 'Very nice, thank you.' The porter left with a smile. I stood petrified in post-petal shock.

As I stared out of the window at the traffic below, the Berlin office of the Kurdistan Regional Government phoned to see if I needed help. No, I was already here, thank you. I called Karda at the British Council, equally surprised that I'd managed it all by myself. By now, I was an Iraq veteran. As hunger pangs and synthetic roses overwhelmed me, fear paralysed me. How could I feed myself without destroying my gut? Fortunately, that same restaurant to which the British Council had taken Phia and me last year, with the great pizza and mammoth fruit cocktail decked out like Carmen Miranda, lay just across the road.

The balmy September had already tempered itself compared to last year's August, the course with the 47-degree garden concert. I planted myself at a pavement table, my foreign manner clearly attracting attention. Those who caught my eye withdrew suspiciously at my returning smile, and if you knew my smile, you'd know what I mean. A Kurdish high school student, hearing me struggle with the waiter to order a kebab platter, offered his assistance in elegant English. Unlike the shisha cafes or executive hotel bars, this substantial restaurant was packed with families.

Family is the core of the Kurdistan region and Kurds are rather like the Hobbits of the Middle East. Members protect and nurture each other from youth to old age, with many of my players marrying and continuing to live with their parents into their late twenties. In a nepotistic society, surnames define futures. Home is mother's cooking, as unlike German food as imaginable. On one hand, Iraqi Kurds don't like to stray far from home, but more so than Arab Iraqis, this tightly knit minority has learnt survival by networking through its diaspora. My players could find me anything and anyone Kurdish. I baptised my arrival in Erbil with another Carmen Miranda cocktail. The waiter indicated with his hands that it would be *big*, and I acknowledged with an insider wink.

I had two precious free days. For the first time, I was able to get Erbil under my feet, taking time to look and feel. Traffic police at check points supervising the bustling roads smiled back at me, a beacon of Scottish whiteness on the barren pavements. In the Kurdistan oil capital, nobody here 'walked'. The splendid Citadel, an imposing circle of sheer stone walls on a mound of rock, stood at the very end of my street.

Climbing the road to its entrance, I followed in the footsteps of merchants from 4,000 years ago. Being Friday, people were praying in the Citadel mosque, and aside from a row of black cars, the streets were deserted. Once, not so long ago, the residents were moved out as UNESCO took over responsibility for the Citadel's restoration. And so, barren houses were left falling apart, with nobody to do the daily repairs. The carpet museum stood at the entrance where, in March, Ilona Shmiel had held her fundraising party for the orchestra's visit to Bonn. In spite of the Mayor of Erbil also being a former resident of Bonn, even she could not break into the quantum universe of Iraqi corruption.

A guard called out to me from afar and ushered me back out of the Citadel, distraught at my explorations. I descended from the Citadel feeling not history, but ghosts of stone and cloth. Walking slowly back to the hotel in the baking noonday heat, a taxi driver pulled over, beckoned me in and drove me back to the hotel for free. In spite of the terrible security situation in Iraq, the Kurds had not lost their sense of hospitality. The next morning, I checked out and headed off to the orchestra's hotel. What existential crises would await us this year?

Two days of relaxing and exploring had chilled me out, so I could welcome the players with a smile. The foyer was spectacular: a large open hall partitioned by deep black leather sofas around coffee tables, three flatscreen TVs showing 'Kurdistan's Got Talent,' Iraqi news and subtitled Hollywood action films, not forgetting the assorted plastic plants draped in Christmas tree lighting. A fountain stood next to the manager's office, tumbling water down a ceramic rock outcrop covered with plastic flowers and a mechanical bird sporadically twisting and shaking in outbursts of digital song. In the West, you couldn't dream up kitsch like this but to Iraqis, this was genuinely intense.

Over the course of the afternoon, from Baghdad, Suleymaniyah, Erbil, Mosul, Kirkuk and Ranya, the players assembled in the foyer, reuniting with hugs and kisses and spreading themselves tribally over the sofas. This year, I decided to leave orchestral management not only to Majid but also to Hassan, now too old to play first flute with us. NYOI's survival depended on their taking ownership. Karl-Walter also arrived to make sure our relationship with the German Consulate and the Goethe Insitut in Erbil ran smoothly. I figured that, in our third year, we'd finally gotten the hang of it. What else could go wrong?

That is, until that first afternoon in the foyer. I noticed tell-tale signs of dismay in the eyes of some of the Kurds; it turned out Majid had organised the Arabs two or three to a room, whereas some of the Kurds ended up six to a room. Majid claimed there was no more space, so I immediately told Karl-Walter, who went up to reception and booked more rooms for us. Problem solved. Except it wasn't really. The budget still had a $20,000 hole, the cost of our hotel rooms for 44 players, 12 tutors, myself and three management for two weeks. Karl-Walter stepped in again to solve this with a loan from the British Council, which the German Friends would somehow pay back. Majid did do a good job of organising the food well in advance, with lunch at a family restaurant close to the great White Mosque. Dinner took place at a food court, where Hassan gave each of us 10,000 Dinar, roughly $10, to buy what we wanted from pizza, salad bar, burger, kebab and fried chicken outlets.

Upstairs from the food court, in a large, entirely male café, I met Hassan to talk about the future of NYOI, with Murad present to give us his own vision. First, in his opinion, the orchestra should all speak Arabic, as they were all Iraqi. We met this one with deafening silence. Also, and here came the icing on the cake, as Musical Director of the National Youth Orchestra of Iraq, I should learn Arabic, and negate the need for translators. I was taken aback by this. He wanted me to learn Arabic so I could rehearse one concert a year? So I calmly replied: 'I've got a great idea. You do my admin for me, and I'll learn Arabic.' They met this one with a deafening silence of their own.

After two years of experimenting, I'd forged the dream teaching team; big Father Christmas Dobbs from New Hampshire, the wonderfully committed Angie Cho on violin, loyal Dave on cello, moviestar Jonny back from 2009 on trumpet and Scottish Sarah on Horn. Daniel from Cologne was really looking forward to teaching Waleed in Arabic. Ilona had proved herself as a solid viola teacher with the right attitude, and got on tremendously well with her viola players. The youngest, Nick Macorison, our bassoon tutor, knew how to drill the players on the basics they both lacked while staying matey. This year's lead wind tutor, clarinettist Dougie Mitchell from the Royal Philharmonic Orchestra in London, led like a dream. I could relax and let all of them get on with the job of growing us an orchestra.

A more senior musician, violinist David Juritz from London, came on board for the first time. Like Dobbs, he'd already touched base with me in 2009, for as well as being a leading London freelancer, he ran a charity called Musequality for music programmes in African schools. By busking Bach in streets throughout the world for a solid year, he'd raised them a lot of cash: like Dobbs and his solo tours of Afghanistan, a considerable class act with a great deal of humility. He began a little out of sorts amongst his young colleagues, but when I told him that peer to peer teaching was part of our strategy he immediately understood.

I also welcomed Christian Kemper, our oboe tutor, to the NYOI family. Getting decent oboes into Iraq proved an enormous stumbling block, which I tried to crack beforehand by borrowing one instrument from Bonn, and another from an oboe professor in America. This latter decision cost me dearly just before my departure. The oboe she had sent was confiscated by customs officials, so I had to hurriedly purchase a special import certificate and pay a deposit which was never returned, before it could be released into my care. The instrument of our first oboist, Du'aa, had already cracked in the heat, and our new second oboist from Suleymaniyah, Musli, possessed something I didn't want near the stage of Beethovenfest. Christian took stock of my efforts and, with a chuckle, said he didn't need the American oboe after all. I hid my dismay and, feeling like Patient Zero in a zombie apocalypse, wandered back to my room and closed the door.

Day one of rehearsals at the Ministry of Culture: during her visit to Erbil in March, Ilona Schmiel had secured us the use of the Peshawa Hall in their compound, but Majid hadn't followed up. So that morning, our musicians arrived unannounced by the busload at the barrier to be met by bemused guards. A few phone calls later, they let us drive in. As with past years, we began with an icebreaker activity on stage, which involved introducing ourselves to each other, and ended with Majid draping an Iraqi flag around Karl-Walter and me in symbolic gratitude. I fixed a smile and froze while Saman and Shwan, our translators, assured me it was unlikely to create conflict.

The Peshawa Hall could take the orchestra, but we needed breakout rooms too, and the air conditioning had been out of order since February. As I sent different groups to different rehearsal spaces, we realised nobody had brought their music stands, as requested, so I found a pile of artists' easels stacked in a corner, and used these to hold the music. As the day progressed, the comedy of musicians playing from easels in 37-degree heat became increasingly absurd. Tired and embarrassed, we received word that the Minister of Culture demanded to see the orchestral management, as nothing about our visit had been put in writing.

While Majid was sorting that out, I held an emergency tutor meeting. We'd go back to the hotel, use their conference rooms, and hold the course there. To hell with the extra cost. That was Majid's problem. In a final attempt to anchor us in success, we came back together and played through the first movement of the Haydn as a full orchestra, coarsely, but in one go. I turned to see David Juritz applauding from the auditorium. At that moment he knew what we were attempting was possible. If we were to secure leave to play in Germany from the Kurdistan Regional Government, as two thirds of the orchestra was Kurdish, we'd gotten off to a bad start. Back in the hotel foyer, Majid negotiated with the diminutive hotel manager to get rehearsal space. Her pluckiness versus Majid's charm completed the tragi-comedy for me. I retired to bed, some things best left untranslated.

Over the coming days, we installed our routine into the hotel's bricks and mortar. Breakfast, warm-ups, rehearsing, lessons, sleeping and coaching chamber music all happened within spitting distance of each other. Majid's room became the course office, his printer spewing out endless sheet music. Jonny's room, 210, opened for business as the tutors' bar, stocked with beers we'd bought in bulk from off-licences in the Ankawa district. We pooled fridge resources to keep our supplies flowing and cool. Room 210 became our haven of complaining, laughter, discussions and beer o'clock as Jonny's wardrobe gradually filled up with empty cans. By the end of week one, half of it was solid aluminium.

Bettina Kolb, who had joined us to film a report for Deutsche Welle, blogged on us as well.

'We're all staying in a hotel on the edge of Erbil. Outside, it's 38 degrees Celsius (100 degrees Fahrenheit), and not much cooler inside. Music wafts through the foyer as I enter – clarinets in room 210, trumpets in 216, and a horn sounds from the practice room.

The young musicians are working one-on-one with tutors from Germany, Scotland and the USA. The 43 musicians and their 12 tutors have been here for a week already rehearsing, as has Paul MacAlindin, their musical director and conductor. It's the first time that these young people, all between the ages of 16 and 28, are performing together. They hail from across Iraq – and from each of the country's major ethnic traditions: Kurdish, Sunni and Shia.

But they've left the political and religious tensions at home. These young people are the hope and the future of their country and also among its best ambassadors – even though it's anything but easy for them.

Getting Western music instruction in Iraq is no simple thing. In Baghdad, it can even be dangerous to be seen with certain instruments on the street. Conservatives strictly oppose classical music, which they regard as a symbol of Western decadence. But for the young musicians in Erbil, playing in the orchestra means finding a communal language that can build bridges in a country fraught with war and conflict. (...)

On my first morning with the orchestra, they've already been practicing together for six days. They don't start with

119

Beethoven but with an African folk song. It's a warm-up where everyone sings, claps, stomps and marches in a circle. Then, the instruments are tuned, and conductor Paul MacAlindin leads them in a rehearsal of Haydn's Symphony No 104. Excitement is in the air as the musicians make last-minute tune-ups, cast concentrated glances at the score and whisper to their neighbours to ask which measure they're starting at.

Time flies by ahead of their first concert together in Erbil, just two weeks after they began rehearsals. It will be a big and long-awaited event. By now the notes are there, but the rhythm is still off during a few passages. The conductor is sweating – and not just on account of the heat.

That night, the young performers had gotten out their traditional Kurdish instruments and played some local favourites – music they have in their blood. Classical music, on the other hand, is something they hear over YouTube or on their I-Phones. It's not part of everyday life (...)

At the end of the day, conductor Paul MacAlindin rubs his eyes, saying, 'Some passages sound so beautiful, some aren't coming together. But I just don't know if the orchestra can hear when they're playing well and with power – whether they hear the difference.'

It's not perfect yet, but they are all very motivated. The musicians practice further on their instruments in their rooms. Even after midnight, Beethoven is still in the air.'

Week one also saw an invasion of German journalists, led by Beethovenfest's Press Officer, Silke Neubarth. Major media such as *Die Zeit*, *Süddeutsche Zeitung* and *Deutsche Presse Agentur* turned up to report on our build-up to Beethovenfest. Two documentary makers, Edinburgh based Gill Parry from last year, and Cam Matheson from Melbourne were also following us. Both were necessary for our PR strategy, and had free reign to film whatever and however they liked, editing the story in ways that could be beneficial to us, or not. A question mark remained over whether they were culturally sensitive enough not to endanger us by presenting an angle that would backlash in Iraq. This had already happened with a film about an orchestra in Kinshasa, capital of the Congo.

I heard this story from an aid worker who was close to some of the players. It featured a particularly poverty-stricken flautist, a single mother with her child. That the film crew followed her daily situation so shamed the other musicians, or perhaps they were envious, that they subsequently mobbed her out of the orchestra. Regardless, the German team had their sexy music story and the film became a hit. Musically, I felt deeply uncomfortable at the way my rehearsing was being filmed. I'd modified my technique considerably to deal with NYOI, and I was giving little that represented my true artistic ability. Amid this menagerie, the feisty hotel manager and her young porters, christened 'The Pinkshirts,' warmed very slowly indeed to the madness we had brought upon them.

Zuhal was ill in Scotland, exhausted with frustration at her new life and unable to take part. We still hoped she'd come to Germany. Ali Authman had written the piano part in his composition, *Invocation*, especially for her. Meanwhile, Karl-Walter Keppler, burning with quest energy, set it upon himself to take off in a taxi with one of our translators, and march from one ministry to the next, explaining why the Kurdish players needed leave from their jobs to go to Germany. His persistence over the coming days paid off as the issue finally landed in the office of the Prime Minister. His gut feeling was that they would allow this, but still no official confirmation was forthcoming. As the German Foreign Office had committed €50,000, their Consulate also wanted to see that the players would get on the plane, knowing their jobs back home were safe.

Meanwhile, I reassured the orchestra that everything had been done by Hellgurd and me, and was being done all over again to get them permission to go. For our Erbil concert we had an orchestra with a majority of Kurdish players, a Kurdish world premiere and a Kurdish soloist for the Beethoven Violin Concerto in Zana Jalal. We'd done everything right in a culture where everything could still go wrong.

121

Bettina wrote: '*Kurdish music is hammering in the afternoon from a little white bus flashing its way around the turns on a four-lane street. The whole bus is shaking because 20-year-old flutist Waleed and his friends are dancing in typical Kurdish style. Those who aren't dancing are clapping and shouting encouragement to the five boys, who don't lose their balance even on the sharpest of curves.*

I, on the other hand, fall on top of the cellist to my left or the violinist to my right again and again as I try to film the scene. But the two young women aren't bothered.

Spontaneous parties of this sort sprout up again and again. That's one unique thing about this orchestra: during rehearsals, they're hungry to learn and concentrated, but as soon as the instruments are put away, they start laughing, talking and celebrating life. They're not defiant, just cheerful.

Ali Authman comes to the rehearsals. The Kurdish composer lives in the Netherlands and composed the work 'Invocation', commissioned by Deutsche Welle. He described it to me as a 'prayer that is intended to foster peace among people.'

Authman is going over a few final touches with the violins – places where he would play the rhythm differently. The exhaustion from the many long days of rehearsals is plain to see. During the short breaks, a viola player lies on the ground and dozes, and one cellist almost falls out of her seat, with her instrument between her legs.

During the lunch break, I accompany violinist Aya, bassoonist Murad and flautist Waleed into downtown Erbil: a young Arab woman from Baghdad with a punk haircut and orange finger nails, a journalist and orchestral musician from Baghdad and a music teacher from the city of Kirkuk (...)

We head to the markets. Juice and fruit stands light up the byways with shades of orange and pomegranate red. Bills are stacked in towers on the rickety tables of the money changers. Merchants cry out their deals in every direction. Mountains of sweets are for sale in every conceivable pastel.

But our conversation is about security. All three of my companions agree that life in Iraq is completely normal. 'Dangerous? No, it's not like that anymore. In the last few years, a lot has changed,' Aya says.

I ask sceptically about car bombs and extremist forces and get a shrug as an answer. Maybe they're just tired of all of the same journalist questions about dangerous living in Iraq, especially in Baghdad. Murad prefers to talk about his fiancée, a Turkish bassoonist that he met in 2010 during the orchestra's summer session in Erbil. 'She is the most beautiful gift of this whole experience,' he says.

Now it's especially important to him to find a place where the two can get married and live together. He doesn't want to bring her back to Baghdad because it would be too difficult for her there.

Waleed heads off to buy some apricot candies for everyone. His priority here is making friends. 'How else can I know if the young people in Baghdad are just as crazy about music as we are?' he says.

And when I ask if people on the street here know who Beethoven is, Aya suddenly sings from the Fifth Symphony, 'Ta Ta Ta Taaa... yeah, of course, they all do that as soon as you ask.' Of course, that's quite a bit different than if you would ask someone in Germany on the street to name an Iraqi composer. But for now, the most important thing is deciding which candies to buy. A little treat to calm the nerves before heading back to rehearsals.

This evening, I'm invited into the home of Alan and Darwn's family. The two brothers play violin and viola. Like two other musicians in the orchestra, they're originally from Erbil. At the door of their two-story home, the family is waiting – a mother, a little sister and two older brothers. They fall into each other's arms, kisses flying back and forth. They haven't seen each other for a week because Alan and Darwn are staying in a hotel with the rest of the performers.

The family shares fresh dates, figs and sweet pastries while they all cheerfully catch up with each other. A picture of their father hangs on the wall, an artist who died two years prior. He encouraged his two sons to learn an instrument and supported them along the way. Their mother, Najat, is visibly proud of them. She's a resolute, warm and open-minded woman with laughing dark brown eyes.

'My sons are going to play in Germany, is that not wonderful?' she says. 'Thank God they can play now.' The two brothers have been practicing for eight years. As an instrument is pulled from its case, their oldest brother jokes, 'Please, not classical again.' Laughter flows – and more sweets – as a full moon shines down on the hot night.'

During our free day, everyone went sightseeing and I stayed in the hotel, enjoying stillness alone. The week's hard grind, correcting the most basic mistakes by the players then consolidating only to hear something else go wrong, had drained us all.

ELEVEN
The sword of Damocles

Along with film-maker Cam Matheson came an old university friend, Mark Edwards, a sound engineer who had promised to record the orchestra professionally. I could not express my relief enough. Himself a fine violinist, he understood the orchestra perfectly. After three years of battling to develop a half-respectable sound with these young players, then watching TV crews come along with no equipment or knowledge of recording an orchestra, and make us sound worse than we actually were, I was sick and tired of filming as a necessary evil. This was one of many quality battles that the orchestra fought hard to improve in our short time together. Only the players' intense motivation to learn as much and as fast as possible kept us going, as every year, the orchestra improved by superhuman leaps.

Mark, in his blog, captured our spirit:

'Today was a day off for the orchestra. Having a day off though does nothing to dampen the motivation for practise, it just makes it a little less formal. We spent the afternoon at the parks in central Erbil. These parks are built on the site of a historic mosque of which only a single massive minaret is left. The two parks are connected by cable-car, so of course the whole orchestra had to go across for a ride. On the way, Cam and I travelled by car so we could get some external shots of 'party-bus' activity. It was quite refreshing to be able to walk in the dark through a huge city park alongside so many other people – young and old – and not feel apprehensive or uncomfortable in any way.

On the return journey, I discussed with one of the translators how Erbil had changed since the invasion in 2003. It was fascinating to hear how much investment has poured into the region and how much the infrastructure has been developed over the past few years – and continues to develop. Even with Erbil's historic past, much of the city is new and it is still growing and expanding. The city has a very relaxed feel about it.

The students' party like nothing I have ever seen – and I have seen some pretty awesome partying in my time. The second the dance CD is playing in the bus, they are up and dancing – the rear axle joining in by squeaking as they drive down the road.

After we got back to the hotel, we were treated to an impromptu performance on the Arabic and Kurdish Zithers, accompanied by some amazing strings and wind playing. After the zithers the dancing and drums came and once more bedtime at 2am.'

Being the orchestra's leader had the disadvantage that I rarely heard the truth about anything. Though I tried to stay as close to the players as possible, the interviews and media feedback were vital for me to catch an objective perspective, and a more reflective voice from the players. I had worked closely with Beethovenfest on our PR strategy and could rattle it off under the worst circumstances, but, sometimes, I needed to express my true feelings. One journalist asked me if I ever felt like giving up. 'Yes, every day,' I replied, coldly and without hesitation.

Bettina wrote: *'Practice, practice and more practice, from 9 am until late in the night. But today conductor Paul MacAlindin is visibly upset with the orchestra. The first violins are too slow, and percussionist Mohammed has missed his entry once again.*

Downtrodden faces all around, instruments resting on knees as composer Ali Authman nervously paces back and forth, right and left. The composer grabs a violin, plays the rhythm, then pats violinist Alan encouragingly on the shoulders. Tomorrow is the big concert in Saad Palace in Arbil.

'Oh well, by the time they reach Beethovenfest, they'll be playing much better. They still have two more weeks,' says Authman.

But the trip to Germany has put everyone on pins and needles. The Kurdish culture ministry keeps delaying an approval to let the Kurdish musicians, nearly all of whom work as music teachers under the education ministry's auspices, travel to Germany for two weeks.

'We need their approval by tomorrow,' says Paul MacAlindin, passing a hand wearily through his greying hair. 'We are supposed to fly out on Saturday, and no one works here on Fridays. I just don't know...' One bright spot, though: the culture minister is coming to the concert. Maybe the music will convince him.

During a brief pause, I chat with Awder, a cellist from Sulaimaniya.

'My former cello teacher is actually a violin player and had no idea about cello. I watched other players online and basically taught myself everything,' she explains. 'Starting in 2008, I had a teacher from the USA, (Bruce Walker from American Voices) and now I'm here for the second time at the summer camp. It's a huge opportunity for me. And the tutors are great. They give us so much time and are so patient.'

During lunch, Awder glances lovingly at a musician named Harem. They've been married for ten months. He is a flute player in the National Youth Orchestra of Iraq and a music teacher.

'No, we don't know each other from the school,' laughs Awder, as I ask whether sparks first flew during one of the orchestra's rehearsals.

I wander through the hotel. Violins are sounding from room 208, and in 207, the violas. In 210, Jonny from Scotland is sitting with Murtada, who doesn't speak any English, and

Frand from Baghdad, who patiently translates the lessons Jonny wants to impart.

But really a translation isn't necessary. Jonny is using all kinds of body language and mimicking the trumpet sounds he wants to hear. Horn player Ali from Baghdad has the fortune of having a tutor all to himself, Sarah, who hails from London. She sends him to the other side of the large conference room to play the same passage two times in a row with differing intensity.

'Do you hear the difference? You have to exaggerate. Because at the concert, the grandma sitting in the very last row is going to want to hear what you're playing, okay?' says Sarah.

Ali nods, takes his horn and gives it everything he's got. He's already risked a lot for his passion for music. The Baghdad resident comes from a strictly religious neighbourhood. Music is dangerous there, since the conservative residents strictly reject it. As such, Ali sometimes practices underneath a towel, an improvised sound absorber. The neighbours aren't supposed to hear that he's a musician.

Some of the other orchestra members have to hide their instruments in trash bags when they head out into the streets. Even though all of them stress that the country has become safer in the last one to two years, real security doesn't exist yet.'

Majid came to me about Frand, our first trumpet. He'd been acting up with Hassan, refusing the money he was being offered to buy dinner in the food court. Majid asked if we could replace him in Bonn as a punishment. I sighed inwardly. This was not an option, as his flight and visa had already been paid for, and booking a German trumpeter would incur even more cost to Beethovenfest. Also, it was a pretty heavy suggestion for something like that.

But face had been lost. He'd also have less motivation to stay in Erbil, and could leave us without a first trumpet for our concert there. The serious scarcity of good young players in Iraq proved our main weakness.

So, Majid brought Hassan and Frand with Dara, another of our translators, into my bedroom, to discuss the problem. Taking adversarial positions across from each other on my twin beds, Majid tried to open a dialogue. Although everyone spoke excellent English, our attempts at calm mediation quickly descended into flying Arabic accusations between Hassan and Frand. I sighed inwardly again. Dara wouldn't tell me what was going on. He just shook his head saying, 'It's personal'.

Eventually, the venting subsided, and I tried to inject some reason: the orchestra had no right to order anybody to do anything, as it didn't exist legally. We were only here because we trusted each other, and we all had a responsibility to maintain that. If Frand wanted to pay for his own dinner, he should politely say 'No, thank you' when offered the 10,000 dinars by Hassan. Nevertheless, Hassan's authority and Frand's autonomy remained wounded. Finally, Dara confessed that there was a long-standing feud between their families. Venting their anger in front of Majid and me had the short-term benefit that we could all get out of my room and back to work. For a few nights, Frand didn't turn up to dinner, and that was all.

Meanwhile, Cam and Mark were interviewing for their film. They loved Iraq's food culture and continued the story of Ali, our first horn, as Mark explained:

The food here in Erbil is, without exception, awesome. We take breakfast in the hotel, lunch at a restaurant called the 'Three Stars' and dinner at a food court called Abu Shahab. At Abu Shahab we can have either Italian, Kebabs or Krunchy Fried Chicken (KFC). Kurdistan's attitude towards Colonel Sanders, the Kentucky Fried Chicken trademark, is obviously one of 'bite me'.

At Abu Shahab tonight we observed one of the waiters (yes, this is a food court with table service) paying his respects to Allah on a mat at the side of the eating area. We were also privileged to interview Ali, who is a French horn player. Without giving away too many spoilers from our documentary, we will tell you a little about Ali. Ali's father was a trumpet player in the Iraqi military during the rule of Saddam. He has always lived around music, which was actively encouraged during Saddam's time. Classical interpretation was not something he was exposed to though, as most music was interpreted in strict – military – time. This was something also reinforced by his tutors in Baghdad, most of whom also came from a military background.

Since the fall of Saddam, Ali has been living in Sadr City. Sadr City is overseen by religious fundamentalists that do not permit music to be played. Ali therefore has to plug up his horn with mutes and dampen the room where he practices with towels so that the sound doesn't get out. The consequences of being heard practicing the horn could be quite serious.

Coming to the NYOI course has opened up a whole new world of both horn sound and musical interpretation to Ali. Here in Erbil, he doesn't have to use a mute, nor does he have to worry about being heard. Quite the opposite, in fact his coach Sarah actively encourages it.

Ali hasn't been overseas before, but words cannot describe the look on his face at the thought of going to the birthplace of Beethoven and playing alongside German orchestral musicians. Now of course Ali does not lament the fall of Saddam – we are yet to meet anyone from Iraq that does – but he really misses the opportunity to play and practise the horn properly – a freedom he does not currently enjoy in Baghdad.

At this point we are really only just scratching the surface of some of the stories of these players, but it's really not hard to see why the motivation levels are so high.

So – any instrumental teachers out there having trouble getting your students to practise? Just introduce them to the story of Ali.

As the Erbil course drew to a close, and the wardrobe in Jonny's room was almost bursting with empty beer cans, we revisited the school used for last year's kids' concert. This time, we put on a much more streamlined show with games and chamber music, including a Ligeti Bagatelle for wind quintet and the second movement of Mozart's Clarinet Quintet. The auditorium filled to the brim with young girls in white headscarves, looking utterly adorable.

Uninhibited, they joined in Jonny's clapping and Dougie's singing games, their teachers watching on apprehensively from the back row. But when Dobbs came on and started his fairy story in Kurdish while plucking away at his bass, even the teachers became enraptured. Music making in Iraq is basically a man's pursuit, girls are discouraged, and we so loved reaching out to these young souls. Afterwards, they inundated Jonny for autographs, his film star looks beating everyone else for popularity.

Our chamber music coaching had slowly built musicianship and self-confidence into our players. Very slowly. We desperately needed to promote mobility of musicians within Iraq, even if it meant travelling along dangerous roads across ethnic or sectarian divides. To me, chamber rehearsals and performances acted as a kind of bricks and mortar for the new Iraq. They were low-budget and highly flexible, attracting new audiences, breaking down language barriers, and uniting everyone under a shared emotional experience that had nothing to do with religion or politics. I hoped dearly that our players would take up the lead when they went home. The prospect itself was hugely exciting.

As the last day of the course fell upon us, Bettina wrote:

An unusual silence fills the breakfast room this morning – a departure from the previous days when laughter and cheerful 'Good Mornings' resounded all around the table.

Tonight is the big concert in Erbil's Saad Palace. Yesterday's rehearsals went well, but the musicians are nervous and quietly munching on cheese, olives and bread. Then the orchestra manager, Majid, calls out, 'To the bus!' And off they go, leaving plates with half-eaten flatbread behind. Once they've boarded, Majid knows no mercy. Two young men carry the big bass drums above their heads into the vehicle. Room has to be made for them alongside the conductor, 12 tutors and 43 musicians. Instruments are stacked one on top of another, and we manage to squeeze ourselves in between.

But this is our first trip together where there's no Kurdish music, no hopping, dancing and singing to set the bus to shaking. It's almost time for the dress rehearsal. Once there, everyone has to pass through security. Metal detectors loom behind guards with red berets, bulletproof vests and machine guns. They open up the violin cases with utmost seriousness – so serious in fact that it's clear they don't know just what to make of the instruments inside.

Before the music begins, conductor Paul MacAlindin lets his orchestra members rehearse entering the stage. There are some little collisions. MacAlindin takes on the role of choreographer. After all, this warm-up is necessary. Beethoven's Violin Concerto isn't the only part of the evening that will require the musicians' full attention.

The Beethoven piece is joined by four others on the programme, including two works commissioned by Deutsche Welle from Iraqi composers – 'Desert Camel' by Mohammed Amin Ezzat from Baghdad and 'Invocation' by Ali Authman. The latter composer is on hand and more relaxed today than before. No longer pacing back and forth, he sits in the seventh row, listening, making notes and looking up again.

Bassoonist Murad, on the other hand, looks upset. 'I've had a sore throat since last night. I don't know how I'm going to play. But I want to no matter what,' he says. He's sitting in his chair in the last row at the rehearsal and fighting on...

Three hours later, the orchestra has transformed itself. The young women are in elegant black outfits, hair done up, lips red. Cellist Tuqa from Baghdad is the only orchestra member wearing a hijab, decorated with silver pearls for the occasion. The young men are wearing white shirts and bowties. In the hotel lobby, they arrange themselves into ever new groups as cameras flash every second, capturing photos for the family or Facebook. The joking and laughter have returned.

Three kilometres away, the Saad Palace is illuminated in a deep red-orange as the sun gradually sinks below the horizon. The uniformed guards are still in place but with reinforcements. The Prime Minister is expected to come.

Once the young musicians have made it to the broad corridors backstage, the violinists and clarinet players begin warming up. At the end of an especially long walkway, flautist Waleed is playing all by himself. A melody flows from his instrument as he paces with closed eyes. He takes three steps forward and a little turn as he continues to play, completely lost in the music.

The concert is slated to begin at 7 p.m., but it isn't until 7:30 that the VIP guests have finally arrived. They are seated in the first row behind little tables bearing cool drinks. The Prime Minister is the only guest who is still tied up elsewhere. But the concert won't begin for a while still. First come the speeches – an Iraqi and a Kurdish flag stand next to the lectern. The orchestra is showing its impatience, but conductor Paul MacAlindin stands stock-straight and still. 'That's always how it is with musicians – they just want to get on stage and play. Nothing else. Just play,' he says.

Violinist Alan is radiant ahead of the performance – 'I'm so happy!' – as I teach him the German phrase, 'toi toi toi.' That's how we wish artists good luck before they head on stage.

We were minutes away from entering the stage, with all the Kurdish Ministers including Foreign Minister, Falah Mustapha Bakir, lined up in the front row. They were here to check us out, and I still hadn't heard anything official about our Kurdish players from them. Chris Bowers, the British Consul General in Erbil, introduced us to the audience. The British took a strong interest because Germany's remarkable investment in us, along with the £100,000 from the Scottish Government, had increased the chances of a UK visit for next year, 2012.

We walked onto the Saad Palace stage knowing we'd learnt the notes and crunched the main musical problems. With a downbeat to Ali Authman's dramatic opening to *Invocation*, and Dave Edmonds playing Zuhal's part on an electric piano, we began. I focused hard on Waleed's counting, our first flute, along with countless dangerous little corners, but we got to the end without falling apart. As Ali walked humbly on stage to take his bow, I hoped that this would help sell the shock of his modernism to an inexperienced audience. We launched into Mohammed Amin Ezzat's *Desert Camel*, a romper stomper Arab fantasy about a camel rescuing his kidnapped girlfriend from bandits in the desert. We delighted in passing snake charming melodies around the orchestra, letting rip in the bombastic fight scenes and revelling in the Bedouin flavours that made it such fun and so very Iraqi. Written by a conductor whose hometown, Baghdad, was under daily terrorist attack and still trying to recover from a six-year war, I found his spirit uplifting.

I also had a tactical reason for commissioning new music. Because we were limited with instruments I could dictate to the composers exactly what to write for, and ask them to be especially creative for the horns, trumpets and percussion, which gave them more substance during the course.

Our next performance, Haydn's Symphony No 104, like Beethoven's 1st Symphony and Haydn's Symphony No 99 in previous years, really taught us how to listen and react together as an orchestra, our chamber music coaching really coming to life in this intricate composition. Here, our brass and percussion would be lucky to play two or three different notes through the whole work, though how sensitive they were to the grand scheme of the composition became the real work for youngsters who'd grown up musically with either 'very loud' or 'stop'.

Spirits backstage remained sky high at the interval. The Kurds hadn't heard a 'yes' from the Kurdistan Regional Government to take leave from work, but we hadn't heard a 'no' either. The players took comfort in this and knew that the answer was going to be last minute anyway. A range of diplomats from Germany,

US and UK were also present to keep an eye on what was happening. By being fair and inclusive, NYOI challenged every status quo in Iraq. We grated quite painfully against Kurdistan's strategy of differentiating itself from Baghdad, though paradoxically also providing us with a safer haven to work in than the capital could ever be. We all sensed the history we were making here, and had acquired a taste for success that couldn't be achieved anywhere else in Iraq.

The second half of the concert was upon us. Bettina continued: *And then it's time. The young musicians make their entrance with pride and composure – and this time no collisions. The maestro lifts his arms, the instruments go up, and 'A Reel of Spindrift' by Peter Maxwell Davies begins to sound.*

Sea salt and spray from near Max's Orkney home juxtaposed with warm glasses of whisky indoors. We stared into the glowing hearth together where driftwood and unopened letters crackled away merrily. The suspended cymbal splashed over the audience and clarinets throbbed a dour drone underneath an unfolding love song in the strings. A final procession of Scots snaps took us down the aisle with Prince William and Kate Middleton, whose wedding the piece commemorated. A quick glance down at the front row confirmed that none of the ministers had left at the interval. Thank God. More importantly, we had just premiered the first work by our Honorary Composer-in-Residence and Master of the Queen's Music.

With the Beethoven Violin Concerto now upon us, Zana Jalal stepped out to perform. He'd made a huge effort to learn it without payment or coaching. Rehearsing with him daily over the two weeks had drummed his notes into the orchestra's ears. This would allow us to make the best of the limited rehearsal time with Arabella Steinbacher, our soloist in Bonn.

Bettina wrote: *'The orchestra plays itself into the hearts of the audience. The mother of violinist Alan and violist Darwn came to the performance and has tears in her eyes. Standing ovations and jubilation follow the show.'*

Fifty minutes later, the final emphatic chords brought the Beethoven to an end and the audience cheered. I turned to bow, flashed my eyes down on the ministers in front of me, and saw one of them giving us a thumbs-up. A minister's wife stood up and applauded Zana with all her heart. After two gruelling years and thousands of euros in preparation, the Kurdistan Regional Government had just given me the green light. Our players could go to Germany without losing their jobs.

After several days of filming, Bettina brought her journey with us to a close:

'The bus has never shaken quite so much as on the ride home. And it's just the start of a long night of dancing and celebrating.

From trumpet player to DJ: Frand from Baghdad with his punky, gelled up hair is spinning Arabic sounds while the not exactly skinny bassist Samir sets his body to moving like a contrabass string. Murtada challenges him to a dance duel. Then Kurdish music sets the rhythm for a traditional Arabic dance known as the Dabke. The musicians form a circle, hand in hand: left foot out, a jump and a bounce, then the right foot goes back, on and on. Every now and then, someone – both men and women, alike – disbands from the circle, hops into the middle and twirls around, cheered on from the other dancers.

By 2:30 in the morning, I'm exhausted and have to head off, but the party goes on.'

The British Council hosted our after-concert reception in the Saad Palace but, much to the tutors' dismay, without alcohol. We'd made it halfway through year three, and the beginning of our diplomatic survival strategy. I, like everyone, felt shattered after a fortnight in Iraq rehearsing our ambitious programme. We now faced another two weeks in Bonn. Just as our concert became the key to unlock the Kurdistan Regional Government's goodwill, so it also unlocked the visas for our 2012 visit, as Chris Bowers, the Consul General and his Baghdad colleagues confirmed to me that evening.

Chris blogged on the Kurdish news site, Rudaw:

'...had a fantastic evening listening to the talented young musicians of the National Youth Orchestra of Iraq the other week. Anyone listening to a National Youth Orchestra can't help but be impressed by the dedication of the musicians and wonder at the hours of practice needed to get the piece exactly right.

But the fact that we were listening to the National Youth Orchestra of Iraq struck me as a triumph of will, inspiration and imagination. And, wow, were they good. The conductor had clearly not asked where people came from or which sect they came from: if they were good enough they played, if they weren't they didn't.

As I listened to the inter-played 'conversation' between the strings and the woodwind instruments in one of the symphonies my mind wandered to Iraqi politics. If the different sections of the orchestra represented different interest groups in Iraq how did the music gel? Were the instruments in harmony? Was the overall product discordant or in tune? Did the public appreciate the performance?'

The orchestra as metaphor for Iraqi politics was pretty idealistic, but also inescapable. Plato once said: 'Musical innovation is full of danger to the State, for when modes of music change, the fundamental laws of the State always change with them.' For those who wanted Iraq to stay divided, NYOI as international diplomat would be music at its most threatening.

TWELVE
The Iraqi diplomats

The afternoon after the Erbil concert, we filed into the waiting lounge of Erbil International Airport. As we slowly boarded the Lufthansa flight to Frankfurt, I bore in mind that, for many, this was their first visit abroad. Strapped into my seat, I cast a glance around the players. Here was a group of people whom I had hand-picked to create a national youth orchestra. Now they were on a plane to Germany. I rarely allowed myself moments of satisfaction, but I was so proud of them. Daniel Agi and I sat across the aisle from each other, sensing the anticipation. Everyone waited with bated breath to see if the plane really would leave the ground and, at exactly the moment when the wheels separated from Iraq, the whole orchestra burst into a huge cheer. Daniel and I smiled at each other. We were leaving behind a world of internal strife, and flying directly into another world, the home of Beethoven. For now, I was relieved.

We certainly managed to sabotage the peaceful flight for the other passengers. Though we couldn't jump up and down the way we had on the buses, we still managed to make the cabin thick with excitement. Endless chatting amongst the players, Waleed showing everyone a photo of himself playing flute in a German newspaper, Dave Edmonds partying in the isle and being told to sit down, Majid taking up a couple of seats and snoring away quietly, every bit of it as unforgettable for the other passengers as it was for us.

Flight LH697 touched down in Frankfurt on 17th September at 8.00 pm, German time. We bustled out of arrivals into a new world, cornered immediately by a Kurdish film team from Deutsche Welle. It had begun. Also lying in wait were the German Friends, who handed out free sweatshirts with our logo on the back, to prepare us for the cool German autumn and impending media storm. Off we went in the luxury buses, gliding down the perfect German autobahn to Bonn where we would meet our guest families for the two-week stay. No partying. Just silence. Even here, some players still believed we were going on a European holiday. Bless. As we rushed through the night, Alan Rasheed, our Kurdish concertmaster, leaned over his front seat to stare at the motorway unfolding before us. Even the simplest things seemed exciting and different.

Eventually, we pulled up in front of the Beethovenhalle in Bonn, piled into the chamber music hall with tons of luggage, and met our guest-families. They already had years of experience hosting foreign youth orchestras at Beethovenfest, and understood the culture shock everyone was going through. Deutsche Welle and I had already prepped them for everything from breakfast to cultural differences. One German-Syrian family could speak two of the six Kurdish dialects, so we gave them the two sisters from Erbil, Saween and Sabat. Wherever possible, we kept friends and family together, but moreover a musician who spoke English could be put up with one who spoke only Arabic or Kurdish, and act as an interpreter for the families. There were so many chances for communication to break down over the two weeks, with the families' goodwill being particularly tested by this long stay; we had to get this part right. Pair by pair, the players, somewhat disoriented, filed off into cars with their families and went home for their first night in Germany. The welcome efficiency of Beethovenfest starkly contrasted with our course in Erbil.

I'd already warned the orchestra about German punctuality and the following morning, remarkably, they all turned up at the Beethovenhalle on time, to begin group rehearsals with tutors from the National Youth Orchestra of Germany. As I handed a player the fortnight's rehearsal schedule, he turned to me, half-jokingly, and said: 'You really don't like us, do you?' 'I do,'

I replied, 'but we're not ready yet. If we're going on stage in Germany, we need all the rehearsal time we can get.'

Of course we weren't ready. NYOI was light years away from any other national youth orchestra, but I knew if we didn't get this exposure somehow, then the players would be stuck in ignorance forever.

Over the coming fortnight, they would get even more intensive care. Sixteen players from Bundesjugendorchester, the National Youth Orchestra of Germany, whom we had invited to play alongside us, would mentor them on how a top youth orchestra musician works. We would also hear world-class orchestras playing in Beethovenfest. They needed some idea of what to aim for: a brutal schooling, an affront to their pride, but the only way to grow. More to the point, without finance from Iraq, the orchestra now depended entirely on foreign sponsors, and we had to deliver what they wanted.

With only Shwan and Saman around to translate, rehearsing several instrumental groups scattered throughout Beethovenhalle became a major collaborative effort. Over the coming days, I noticed the German tutors making the classic mistake of thoroughly lecturing the players, knowing that about 80% of what they were saying would be lost. As Du'aa said to me: 'Even if we understand the English, most of us don't understand what it means as musicians.'

That worry aside, my next task was to go immediately to Berlin, where we had a live TV interview with German-Iraqi presenter Dunja Hayali the following morning. Zana, Tuqa and Saween, our Kurdish singer, had been flown to Berlin that evening, while I was doing a talk on the orchestra's visit in a pub for the Friends of Beethovenfest. Having missed any later flight, I went straight onto a train in Bonn to connect with the overnight express from Dortmund to Warsaw. Katharina handed me a box labelled 'Scottish Conductor Survival Kit,' including chocolates and a small bottle of whisky, which I wolfed down in the sleeper car to get me through the night. The train arrived at Berlin Ostbahnhof two hours late, and I stumbled into a taxi for the hotel.

Having checked in at 6.00 am, I crawled under the shower, tried not to look too bedraggled in my Beethovenfest T-shirt, and went back down again to a surprised receptionist 45 minutes later to check out. The three players and I could finally sit down together at breakfast. Tu'qa, who only spoke Arabic, and Saween, who only spoke Kurdish, watched quietly on as Zana and I talked about the Erbil course, and Karl-Walter's incredible role in it. For three years, we'd been living on a knife-edge, and finally we were in Germany.

When we got to the studio, we began to enjoy ourselves chatting away in make-up, and before we knew it, it was time. Zana played Bach, and Dunja Hayali interviewed me in German and Tuqa in Iraqi Arabic. Tuqa was so taken aback, she managed just a couple of words and smiled sweetly – not the feisty young cellist I knew. We rounded off with Saween resplendent in Kurdish dress, singing a traditional song in her pure, non-vibrato voice, ornamenting with mesmerising glottal inflections, while Tuqa and Zana accompanied on cello and violin. This was the last thing the producers wanted for a morning magazine, but we were very chuffed to have sneaked in something authentic.

As we drove back to the airport, I let Zana know he'd just performed in front of 2.6 million Germans. Meanwhile, Deutsche Welle filmed our players at breakfast with guest families in Bonn, watching us on TV in Berlin. The media circus was in full swing.

I wanted to expose us to as much media as possible, because a month was very little time to learn how to deal with it. Not only did we need major coverage to survive, we also needed to learn our boundaries and refine our PR strategy for the future. This could only be discovered by opening the floodgates in Beethovenfest and coping with it all. Everybody rose to the challenge remarkably. As Silke Neubarth, Beethovenfest's Press Officer, said, 'They're all media stars, every single one of them'. And she was right. Interview after interview showed them dancing, playing, smiling, and talking eloquently about Germany and Iraq. Everyone was a character. No other youth orchestra that had visited Beethovenfest came close to our ability to put ourselves out there with such personality. Iraq couldn't have wished for better ambassadors, if indeed Iraq had wished for us in the first place.

Of all the players, Hellgurd absolutely loved the camera. Coming from Ranya, a small Kurdish town that had led a revolt against Saddam Hussein in 1991, he'd developed a gentle and sophisticated English sense of humour, taught himself viola in a dreadfully equipped Institute of Fine Arts, and managed to convey the softly spoken sorrow of the Kurds through his black, heavy eyebrows. In spite of me denying him rehearsal time off, Deutsche Welle still managed to make a little film of him visiting famous landmarks of Bonn. His relationship with Germany had begun to change his life.

Monday 19th September, and our players teamed up with musicians from the Gürzenich-Orchester in Cologne for one-to-one coaching. Gürzenich-Orchester had already been to Suleymaniyah in March, to stage Iraq's first ever opera, Mozart's *Il Seraglio*, with Cologne Opera in Telary Huner, our birthplace. Back then, I'd collaborated with Gürzenich to create an impromptu workshop for any players in town who wanted free lessons. Now, I was delighted to delegate everything to the incredibly hard working team at Beethovenfest, while I had the evening off.

Our musicians soon mastered Bonn's public transport system. Once the post-war capital of Germany, the city had become a gentrified haunt for bourgeois students and the elderly. My players loved the quiet, clean streets, the freedom to move around without military checkpoints, and a warm autumn that supported their music making. Finally, they had a chance not only to play in tune, but also to learn what 'in tune' meant without the Iraqi heat and air conditioning expanding and warping their instruments. For the first time in their lives, they had a brief window to find out what it meant to be normal musicians.

The first few days without the German players went well in spite of communication issues, as the tutors started polishing the foundation we'd laid down in Erbil. On Tuesday of our first week in Bonn, the 16 young players arrived from across Germany to work with us on our final build-up. We normally began each course with an icebreaker, but had never done this with foreigners. Having just come back from a visit to Beethoven's birthplace, we readied ourselves to meet the Germans in Beethovenhalle for the first time.

I asked everyone to gather in a big circle. Our singer and second violinist, Saween, stood with me in the middle to demonstrate a game I'd invented. I asked her in English what her name was, where she came from, and what she played. She had to answer in English, with me coaching her. She then asked me the same questions in Sorani Kurdish and had to coach me to reply in Kurdish. Language separated us, so it made sense to use language teaching to bring us together. My little game turned out to be slightly too ambitious as we faltered and broke down into laughter. Everyone knew what I was getting at, and we all started introducing ourselves to each other in English, German, Arabic and Kurdish with hilarious results. It was the linguistic version of dodgem cars at a fairground.

When that all wound down, Waleed jumped into an open space, wordless and utterly electrifying, eyed the German players intently, and started dancing. He'd already orchestrated that Sherwan strike up a rhythm on his daff, and off they went. The rest of NYOI joined in as if a giant party switch had just been flicked. The Germans stood in a row against the wall, looking on in bewilderment. Sönke Lentz, the Director of Bundesjugendorchester, joined in with me to try and encourage them, and slowly, one by one, they let themselves be pulled into the gigantic circle dance. I could see this was not what they'd signed up for!

Once the German players finally sat down to join in on our rehearsals, a number of incredible things started to happen. First, we became bigger and more secure for the large stage in Beethovenhalle; we were now an orchestra of 61 players. The Iraqis felt the discipline and musicianship of these young players sitting right next to them, who acted as guides to orchestral behaviour. These amazing young people from Germany and Iraq were using music, body language and eye contact to communicate with each other in the most complex ways. Most of all, we were making new friends, putting cultural differences aside and getting down to the job of making the concert happen.

Thursday 22nd September, and our first test together arrived: two kids' concerts in the chamber music hall of Beethovenhalle. The whole orchestra sat together in front of a packed auditorium of kids from primary schools in Bonn; an adorable collection of multicultural faces, with some girls wearing hijabs like Tuqa, reminding us of our kids' concert in Erbil. But there was no Murad. Our first bassoon was absent. He came into the packed hall five minutes late without a word, unpacked his bassoon as we waited, and sat down. I was furious.

As Music Director, I moderated our programme, a mish-mash of musical warm up games for the kids and players to do together, along with chamber music taken from the Erbil course. We performed the Kurdish song that Saween had sung earlier on TV, then came the wind quintet.

This group was precious to me, as under no other circumstances would an Iraqi flute, clarinet, oboe, bassoon and horn ever sit down together. First, these players lived too far apart and second, most of the players disliked chamber music because it forced them to make sense of what others were doing. Chamber music is dangerous for your ego's health.

Lastly, oboists, bassoonists and horn players in Iraq were incredibly rare. Fewer than five of any decent standard existed. Murad sat down with the other four and played the Ligeti *Bagatelle* like a dog while our lead bass, Samir and I looked at each other, shaking our heads. Through NYOI, he had found his wife, Burju, and acquired a better bassoon which was getting serviced at Beethovenfest's expense while they lent him another instrument. I expected an apology, and got none.

We moved swiftly onto dance music from our Kurdish trio. Then Waleed readied himself to come on and perform the first movement of the Mozart flute concerto, with German and Iraqi string players backing him.

I introduced him to the kids: 'Waleed speaks Arabic, Kurdish and Turkmen, but today he's speaking Mozart'. Waleed, our most outgoing musician, played with an expressive innocence that filled the hall with spontaneous joy. His long, slender form ebbed and swelled as a cat would stretch in ecstasy. When we talked afterwards, Joachim, our German wind tutor, said: 'It wasn't perfect, but it was nice. Just do it.' In the risk-averse home of classical music, German students found it hard to 'just do' anything.

To finish off, we gave the kids our first performance in Germany together, Mohammed Amin Ezzat's *Desert Camel*, whose vivid imagery and catchy Arab melodies went down terrifically well, and ensured the Arab players felt musically represented. *Desert Camel* proved not only the archetypal Iraqi piece, but perfect for kids. I had the task of telling the kids its story in German, which, according to Mohammed Amin's programme note, goes something like this:

'*Desert Camel* is a dramatic piece that talks about a camel with his lover. He is like a desert ship because of his patience, courage and his ability to withstand the open desert, the isolation and estrangement at the crossroads of the elements; the intense sunlight and the darkness, the terror and the fear, the calmness and safety. There are no barriers between him and the rest of the world in his struggle to survive. The music, beginning with a theme played by the oboe and bassoon, describes a young camel in the desert reflecting on the beauty of the calmness and serenity, the fear and caution of life in the desert. Then, the music rises as if describing the entrance of caravans of camels.

'Suddenly, everything disappears except the camel and his sweetheart, whose image of remaining in the desert alone is expressed by an oboe solo. The struggle starts with the appearance of evil bandits, climaxing with his lover kidnapped, as he falls, wounded and unconscious, in the desert. In this new landscape, the atmosphere and the music change rhythmically and harmonically to give a sad tragic sense of loss of his sweetheart.

'Urgently, he starts looking for her, and suddenly the music changes with a gradually building dance rhythm. He sees that there is a gathering and celebration in the distance, and on approaching them, he sees his sweetheart being humiliated and jeered by a crowd. He manages to rescue his lover, pursued by the bandits, and battle commences for his camel sweetheart. He ends triumphant, the evil gaze of the wicked bandits no longer persecuting his beloved.'

Our day off arrived on 23rd September, a Friday of course, to stay in tune with the Iraqi weekend. I remained in Cologne, alone in the local park, sunning myself on a grassy bank, as far away as possible from the players' day trip to the city centre. Naomi Conrad and Rim Najmi blogged on them for Deutsche Welle:

It's a warm, sunny Friday in Cologne's main pedestrian district. Shoppers laden with plastic bags and students pushing their bikes have gathered around a group of musicians playing Vivaldi in a quiet alley off the city's bustling shopping street.

'I've never seen any street musicians in Baghdad,' Aya Isham shrugs. She certainly would have an eye for them. After all, she's a member of the National Youth Orchestra of Iraq, playing at Bonn's Beethovenfest on October 1.

She and her group are trying to live a normal, modern life in Iraq —despite the ongoing violence, and restrictions placed both on women and musicians. Founded in 2008 by an Iraqi émigré in the UK, the orchestra is made up of 45 young Arab, Kurd, Shiite and Sunni musicians, exemplifying their complex, diverse society. For many, the trip to Germany is their first time away from Iraq.

With that distance, violinist Aya recalls the period of Saddam Hussein's regime. Even then, before the war and the ensuing violence, the bombs and the suicide attacks – when it was still relatively safe to walk down a street in Bagdad – she says there were no musicians playing outside cafés or shops.

She's so enthralled with the street musicians in Cologne, she has to film them using her lime-green, flashy smartphone.

'He's really good,' she says, without taking her eyes off the violinist, a tiny figure frantically fiddling away, building up to Vivaldi's crescendo on her phone screen. 'I wish I could take him back to Baghdad with me,' she muses. She and her fellow members of the Iraqi National Youth Orchestra are on a gruelling schedule during their two-week stay in Germany, rehearsing almost every day until late at night to prepare for their concert.

Back in Iraq, rehearsals are normally conducted online, via Facebook and Skype, or recently, in the more secure, semi-autonomous, Kurdish area in the north. But right now, Aya is enjoying a day off from rehearsals with her friend, Du'aa Azzawi, an oboist in the orchestra. They're headed to a music shop in Cologne's city centre. They need to buy a supply of oboe reeds and violin strings. There are no music shops in Baghdad, so the members of the Youth Orchestra have to make do with patched-up, old instruments, handed down by friends or sent by relatives and supporters from abroad.

In the 2003 invasion to topple Saddam Hussein, Du'aa was sent to a different city to stay with her mother's relatives. But when she returned to Baghdad, she discovered that someone had broken into her school and destroyed all the music instruments. Schools there reopened among the debris and destruction of the war and continuing sectarian violence. Du'aa's oboe teacher, like many educated Iraqis, had left the country in the first days of the war. So she, like many members of the Youth Orchestra, had to teach herself how to play her instrument.

Despite continued violence, other things have changed over the years. Western styles, for instance, have permeated some of Iraqi culture. Take Aya. Her hair is cropped short and dyed a colour verging on orange. She wears a short black skirt and beige leather boots; her Arabic is mixed with American English. 'I'm the only woman with short hair in Baghdad,' she claims, proudly and defiantly. She poses for a picture with the violinist street musician. She bought her new boots and skirt in Germany, sneaking out in-between rehearsals.

She also admits that she walks around Baghdad in short skirts and boots. Isn't she worried about getting harassed? 'Well, there are many, many other problems on the street,' she points out. 'I don't care. I just want to enjoy my life.' And no, she doesn't hide her short hair and pierced ears, four rings in each ear, under a scarf.

But even her liberal family, who allows her to travel, play music and mix with men, cannot allow her to walk around Baghdad without a male chaperon. 'I can't go out on my own,' she explains. Every time she wants to leave the house, catch a taxi or go shopping, she has to take someone along with her – a male relative, her father or a friend. And, she adds quietly, not every part of Baghdad is safe enough for her to visit.

She gingerly prods her new piercing: a small silver stud, just below her lip. She had it done just a day ago. When she gets back to Iraq, she will have to take it out. She will wear it at home, maybe at a friend's house in the evening, but not out in public. There are still limits as to what is possible in Baghdad.

'I just want to lead a modern life,' she comments. She says 'modern,' but could also mean 'normal' – a normal life in which she can stroll down a busy shopping street by herself or with friends, listen to musicians and buy violin strings and music scores.

Life in Baghdad, after all, is still not normal. Aya says things have improved, but there are continued suicide attacks, bombs and insecurity. 'But nothing as bad as the worst years,' she recalls. She remembers going to school back in 2006 and 2007, seeing corpses along the road. She used to come home crying, overwhelmed by all the horror. Back then, musicians were afraid to walk around with their black instrument cases, lest they be mistaken for makeshift bombs. Today, Aya says, the city is slowly being rebuilt.

Du'aa, for her part, is proud that she's making money as a musician. Not many of her friends have salaries in a country where some Iraqis still object to Western music – and female musicians. But, 'at our last three concerts in Baghdad, there were so many people there, they couldn't all sit down.'

To her, so many people crammed into the concert hall was a sign that Western music, and the musicians playing it, are being more widely accepted. Only one of Du'aa's aunts has complained, saying she should find a better-paid job. She grins like any Western musician, laughing off a concerned relative's plea to get a job with a secure income and retirement plan.

Right now, anyway, Du'aa has other worries – the music store on a side street in Cologne has closed and moved to another part of town. What other option but for her and Aya to grab some lunch and do more clothes shopping?

'I love shopping,' Aya says. Iraqis, she explains, have started buying expensive clothes. Under Saddam Hussein, it was impossible to find expensive labels – Gucci or Louis Vuitton, for example. But nowadays, Aya adds, Iraqis are flaunting expensive clothes and labels, following the latest fashion trends. She and Du'aa walk into a shop selling fluorescent-coloured donuts. There are no donut shops in Baghdad, no McDonald's, no fast-food shops – and no pedestrian districts where young people wander in and out of shops without chaperons or fear of explosions.

A take-away iced coffee in one hand, a half-eaten cinnamon donut in the other, powdered sugar on her tiger print shirt, Aya strolls down Cologne's shopping street, laughing and chatting with the other musicians from the National Youth Orchestra of Iraq. Four of the Kurdish members are wearing Kurdish national dress: baggy grey or dark blue overalls, broad, colourful, fabric belts, rounded off with turbans or knitted caps – and luminously white gym shoes. Passers-by glance surreptitiously as the mixed Arabic-Kurdish group poses in front of a shop window selling beach accessories and necklaces. Aya and Du'aa, meanwhile, disappear into a store – two young women, shopping, on a bright, sunny morning.

After this brief respite, we drank our milk, and got back on our horse.

On Saturday, we rehearsed. Samir and I talked about the players who had deserted us in 2010. Playing the diplomat, he told me: 'The guys in Baghdad really regret not being here with us.' 'Of course they do,' I replied. 'We're here and they're in Baghdad! The orchestra is educational, not a travel agent.' Banned by Majid and Zuhal, of course they wanted to be in Germany, and of course we couldn't let them. Anyone who felt like walking out on us and putting a project costing this much at risk, couldn't take part.

There were some things the players really disliked. One was German food. Another was the endless rehearsing. Much of the time, I just had to guide them through how they fitted into the whole sound. Beethoven and Haydn were robust enough composers to help with that. Nevertheless, I either ended up conducting like a pantomime dame or a traffic cop to get my point across. This was not how I wanted to work on the stage of Beethovenhalle. Normal rehearsing sometimes worked, sometimes not. Iraqis learnt by rote, a heavy mentality that took us two steps forward and one step back. Thank God the German players helped us as servant-leaders, and the engine of the orchestra started to make good, steady progress.

Meanwhile, power games were afoot. The German Friends started believing they were the orchestra, and that anything going on in Baghdad with Majid was on a hiding to nothing. To all intents and purposes, they were right. Majid had attended a seminar on how to set up a charity, and was central to co-ordinating the Baghdad players for NYOI, but until we had official recognition from Iraq, there was little he could do. Meanwhile, the German Friends and particularly Karl-Walter had solved many big problems, played a vital role in our visit, and donated hundreds of hours of work. But they were not, and could never be, the central administration of the orchestra. They weren't Iraqi.

Our survival depended on major project partners with great political connections and large amounts of cash. Jumping from country to country wouldn't last. Only through central funding from the Ministry of Culture in Baghdad could we become as sustainable as the Iraqi National Symphony Orchestra. Tensions mounted between the German Friends, and Majid and Hassan, who were left redundant when Beethovenfest took over running the course.

While this looked bad to everyone, I sympathised. You can't drop even experienced managers into a running system in a different culture, without some kind of preparation.

Majid and Hassan did find something to do: put a spanner in the works. They sat down with me and the Regional Representatives round a table in Beethovenhalle's canteen. Now came the bombshell. The Baghdad players wanted to be paid for their work. Why were we hearing about this only now? I was lost for words. Everyone had known for months that they were going on an all-expenses-paid trip to Germany and the orchestra's primary goal was educational. That the players from Baghdad played professionally in the Iraqi National Symphony Orchestra didn't, to my mind, change the fact that they desperately needed training, and like every other national youth orchestra, wouldn't be paid. But they thought otherwise. Their Ministry of Culture contract stated that if they were given leave to miss a concert with the Iraqi National Symphony Orchestra, as was the case here, then they would not get that month's salary.

Matters were complicated by the fact that the Kurdish players, who'd been granted leave by their government, were still receiving their salary for September. The Arabs wanted to be paid too, and expected Beethovenfest, who had no budget for this, to foot the bill. The issue ended up being escalated with the German Embassy in Baghdad trying to sort something out with the Ministry. Inwardly, I was furious. It felt like I'd brought myself to my knees to give them an experience beyond their wildest dreams, and still they wanted more. It was hard to cope with how brazenly irrational this felt.

Sunday 25th September was a rehearsal day, and we walked onto the main stage of Beethovenhalle for the first time. Finally, we'd reached a hall whose acoustic was built to enhance the orchestra, and I fell in love with performing all over again. The vast sea of seats, the wooden floor and the giant Beethovenfest banner lit by the working stage lights lifted everyone's spirits. It slowly dawned on them just how valuable their work to the festival and Germany was. Sitting next to each other for a solid month, weathering all manner of challenges, no musician had ever felt this wanted before.

In this final week, the orchestra gelled into a new, stronger musical personality. We were right to give everyone two weeks to get used to Bonn. The German players, already experienced world travellers, brought their own sense of humour and discipline to their Iraqi counterparts. A concert like this would have taken them two or three days to rehearse, so their patience also played a crucial role in nurturing us. Playing in an orchestra is like making love. With so much emotional energy pulsing between the players, few collective experiences are as intense and intimate as this. Every little change you make leads to a thousand miniscule adjustments from everyone around you. While I stood up and dictated the beat, these two radically different groups of players intuitively negotiated to build a new National Youth Orchestra of Iraq. This was the kind of reconciliation and mutual respect that couldn't easily be put on a funding application, or explained to ignorant foundation secretaries, but it was the essence of our existence. And it worked.

By Friday, the day before the concert, we were thoroughly prepped for the arrival of our soloist, Arabella Steinbacher. She'd just come in from the United States, and was flying onto another gig almost immediately afterwards. Normally, she'd get only the afternoon of the concert to rehearse with the orchestra, but under these special circumstances, Beethovenfest programmed us to work with her the day before as well.

That morning, Salar, a new violinist, came up and asked: 'Is that the soloist?' 'Yes' I replied. 'Oh my *God*!' he uttered, walking back to his seat with eyes popping out of their sockets.

The soloist was a woman, and a particularly beautiful one at that. Throughout the morning, she gave us her constant loving attention, making sure she always played to the orchestra, maintaining eye contact with each of them. The generosity which had led her to accept us, now shone out through the hall. After so much effort, we needed this. Sometimes, the players just couldn't react to her finely shaded interpretation and my accompaniment of her. So she changed it to work for them. I was impressed, and they were in awe.

Finally, on Saturday 1st October, we reached the end of a weary journey that had begun on the sofa of *Telegraph* critic Michael White in 2009, and ended with a sold-out concert in Beethovenfest, one of the most prestigious festivals in Europe. From a three-hour general rehearsal in the morning, I went straight into a live radio interview. As I fought my way through in dazed German, Ilona Schmiel, sitting across from me in the studio line-up, motioned her hands in a sleeping position next to her face: go somewhere and lie down before the concert. I did. After one month of rehearsing the same music over and over again in Iraq then Germany, there was little else to do now except crash, conduct and crash again.

With the arrival of German President Christian Wulff, we completed the complex tapestry of cultural diplomacy. In an interview with Deutsche Welle, he declared: '*It is such a great symbol of hope that the different groups from Iraq increasingly understand and relate to each other better. With western music played by an orchestra of Arab and Kurdish musicians it is possible to show that music connects people.*'

Getting into Beethovenhalle after a late lunch, through the bag checks, security tags and bodyguards for the VIP visit, we felt as if we were safe and sound back in Iraq. The President and his wife made their first pit-stop to be photographed backstage with the orchestra. We chatted away pleasantly, knowing that this was the biggest and best thing to happen to German-Iraqi cultural relations for a long time, and the regimes in Baghdad and Erbil could bask in our success while avoiding any real responsibility. The Iraqi Ambassador to Germany, standing next to us in front of the cameras, with slight hesitation offered me his hand in congratulaton.

In the couple of hours before the concert, I met the Music Director of the British Council, Cathy Graham, and Dr Al Shaikhly, Chair of the British Iraqi Friendship Society. They had come over from London to hear us and see how to take next year's UK visit forward. I then went to a hotel foyer round the corner, where I met Pierre Barrois, Director of the Orchestre Francais des Jeunes and Dominique Bluzet, Director of the Grand Theatre de Provence. They were checking us out for an invitation in 2013, when Marseilles-Provence became Cultural Capital of Europe. That Pierre was also a great colleague of mine in the European Federation of National Youth Orchestras was more than instrumental.

The orchestra, stunning in their concert outfits, tuned up backstage, stepped fearlessly out in front of the full house and sat quietly, cooling their heels. The Iraqi Ambassador stepped up to a lectern and introduced the concert in English, followed by Saman and Shwan reading prepared translations in Arabic and Kurdish. God knows why. After that, I banned all speeches before concerts. You can only kick a political football so hard before it deflates.

Finally, I got to go on and deliver the upbeat for Ali Authman's *Invocation* with a German percussionist playing the piano part written for Zuhal. Ali's dark, bold modernism, just within reach of our players' abilities, gave Bonn's sophisticated audience something of what they had come to expect from 'Orchestercampus'. Ali had grown up in Suleymaniyah, studied music in Baghdad and completed his Masters in composition in Holland. His was a language of reconciliation between East and West:

> 'The first Big Bang and the beginning of the white and black creation; it is a beginning time for the invoked voices by the human being and resorting to nothingness. Once angrily, once like a loser and once more for invocation and praying. An invocation which is asking to remove the differences of the human being like color, language, thought and beliefs.'

Then, with Mohammed Amin Ezzat's *Desert Camel* which Michael White from the *Telegraph* described as: *'a programmatic piece about a lonely camel in the desert that sounded like the score to a 1950s Ali Baba film,'* they got treated to a portion of Arab Iraq. Finishing the first half with Haydn's Symphony No 104, we found our groove and powered to the end, the perfect catalyst for our intense joy at being in Beethovenfest.

In the second half, the star of the show, Arabella Steinbacher, came on in a bright red dress and suddenly, the orchestra sounded completely different. As Michael continued to write: *'Her presence raised the stakes considerably, and she did it with an admirable amount of generosity and class: not every soloist I can think of would have been so accommodating.'*

Too true.

Unforgettably, Arabella came into her own with the cadenza, a moment of solo evangelising where she soared like an eagle through the hall. The audience watched the guys in the first violins' jaws drop, Arabella standing right in front of them, eyes closed in deep absorption. From the podium I smiled at our second horn, Ranya, who smiled back, tears glinting in her eyes. This meant the world to a female Iraqi musician, a supreme statement of equality and transcendence. As the orchestra rejoined Arabella for the final passages, and her sweet tones lifted the audience up towards the closing phrase, we bounced off the last two chords with triumph and the audience roared. They too had never experienced anything on stage like this before. The orchestra of the impossible had somehow done it again. Nobody knew precisely what to call what we'd done, but who cared?

In the closing lines of his review, Michael White concluded: *'The speech-making in Bonn was heavy with portentous, reverential intonations of the title 'National Orchestra of Iraq'; but the fact is, these words have no meaning, because the band still has no legal or official status. Two years on and it remains de facto: still no more than emails on Paul MacAlindin's laptop. The Iraqi government, British Council, and whichever other parties claim an interest, need to do some looking into that.'*

Indeed, and this was exactly what Cathy Graham and the British Council were trying to change.

THIRTEEN
The British apotheosis

When our lives are torn apart, we can find ourselves spending many years trying to reconcile the irreconcilable. Bad things happen to good people. I was fortunate to have a mother and father who loved me tremendously, and who let me follow my artistic instincts from an early age, though there were no family musicians as such. Dad, a journalist, had grown up in a stable home in St Andrews, where his father was Master of Works at St Andrews University. This put him in charge of the repair and maintenance of the university's buildings. Mum grew up not far away in the Bow of Fife. The oldest of three sisters and a brother, their mother and father had managed a farm, one of a handful of houses that made up the hamlet of Pickletullum. It was so small, on driving though, Mum taught me to say, 'That's the Bow of Fife... that was.'

One day, aged five, I announced to Dad that I wanted to play the piano. A piano was purchased, along with lessons, which took pride of place in our small flat in the coastal village of Aberdour.

When I was seven, we moved to the ancient capital of Scotland, Dunfermline. There, I became 50% of the male ballet dancing population of the Kingdom of Fife. Miriam Holroyd ran the Victory School of Dance, a grand lady who made her living teaching all manner of dance classes as Mrs Askew, a chain-smoking pensioner hunched over a piano, dutifully launched into the repertoire for putting us through our Royal Academy of Dance exams. Between them, they definitely had a 'marriage of convenience,' but soon my body was carried away by the poise and élan of ballet. We dancers have a saying, 'Between the leap and the floor, is God,' and I felt that leap in every lesson. Miss Holroyd's cool professionalism masked her deep love of teaching me to dance. We worked together for 11 years.

At 11, I started at Dunfermline High School, a factory processing some 1,800 kids, whose music department quickly became my refuge. The slightest sign of weakness was harshly attacked, the staff embattled. In my school magazine article about J-Block, 'J For Junk,' I quoted one teacher as saying, 'This school was built to be systematically destroyed by children.' The catchment went down to Rosyth Dockyard and Spam Valley, a new housing estate occupied by young families who had invested so much on their home, it was said all they could afford to eat was spam. Many were expected to leave school and start working at the dockyard. So a musical, ballet-dancing boy with an unusually large vocabulary and an accent that didn't fit, was an easy target for a harsh regime. I reckon about a third of us should have been locked up in secure accommodation to protect us from the other two-thirds.

The performing arts became my salvation. We had the Carnegie Youth Theatre, a hugely successful company that made starlets of us local kids. Dramatika, Mr Cauldwell the Latin teacher's theatre club, put on anything from Ibsen to saucy Feydeau farces. Then of course we had school musicals. I found countless opportunities to dress up in other people's clothes, speak other people's lines, and finally be myself without fear of attack. I specialised in transvestites and pantomime dames. The stage was a force field that provided me with rich comedy roles to inflict bawdy humour, much of it in drag, on the very people who were attempting to crush my spirit in the corridors of learning. There, I could wrap a full house round my little finger with unbounded absurdity. Throwing the public into psychological tailspins, I struck back and regained control. The theatre became a womb to give birth to my power.

Both my parents really loved me and let this little soul, who had decided from an early age who he was, simply be himself.

But, as was common in their generation, love played no role in marriage. Mum was expected to find a husband with a steady job, and Dad a wife to build a family with. The children of such marriages found themselves blackmailed into becoming the sole reason for keeping these two adults, and thus their entire world, together. In my case, divorce would be loss of face for my Catholic mother and my socially active father. On top of that, all three of us were trapped in a downward spiralling calamity, the worsening of my mother's untreated schizophrenia.

This started to manifest itself in disturbing letters sent to school and to the Carnegie Youth Theatre. Jeans that were too blue were deemed cancerous, as was sitting directly in front of the TV. I was to be home at a precise time, to be fed burnt food. By the time I was 16, I was barred from going to parties. If I accepted a hot drink from her, it would contain the vestiges of a half dissolved Tenormin, prescribed for my father's high blood pressure. Never once allowed to close my own bedroom door, she would creep in at night and open the window, convinced I wasn't getting enough oxygen. This would trigger asthma attacks that were only diagnosed years later. I would wake up with a start in the middle of the night to find her standing over my bed, staring coldly down at me.

The worst part was hearing her barricade herself into the kitchen to talk to herself, sometimes to cry, and often to scream at the voices in her head. In the ironically labelled 'quiet room' next door, I was trying to get on with composing and piano practice.

Throughout my adolescence, Dad and I would get ourselves out of the house as much as possible, he to tennis, badminton, golf, me to ballet, piano lessons, youth theatre. As long as the law stated that Mum was not a physical danger to herself or anyone else, treatment could not be imposed, and in her suffering mind she was not ill. The disease was defending itself. As the most stubborn member of her family back in Pickletullum, no one could convince her she had a problem. On the contrary, she was telling us to get psychiatric help.

The illness was distorting her intense love for me into manipulation, delusion, paranoia and shame. Our lives were being slowly destroyed, but all we could do was work around it. Outside the home, she barely interacted and was gradually ignored, a common situation for Scots with mental illness in the 1980s. Our family's mounting history of emotional abuse was invisible to the law, the medical profession and society. Until one day.

My fifth and penultimate year at high school saw me particularly drained by bullying. My grades were suffering, and Mum's illness was climaxing in new and awful ways. She was determined that I should not grow up, as my impending adult life would be her world-shattering loss. The school had been invited to a performance of its orchestra in a friendly competitive play-off with the orchestra of Queen Anne High. This was set to take place in the neighbouring town of Kirkcaldy. Three days of rehearsal were organised, and every participant got time off other classes to rehearse. I played in the percussion section, and sang in a quartet. I told mum this and woke up on day one of rehearsals to discover she was refusing to let me go. Through the irrational conversation, I managed to work out that, in her mind, Kirkcaldy was riven with AIDS and my presence there might lead to me standing on a piece of infected spit lying on the street with my shoe, and so catch HIV.

Dad was at work in Edinburgh. She locked all the doors and barricaded me into the living room. I broke the rusty nail that had bolted one of the windows, leapt out onto the front garden and ran to school. I arrived late, out of breath, and through my wheezing told the story to the Head of Music, Mr Greenaway. Since I was usually punctual and enthusiastic, he said nothing and let me carry on with rehearsals. Day two was the same as day one, except this morning she barricaded me into the kitchen. I pushed the washing machine in front of the door to prevent her coming after me, forced a window open onto the back garden, leapt out and ran to school, late again. I was greeted with some incredulity, but allowed to rehearse. Each of the two evenings I told Dad what had happened and he reacted with silence. Probably disbelief. Certainly helplessness.

On the morning of day three, Mum and I had a bitter argument and began fighting each other in the living room. She stormed out and locked me in. For the third time, I forced open a window, and ran out through the garden. By now, I was belting along the road at breakneck speed, breaking through adolescence and into the free warrior spirit of a young man. As I made it to school, two double-decker buses awaited the school orchestra in front of the main building. We all piled on board, preparing for the big adventure. And then she appeared. I escaped to the top deck, right at the back, surrounded by other pupils. Up she came and said: 'Come on, Paul, we're leaving.' I looked her in the eye and, with cold decisiveness, replied: 'Certainly not'.

That was the cut that changed everything. With nowhere else to go, and two busloads of kids needing to depart, she managed to keep three Deputy Rectors and the Head of Music on the pavement in front of the school, arguing with her for 45 minutes as the orchestra peered through the windows at the spectacle. Mr McParklin, a raven of a man who proudly stalked the corridors in his black rector's cape, could actually be heard asking her if she wasn't afraid I would run away from home if she carried on like this. A noble attempt to stand up for me in a clearly desperate conversation that, as I stood in the doorway of the bus, could only lead to another defeat for sanity. But the illness had broken cover spectacularly, in so doing defeated itself, and the buses eventually pulled out with me on board.

She followed us in a taxi to Kirkcaldy, and was seen by staff of the Adam Smith Centre, where we were performing, walking around inspecting the air conditioning, presumably to check my oxygen intake again. But there was no further interference. That afternoon, Dunfermline High School Orchestra was trounced by Queen Anne High, but as we travelled back home and for the coming days and weeks, the kids, and soon the entire school, had much more interesting things to talk about.

Back home in the evening, Dad, who had been phoned by the school, came back from work, walked straight in and without saying a word to Mum, turned to me and, using words that oddly mirrored hers, asked: 'I'm leaving, Paul. Are you coming?'

Thus, Dad and I began our new lives. The myth of my parents' marriage, our lower-middle class stability, the facade of normality were exploded by an act of mental illness and a reaction of adolescent defiance. My initiation into manhood was unplanned, public, messy, but most of all, self-made. Everyone was at a loss as I grasped in the dark for a new life. Bullying stopped overnight. I continued my refuge in the music department, got an unconditional offer to Surrey University, a merciful 600 miles south of Dunfermline, and faced the incredible task of rebuilding my life. Mum, Dad and I would live the next 25 years with the guilt, shame and shock of our family's irreversible destruction.

Thus, performing arts became a shield to protect myself from the violent madness around me. They were healthy mechanisms for converting this energy into creativity and eventually, with the Carnegie Youth Theatre, musical direction of my first shows. By the time I left school I could sing, dance, make music and deal with madness, all good basic training for the Musical Director of an Iraqi youth orchestra. As I look back, I realise Mum was sick but, for allowing our incalculable suffering, society was mad.

After Beethovenfest there was no such thing as business as usual. The critical elements of running auditions online, fundraising, presenting NYOI abroad and sorting out the thorny visa process for the UK were different kinds of hurdles from Germany, but we went through not dissimilar motions. With the expertise I'd built up, I was involved on many levels, while countless people led or assisted behind the scenes. The German Friends continued financing my work at their better-than-nothing rate of remuneration. I was alive, but always choking. However, this year, some elements changed dramatically. And I was ready for battle.

First, I dropped the idea of a course in Iraq, because nobody wanted to pay for it. Instead of pounding away at one programme for a month in two parts of the world, I designed a single three-week course in Edinburgh, with community outreach and visits to the International Festival. Keeping NYOI in one place would, I believed, bring us good concerts, great coaching with local tutors and maximum media exposure at minimum stress.

This solution for the quality I sought, also proved the most cost-effective.

Second, there was no one like Beethovenfest to organise us. The Edinburgh Festival Fringe gave us an official invite, but with over 2000 other shows to present, their help limited itself to advertising and selling tickets for our concert. Everything else, from accommodation, food, transport and health insurance to concert hall bookings, budgets, publicity and print had to be managed by a team of freelance project managers, led by Becca Lawrence in London. Local PR firm Material was briefed to maximise media coverage at minimum interference to the course. British Council Scotland became the project banker for funds from the Scottish Government, and Cathy Graham oversaw the project from British Council London, especially the fundraising with Becca. I worked tightly together with them on this, using my original research in 2010 and the contacts I'd built up through the British Iraqi Friendship Society and the Iraqi British Business Council. Still, our successes were hard won.

From all our gold digging, Creative Scotland and the A.M. Dommett Charitable Trust gave us their support. Of course, many did not. By far my favourite rejection letter, one that will live with me to the grave, explained with consummate sensitivity: 'Sorry, at present we do not fund cross-ethnic quasi-classical music as there is so much to do in the purely classical field.'

That was that then. We did get a terrific sponsorship of £20,000 for the London concert from Majid Al Jafar, the CEO of Crescent Petroleum. We'd met two years before at his seminar on the Future of Iraq's Oil and Gas. Dr Shaikhly at the British Iraqi Friendship Society had indeed come through for us.

As part of the deal, the Scottish Government wanted a performance in the Edinburgh Festival Fringe, so I targeted their last weekend, Sunday 26th August, one week after Ramadan. Simply put, we could never perform during Islam's holiest month. However, we could rehearse through Ramadan, because work was sacred and this was acceptable to the orchestra. We also planned a preview concert in Glasgow's Royal Conservatoire of Scotland the night before. After Edinburgh, we were set to perform in the Queen Elizabeth Hall in London, a joint British Council and British Iraqi Friendship Society event. Then home. No concert in Iraq. I was sick of Iraq. I was sick of working through continual crises no matter how well we tried to prepare. I was sick of trying to drum up big amounts of cash amid their political strife. If the Ministries of Culture in Baghdad or Erbil wanted us to perform there directly afterwards, they could pay for and organise it themselves. I knew they couldn't and wouldn't.

With few tangible indications for success, a project like NYOI could only be achieved on blind faith, and having learnt over the years to get results on pure emotional stamina and hard work, it seemed to be working.

However, simmering away in the background was the British Council's strategy of helping the orchestra set up its own NGO in Baghdad. The Director of British Council Iraq, Brendan McSharry, had helped Majid, Hassan and Shwan set up an office with furniture for them to get down to business. The rules for creating an NGO in Iraq required that the board set up a website, office and bank account before registration. In Iraq, I could have walked into a bank and opened an account under the name of Barack Obama if I wanted.

The British Council flew Majid and Hassan across to the UK to have meetings in London, Edinburgh and Glasgow with the project team, myself and Zuhal. They had correctly analysed that NYOI desperately needed international mobility to survive. The orchestra had me running around the world for them, often at my own expense, but the Iraqi team was hindered by the world's least popular passport and a government that made it almost impossible for them to set up a legal entity. For me, it still came down to passion and hard work. As I said to Cathy Graham about Majid: 'Look, it doesn't matter where you are. You still have to go through the shit to find out what works. And he's not doing that.'

It was easy for me to mount a neo-liberal high-horse and declare that I'd managed to keep the orchestra going all these years with just a laptop. This belied the reality that I, a British citizen living in Germany, was in a vastly more privileged position to act than they were. Still, passion, hard work and the ability to ride out disappointment were universal human attributes that could be learnt.

During Beethovenfest, after a day of swatting journalists like flies, the Director of Bundesjugendorchester, Sönke Lentz, offered me this advice: 'A national youth orchestra course should be like a little utopia. There should be nothing to disturb it. You should be able to rehearse as much or as little as you want.' I loved the sound of that: very much the German philosophy that good management should be neither seen nor felt, and took this to heart for our British visit.

Thus, we found our perfect home from home in Jewel and Esk College, a campus on the outskirts of Edinburgh in the borough of Portobello, where Mum also happened to live. Their modern, on-campus accommodation offered us the peace we needed to work, a student canteen, rehearsal rooms, fitness centre with pool and a 22-minute bus ride to the worldwide mayhem of Edinburgh's Festivals.

NYOI's local earth mother was, of course, *la Capona* of the Edinburgh Youth Orchestra, Marjory Dougal. A powerhouse in her own right, she'd run them for over 30 years, and knew everything about musical life in the town. When she, Zuhal and I met in Edinburgh back in 2010, none of us imagined how we could bring the orchestra here. Now, with immense amounts of collective willpower, we were on course. We set the Edinburgh Youth Orchestra to play the same role as Bundesjugendorchester: supportive string players, youth orchestra mentors and city guides through the chaos of Edinburgh Festival time. I was worried the Iraqis would get lost. We scheduled the Edinburgh players to start with us in week two, after we had solved our own musical problems in week one.

As for the programme, I decided we were already overjoyed with joy, and to mature, we needed to play to the orchestra's darker strengths. Given the players' backgrounds, there was definitely murkier psychological territory to explore. We were also invited to the wacky Fringe and not, thankfully, its considerably more conservative partner, the International

Festival. This year, we would show the world how sophisticated, diverse and innovative we could be. I found Karzan Mahmood, a Kurd living in Stockholm with a Swedish passport, and Osama Abdulrasol, an Arab living in Antwerp with a Belgian passport. Both had grown up in Iraq and developed as composers in Europe. Both knew how to write for orchestra, didn't need visas to enter the UK and had minimal travel costs. Perfect.

Max's *Reel of Spindrift, Sky,* written for us in 2011, made the ideal concert opener. His dual status as anti-war protester and Master of the Queen's Music made him a superb figurehead.

Next, I had to decide, with four horns as a game changer, what our symphony would be. This part of the programme had to fit the pedagogical needs of the orchestra. Besides, with limited forces and abilities, we had little choice but to find something from Haydn to Schubert. Tchaikowsky was out. After much deliberation, I plumped for the complexities of Schubert's 4th Symphony (the *Tragic)* over his 6th, which I was sure would drive me nuts with boredom after three weeks. Our first programme without our old friend, Beethoven, I felt as if we'd evolved a little.

This left the matter of a soloist. Marjory suggested Julian Lloyd Webber, as he had close ties to Edinburgh Youth Orchestra and had also taken an interest in NYOI back in 2009. I agreed. We needed a major musical presence on stage, not just for Greyfriars Church in Edinburgh, which was a 550-seat venue, but also for the 950-seat Queen Elizabeth Hall in London, performing the day before the Paralympics opened. Julian, with his El Sistema education work in England and international cello career, was the perfect artist to fill those venues and deliver our common message of music education and reconciliation. But Elgar's Cello Concerto was out of the question. On one afternoon's rehearsal with Julian, we'd never pull such an intricate piece together. Instead, we chose the Fauré *Elegy*, an easier seven-minute study in mourning which at once shared the sense of loss in the key of C minor with Schubert's *Tragic* Symphony. I spent a good half hour worrying if putting these two works next to each other in such a dark key would overwhelm the audience. Silly me.

The second half of the concert now seemed clear: Fauré followed by Schubert. The first half, entirely new works written for NYOI, still needed a counterbalance to Julian's intense seven minutes of Fauré, perhaps another soloist, but definitely not classical. I remembered Dr Shaikhly's words to me back in 2010. Weaving traditional instruments into the orchestra was a strong move. So, through the British Institute for the Study of Iraq, I touched base with Khyam Allami, a contemporary oud player in London who led the 'Sounds of Iraq' project. His team digitally archived Iraqi recordings dating back decades with help from the British Library and British Council.

My gut told me that we needed a brand new oud concerto, and that my old mate in Glasgow, Gordon McPherson, was going to write it. Gordon, it turned out, leapt at the chance, as Khyam was also the drummer of Knifeworld, his favourite London indy band. So, by February, Khyam was on his way up to Glasgow to help Gordon get his head around the oud, Middle Eastern tuning systems, ornamentations, riffs and so on. The programme worked, at least on paper.

All through this preparation, my heart was thumping as the possibility dawned of being accepted, albeit temporarily, by Scotland. Gone were the Machiavellian plonkers trying to twist me round their little fingers. They were still around somewhere, busy controlling someone else. With Becca and her team, the British Council, Edinburgh Youth Orchestra and the Scottish Government all working to bring NYOI to Britain, I finally felt I could just get on with the job of producing a concert. Really, I was also the middle-man between them and Iraq. Majid and the Baghdad team would clearly never manage the complexities of taking this orchestra abroad by themselves.

I relished my meetings with civil servants, directors, diplomats, finally stepping out from under the shadow of Peter Maxwell Davies to become somebody worth doing business with on equal terms. I had defeated the petty, the stupid and the envious, who suited themselves to believe I was with him to further my career.

The Scots put-down, 'Ah kent yer faither,' or 'I knew your father,' meaning you cannot escape the gravity of your perceived past, no matter how hard you try, held no power over me anymore. Moreover, I was already proud of Dad. Peter Maxwell Davies was 34 years older than me and he was not my father, though he was the man I fell in love and shared nine years of my life with.

The two lovely brothers from Erbil, Alan and Daroon, didn't stand alone in regarding me as a father figure. As a gay man, my parenting potential had never ever crossed my mind. Instead, I'd already played a pivotal role in shattering my own family, by self-initiating through a school orchestra on a bus when I was 17, the same age that Zuhal had founded NYOI.

This gave Majid's rallying cry, 'To the bus!' a whole new slant. Now, in spite of all the professional distance I could muster, I had become a parental role model to young Iraqi musicians who, in return, were giving me a depth of family and reconciliation more profound than my own.

Through that, I could share my knowledge of being a musician, proud minority and leader. I knew that every step on our journey together led them through a passionate rite of passage out of the despair of war, and into their own birthright as musicians, whole and brilliant under the spotlight, finally together in peace. All along, my maternal craziness had driven the project from year to year, while my paternal leadership created the framework that transformed us into an orchestra. How dare I help others transcend themselves and threaten the broken *status quo*? Had Scotland taught me nothing?

Scotland transforming Iraq, Iraq transforming Scotland, sat at the heart of my strategy all along. The sounds of countless Scottish composers whose work I'd supported, had burrowed deep under my Celtic skin. Their shards of yearning beauty found new meaning through the raw voices of my Iraqi musicians. And being allowed to conduct Schubert in my own country, albeit by creating a youth orchestra in a middle–eastern conflict zone, felt indescribable.

Many across Britain who had railed against war in Iraq sought penance, justice and reconciliation. NYOI provided a step closer towards the people they had hurt. To us, it meant vital access to great teaching and being embraced as international artists amid the hubbub of the Edinburgh Festivals and London's South Bank. Bringing the orchestra triumphantly to Britain closed not only the circle of justice for Iraqis that began with a lunch in Edinburgh in 2008, but also vindicated me after years of alienation and rejection. And the more our visit revealed itself to me, the more my pronouns, 'they,' 'I,' 'we,' melted into each other.

I boarded the flight to Edinburgh, about to experience a very human phenomenon I'd learnt from Iraq. My world was already dividing itself anew into those who could handle what we'd achieved, and those who couldn't.

FOURTEEN
On the fringes of Edinburgh

The orchestra's journey at the beginning of August 2012, had been long and fragmented, from insane 55-degree heat in Baghdad to the 16-degree summer of Edinburgh in one day. The Baghdad players had to sit in a bus overnight for five hours and rendezvous with the others at Erbil International Airport. From there, they flew to Amman, Jordan, and on to London Heathrow. Then, they connected to Edinburgh, arriving late evening. Karda Hawree from the Erbil office of the British Council accompanied them, texting me along the way. When they finally arrived at Edinburgh Airport they were tired but excited. Our project manager, Becca and orchestra manager, Polly, got them onto the bus, with Gill Parry holding the camera to record all that was going on.

Since 2010, Gill's presence had been constant. In making her documentary, she was following the golden rule; just keep it rolling. With enough patience, one never knew what one could capture. Everyone gave a weary little cheer as I counted the players onto the bus and again sitting down. All 55 had made it from Iraq. While I rarely dropped my professional guard, they were now family. Off we went to our new home at Jewel and Esk College.

That first evening in Edinburgh, the players filled the residency with excitement. We'd put them in single-sex corridors, taking special care to set up quarters for couples like Murad with Burju. They had fallen in love during the 2010 course, and finally got married. She was also a wonderful musician and a stabilising force for the wind section's bass line, as well as for her husband. I also slipped a third bassoonist into the course, Ahmed, also from Baghdad. He'd managed to get on a six-month programme, learning bassoon in Italy, and improved beyond belief. To say that Murad, the Bassoonist of Baghdad, felt threatened, was putting it mildly. He and Burju were now spending as much time in Turkey as Iraq, so given the handful of bassoonists left behind, Ahmed needed as much love and support as we could possibly give him.

Most important of all, Zuhal had come over from Glasgow to rejoin us after missing last year at Beethovenfest. Her friends from across Iraq rejoiced at seeing her again, and we felt complete. The orchestra settled to its first night in Scotland; for me, a simple victory for an already incredible journey that I'd begun in an Edinburgh pub, back in 2008.

Next morning at breakfast, familiar, disoriented faces assembled in the glass-walled canteen, the clouds so low you might touch them. After the campus induction with the trusty Saman and Shwan translating, we herded everybody onto a coach for a tour of Edinburgh. Saman and Shwan were given a list of notable landmarks to interpret into Kurdish and Arabic *en route*. The tour could more easily have been summed up as: 'On your left, rain. And on your right, rain.'

Having enjoyed homestay in Germany, the orchestra found getting used to campus life in Edinburgh to be a succession of culture shocks. The first was that everything worked. Secondly, everything was clean. Third, we were bound to the hilt by rules. Jewel and Esk had a strict no-smoking policy under Scottish law, no football on the lawn and no noise after 10.00 pm for other students and nearby residents. This sent Waleed, who wanted to practice into the night, crazy with worry. And what about partying, which always meant live music making? Their body clocks woke them up after 10.00 pm, when Iraq was cool enough to go outside. Faced with a completely different sense of time, daylight, temperature and my draconian punctuality, they wandered around dazed and confused. We slapped a fine on them for every minute they were late to rehearsal, which brought in bountiful cash in the first week for bare essentials like washing powder and cello mutes. And they didn't like the food. Again. Some of them seriously suggested we bring their mothers to cook next time.

After a full day and a half of rehearsal, we made it through the last movement of Schubert's *Tragic* Symphony and *For Dilan* by Karzan Mahmood. Though the Edinburgh tutors couldn't believe me, we sounded much better on day one of this year than day ten of last year. Music in Iraq was definitely improving between courses.

I felt we were ready for even more challenging and diverse compositions. Osama Abdulrasol's *Habibu* told the wonderful story of an Iraqi poet, Rabbia Aladawyyia, born somewhere between years 95 and 99 of the Islamic calendar. Aged 10, she was kidnapped by a gangster and made his slave. Being extremely beautiful and a great singer, she was sold to a wealthy man, and she grew up to become the queen of his harem.

However, Rabbia fell in love secretly with God. Since Islam forbids the personification of God, she used to go secretly to talk to her lover in a very poetic language and sing for him, *Habibu* – anonymous lover. In her late 20s, her master heard her reciting one of her poems, *In love with God,* and freed her. Rabbia, now a Sufi mystic woman, departed the city towards the desert to unite herself with God. Afterwards, the same people who came to her performances gave up their lives to follow her into the desert.

It astounded me that, like every Arab Iraqi composer I knew, Osama wrote us an upbeat and deeply traditional work, even after living for so long in Belgium. It seemed the romantic Arab heart always longed to relive the greatness of its past.

Karzan Mahmood, on the other hand, wrote *For Dilan*, whose edgy modernism I'd heard from other Kurdish Iraqi composers. His dedication of this abstract work to his new-born son, pointed to the future in a musical language that had cut itself free of the past. I felt torn between another missed opportunity to showcase traditional Kurdish music, which he certainly knew how to do, and his right to express himself. The very absence of tradition did speak strongly to the thousands of Kurds who

Saddam Hussein had murdered and buried in mass graves and, with them, centuries of oral tradition. Modernism and mourning marked the contemporary Kurdish sound.

Musically, the orchestra just hated this piece, though technically, it was playable. It seemed a shame they'd flown so far to play music they couldn't understand. Though we couldn't really explore musical finesse from either of these two composers, spending all of our time just getting it right, we could at least show Britain just how radically diverse Iraq was.

The tutors and I really dug deep into the players' musicianship with our first attempt at romantic music, Fauré's *Elegy*, and Schubert's *Tragic* Symphony, an exquisite, and hugely rewarding late classical work. I cared passionately that each part of the programme gave everybody something challenging to do. We'd spent a lot of money on each musician, so they were going to play as much as possible.

That evening of the first rehearsal day, Becca and I took some of us into town for our first event, and quickly got soaked to the skin. Scots like me, growing up in the rain, had developed a semi-hunched posture as we huddled along the street, but the Iraqis were enjoying it, faces lifted heavenwards after leaving behind 55-degree heat. For our oboist, Du'aa, rain felt like taking a cool shower on open roads.

Eight of our musicians plus Zuhal, Saman as translator and myself, turned up to the Spiegeltent in George Street, a mobile festival venue for music and cabaret. Fiona Hyslop, the Cabinet Secretary for Culture and International Affairs, was set to attend this British Council press launch of our visit. But Fiona was late, caught in the rain.

On with the show. Marjory presented four of her players from the Edinburgh Youth Orchestra performing the famous Iraqi lament, *Che Mali Wali*. The Austrian conductor, Hans Graf, a former Music Director of the Iraqi National Symphony Orchestra, had arranged this for string quartet in the 1980s. Somehow, he'd managed to crystallise all its earthy sorrow into a Viennese salon piece. Then, Sherwan on the daff, Ballen on clarinet and Rebaz on violin performed a lullaby from Hallabjah followed by a jaunty number about a girl. Our audience sat around respectfully listening, completely missing the point.

We ate, played and danced as a family, so I had to bring the select audience to their feet in a circle, holding hands in the middle of the tent, and cued the guys to start again. Dignitaries, civil servants, journalists and Iraqis all bobbed up and down, occasionally in time, to the hollering clarinet, wailing violin and tremulous daff. Still, the Minister was nowhere to be seen. I whetted their appetites with the story of NYOI, my first contact in a newspaper in the Barony Bar, now coming full circle to our Edinburgh visit. Zuhal and Saman filled in on my filling in. For the first time in years, I felt respected, supported and confident in Scotland.

Being orchestra spokesman was fun, but it also made for a much better double act with the amazing Zuhal. She had shed the teenager, gone through a painful rite of passage in Scotland, and now stood alongside me as a genuinely confident, empowered young woman.

Fiona Hyslop finally arrived. Her journey through the rain to get here on time had been a challenge, she said, but this was nothing compared to the journey of the National Youth Orchestra of Iraq to Scotland. Too true. Now we wanted to deliver a concert that everyone could be proud of. We also needed to tell the story of another Iraq, a country that had been so intensely reported on, about which we still knew nothing.

Back on campus, I set up a tough daily schedule. Every morning, for half an hour, our lead wind tutor, Dougie Mitchell, warmed up the orchestra with stretching and group improvisation. Then followed individual lessons and group coaching for the wind, percussion and strings. At noon, we broke out into chamber music practice with the tutors. We gave ourselves one and a half hours for lunch, then through the afternoon, more group rehearsals and a full orchestra rehearsal at the end. After dinner, tutors carried on giving individual lessons into the night through the translators.

We had tremendous fun with Dougie's warm-ups. As the players came from such a different culture, with improvisation at its heart, we could get away with the craziest things that conformist youngsters in the West would stick their noses up at. Our group jam sessions involved everybody, violas beginning with a clapping pattern, violins fitting in a riff on three notes, basses slapping out counterpoint, then one by one, winds jammed freely on five notes, before the whole orchestra punched out a riff in unison. After a few practices, Dougie could step off the podium and let Samir, Zuhal or others direct the jam session. These great exercises tapped into the ensemble's raw creativity and built trust.

Often, my full orchestral rehearsals became mired in learning by rote and correcting mistakes. So I sometimes stopped and pretended to look down at the score, waiting for them to start chatting away with each other. As I let that bubble up to the surface, I could feel them freeing their inner chaos, and mould it into the next rehearsal segment. And what a terrific energy to work with it was.

However, even with a dramatic improvement in the weather, intense rehearsals and culture shock took their toll. We'd never had people getting sick before. This was tummy, headache, nose sick, which our project team had to take seriously, and drive them down to casualty. Polly, our orchestra manager, came back from these trips reporting much ado about nothing. Nevertheless, the players had discovered a great way to skip rehearsals and sample the comparative luxury of our local hospital waiting room. Before long, I was asking, 'OK, so who's going to Disneyland today?'

Dougie, myself and the other tutors, were clearly relieved to be finally doing an NYOI course in Britain, rather than crisis managing in culturally arid Iraq. Indeed, I was experiencing the slightest tinge of revenge. Here, the management and accommodation worked and the pubs along the waterfront definitely worked. It felt weird, in a good way, rehearsing the National Youth Orchestra of Iraq then going straight out for a pint with the tutors, or starting a barbeque with players on the beach. For many who'd never seen the sea before, going down to the Portobello sands brought them a sense of peace and freedom. Along the promenade, the guys invented their own bullish leapfrog game to see whose testosterone launched them the highest, while the girls cheered on. Even the simplest things felt ecstatic.

However, when it came to more complex activities, like the Edinburgh Festival, they took more persuading. Ignoring the offer of free bus tickets into town, many favoured the college's Internet terminals, surfing at every opportunity, or chatting with friends in Iraq on Facebook. Coming from a culture where going out was too boring, hot, or dangerous, this was how young Iraqis socialised. We saw this coming, and organised free tickets donated by the Edinburgh International Festival so we could go out together and listen to great orchestras. Much more than a music course, we had begun a three-week-long initiation with the first step – separating from Iraq and breaking down old realities. Very soon, we grew sick of sitting around in stifled anguish on campus. Edinburgh's draconian campus life was suppressing the Iraqi party gene, which needed to be expressed if we were to keep our sanity for three weeks.

On Wednesday evening, the orchestra made it down to the beautiful Portobello waterfront, where the landlord of the Dalriada pub donated us a room for partying until the wee small hours. As a firm supporter of traditional music, he was delighted to help. I turned up just as the room was shaking to clarinets and bodies already whooping wildly, and got caught in a whirlwind of intense alpha male dancing, every inch of floor being turned into a hotplate of jiving feet.

The fire alarm went off. Did we have a smoker in the toilets? Despondent, we all shuffled out onto the street. Partying was not an added extra, but an impulsive duty. How could we keep on being told to stop? After a few minutes, the landlord came out smiling sheepishly to clear up the mystery. We were partying too hard, and our collective body heat had set off the alarm. Oh boy. It seemed we couldn't win. How could I tell them to tone down the partying until the next Scottish heat detector sabotaged us? We needed to find yet another solution.

Our three translators, Saman, Shwan and Dara embodied the lifeblood of our communication. Anyone trilingual in Arabic, Kurdish and English was of above average education in Iraq, and their dedication and intelligence kept us afloat through otherwise hard rehearsals and sensitive situations. They didn't just translate, but also facilitated communication among people who otherwise might not trust or respect each other.

Their power was never more evident than one evening, when five of us, Sherwan, Rebaz, Ballen, myself and our translator, Saman, visited the Scottish Arts Club to talk about the orchestra. Through Saman, the guys movingly described the serious shortfall in Iraqi music education, how they could only learn properly through NYOI, and how music meant so much to them and their families. Before performing a lullaby from Hallabjah on the violin, Rebaz told us how this reminded him of Saddam Hussein's chemical attack on his city and how his relatives had been among the victims. The orchestra contained many non-English speakers who journalists tended to ignore, but their stories and performances still evoked life as a musician in Iraq.

Samir, our principal bass since the beginning, had become very attached to his teacher, Dobbs, in previous courses. This year, Marjory asked Ninian Perry from the Edinburgh Youth Orchestra to coach him and Chia. I knew Ninian of old, and a more experienced bass teacher in Scotland was hard to come across, but the look of betrayal on Samir's face when he saw he not only had no Dobbs, but would also be playing next to a well-pierced rocker by the name of Daniel, will remain long in my memory. Of course, it really didn't take long before Daniel and Ninian won him over. After a week, he softly confided his verdict to me. Dobbs was a '10' but Ninian was a very close '9.9'. Well, thank God for that.

Samir and I became much closer in Edinburgh. We trusted each other about many things, and I felt surprised and honoured that he sometimes used me as a mentor or sounding board. He always came back to the same tragic theme of Iraq: a land of broken people who cared about nothing, while he always tried to go the extra mile. Looking at myself, I didn't have the heart to tell him that people who cared rarely came off well in the end. I think he knew.

One day, he took me aside and asked if I could give him feedback on his performance of the Koussevitsky bass concerto. Sure I could, so we fixed up a lunchtime practice room. I knew he wanted to play solo with NYOI, and demanded a clear yes/no answer as to whether he was wasting his time. As he played with all his heart, so I listened with all of mine. He already held a prominent position in the Iraqi National Symphony Orchestra, and a full-time job as a medical service engineer for a hospital equipment firm. Samir had, with precious little support, become a virtuoso, but, leaning into his bass as a mother would cosset a child, he wasn't outgoing enough to be a soloist. Nor did he want to teach back in Baghdad. He felt, with some justification, that he would simply end up passing his mistakes onto others, and turned people away at his front door, telling them to learn violin instead. I asked Ninian to talk with him about this. Everyone found life tough in Iraq, and NYOI could never offer enough support, but Samir was still the best-educated bass player in the country, thanks to us. As I watched him coach our chamber music rehearsals, I knew he could be a great teacher.

As our first week came to a close, he wrote in our blog:

'A Flower Born in a Suffering Country

'A small fairy tale in the mind of a pure, kind young girl started to become a flower born in a suffering country.

'It is fighting for life and passion to give the scent of freedom and music to the world.

'With love and determination, this flower reached Scotland to wear the colours of its mountains, breathing the spirit of the happy Edinburgh Festival, being watered from its rain, nurtured by honest and loving gardeners and sleeping on the glorious stories of Edinburgh Castle.

'I am lucky to have been a small root from that flower for four years, feeling it, supporting it, drawing emotions and giving my soul happily so that she can stay forever.

'This flower is called NYOI.'

Samir's English, as well as his humility, would put many Brits to shame.

By Thursday, the end of week one, we'd covered all the new works and the Schubert. It now remained to introduce the Edinburgh Youth Orchestra players to our rehearsals. After discussing progress with the tutors, I set up the schedule for week two.

We finally reached our first day off, Friday 10th August. *Orchestra of Dreams,* Channel Four's news segment on us, aired that evening. With it came the first taste of some tough questions. How did it feel accepting money from a government that invaded Iraq? Was this guilt money? Zuhal and I were taken aback but also grateful for the provocation, which helped us read the visit's political undercurrents.

I trusted the players to speak openly and honestly to camera about the visit. On the Channel Four blog, 18-year-old Mohammed Al Saed on third horn said: 'It's beautiful and there are things here that you can't find in Iraq, and the people are different.' Tuqa also noted, 'Here they appreciate musicians a lot more than in Iraq.'

'Wow', continued Bashdar, one of our cellists. 'The musician's life is so beautiful because they're travelling the world, they meet the professional teachers; they can travel around to play concerts everywhere. But this orchestra has made my dreams happen, I'm now fulfilling my dreams and I'm so grateful to this orchestra.' Knowing how friendly and accessible the players came across, I felt I had to make sure we weren't being compared to British youth orchestras.

'A youth orchestra here has the foundation of an education system underneath it so that the kids get decent lessons and they have school orchestras, county orchestras and then the national youth orchestras. We're the National Youth Orchestra of Iraq and there's nothing underneath. So we're at the top of a pyramid of air.

'In terms of the motivation however, all of my tutors and I agree that we cannot find students in Europe who are as highly motivated as these young people because of what they've been through and the way they use music to really protect their souls from the violence and chaos around them.' Nobody knew I was talking partly about myself 30 years ago.

Meanwhile, our tutors were utterly bowled over by the whole experience. I asked Sheena MacDonald, who was teaching Waleed and Chro flute, what she thought:

'I've coached many youth orchestras and ensembles in my time, but I have to say that life as a tutor on the National Youth Orchestra of Iraq course is an extraordinary experience! At the introductory staff meeting we were given an idea of the musical and cultural background of the students, many of them learning without a teacher, dependent on YouTube and the web for musical ideas and recordings. There is no way you can prepare for the difference in culture or understand the day-to-day dangers and difficulties of living as a musician in Iraq. Grim, you think. So what do we find? A passion for music that is quite physical in its expression, an intense focus on learning, practice that goes on through the night, and a joy in playing that is quite unlike anything I know. There is so much laughter and an almost tangible feeling of pleasure in life. How do you carry on then when you find your friend has been blown up by a bomb while you are away? You just get on with it...

'As a teacher I'm amazed at the levels these players have attained without much in the way of lessons. Ensemble experience is very limited. You hear the right notes, but not necessarily accurate in tuning, rhythm, and very often ignoring any rests. Music is more about expressing one's own feelings rather than being aware of other players and responding to them. Eye contact barely exists, and that extends to the conductor's beat on many occasions! In rehearsal I see wind players staring at tuning machines propped up on the stand, rather than listening to the pitch. So many contradictions! As Westerners we take for granted our weekly lessons from experienced players and lots of orchestral and ensemble opportunities. We don't realise how much it has benefitted our playing till we hear what it is like when you don't have this luxury.

'There have been some lovely moments... the huge smile on a clarinettist's face when he played his newly repaired instrument. He beamed from ear to ear and played for ages, astonished at how easy it was... the joyous and exuberantly abandoned dancing of Waleed and partner at the introductory warm-up session with Edinburgh Youth Orchestra strings. Trying to get across the idea of emphasis in a Schubert snippet, I said to Waleed ' I *love* you'. His immediate response was: 'And *me* too!' The discussion we had about the contemporary Iraqi composer's intentions, how we can interpret from the written musical directions. '*But he is not here! He cannot tell us how to play it. We must play exactly what is written, loud here, soft there!* 'My response was that Schubert couldn't be here either... but we were poles apart, and the cultural difference that things are black or white – no shades in between – was difficult to surmount. Buying a new instrument while in Edinburgh... how do you explain that we just don't haggle! It's a rollercoaster, and I don't think I want to get off!'

When Sheena referred to losing a friend, she meant Waleed's best friend in Kirkuk, who was murdered by a car bomb a few days after the course began. Waleed Ahmed Assi came to us in 2010 aged 23, as our second flute in the Erbil Course in Saad Palace. Coming from Kirkuk, he proved to be a very interesting guy.

Kirkuk lay in the so-called disputed territories that both Arabs and Kurds claimed as their own. Both were more interested in the very rich oil fields of Baba Goorgoor; 'Father Blaze' in Kurdish, because the area has been famous since biblical times for its eternal fire. Many believe it is the very same fiery furnace from the Book of Daniel. Women visit the eternal fire to pray for a son. The city itself had a much richer heritage dating back 4000 years. Even today, Arabs, Kurds, Turkmens and Assyrians live and work side by side in Iraq's most ethnically diverse city.

Waleed was unique in NYOI, being able to speak Arabic, Kurdish and Turkmen. His strong, outgoing personality made him many friends throughout the whole orchestra, and our gathering of professional teachers and young musicians from across Iraq, who would never otherwise meet, bowled him over.

When he was 19, he already had a career as a professional footballer. This ended one day when, while watching TV at home, he came across a performance of Bach's second orchestral suite. He sat spellbound, never having heard or seen anything like this before. Clueless about what the solo instrument was, he had to ask a friend. That, said his friend, is a flute.

Over the months, he scrimped and saved to pull together $90 for a cheap Chinese import that would get him playing. With the Internet as his teacher, he downloaded as much fingering and advice as he could, and practiced for months, learning to read music along the way. Sometimes, he'd hit a road block and realise he'd been teaching himself incorrectly all the time, and had to start all over again. When practicing at home started to drive everybody mad, he found a derelict building with no window or door frames, and played there for up to 15 hours a day.

He managed to find a teacher and took the bus up to Erbil, about one and a half hours north of Kirkuk. His intensity also ended up threatening older, weaker musicians, so he ended up relying on himself again. Every year, he gave a perfect audition to guarantee a place in the next NYOI course, so he could work in Arabic with our flute teacher, Daniel Agi. Much of what he said could equally describe a young musician in a remote part of Scotland, who has maybe two or three Skype lessons, reinforced by one face-to-face lesson per month. But Waleed was living in Kirkuk, with a history of ethnic cleansing, Saddam Hussein's Arabisation programme from 1991 to 2003, and continual terrorism from then onwards. He left the dark side of Kirkuk at home. Like many other players, he had become nonchalant about violence. It was part of life, and it could take away theirs at any time. But they were not complacent about peace.

A few days after a devastating bomb blast in Kirkuk, he and his friends walked out to the middle of the blast zone, set up their music stands, and reclaimed the space through music for their town.

After our Beethovenfest performance, his tears of joy could no longer be contained. The relief at being valued and treated as a normal artist and human being was too much. A few days later, he played his Mozart flute concerto in an open-air concert, at the invitation of the German President, before flying home. The freedom to express himself through music without fear had set his dark eyes on fire and, like Hellgurd, ignited a leader. More significantly, he became Kirkuk's first flute teacher.

On 31st March 2012, he launched his own ensemble, named after Kirkuk's eternal fire, the Baba Goorgoor Chamber Orchestra. The Kirkuk public library became their makeshift concert hall, where he stood tall and straight in a white waistcoat, conducting local players, performing local composers. He told the English language website, *Kirkuk Now*: 'We want to tell the officials that Kirkuk is the capital of culture in Iraq. It can't be politicised. We can show its beauty through music and prove that it's a capital of culture in Iraq.'

By the time we were ready to receive the Edinburgh Youth Orchestra players into our ranks, the indomitable spirit of Waleed and the orchestra was in ascendance, and they were deep into their transformation. They were shedding their delusions of what was musically right and wrong, as well as who was of value and who was not. They had dived headlong into a new and difficult world, and were working hard to bring their message of hope and acceptance for Iraq, to Britain. Yes, it was painful for them, but they had good people guiding them with love and skill. I didn't want to be a father figure to these extraordinary young people, but it was too late to change that now.

FIFTEEN
Reconciling Scotland

On Sunday 12th August, the Edinburgh Youth Orchestra players and oud player Khyam Allami arrived at the course. As with Beethovenfest the year before, the new players sat on the inside of each string desk and the Iraqis on the outside, not just to support, but also to make sure that the orchestra actually looked Iraqi in public.

The Edinburgh players were somewhat similar to the Bundesjugendorchester: largely female, younger than us but, unlike the Germans, were mostly local and often late. They were obviously unaccustomed to trilingual rehearsals and the slow rate of progress. Just like Bundesjugendorchester, they had to learn how to support us with patience and humility. Marjory, who turned up every day, kept them pretty much in line, but I also sensed they hadn't fully grasped that they were role models for my players, and a couple of them needed to grow up fast.

Having said that, once Marjory and I had words, they started turning up on time, and taking the job of helping us to build a new sound seriously. The most ironic culture shock for them was the prevalence of new music, especially from Gordon McPherson and Peter Maxwell Davies. It took the National Youth Orchestra of Iraq for young Edinburgh musicians to play Scottish orchestral music. I knew the establishment here very well. In spite of the fact that Scotland was some 70 years ahead of the Iraqi scene, classical music remained conservative, repeating the past with little variation, as often as possible.

Khyam Allami came up from London to rehearse Gordon's oud piece, *Blood Dance* with us over the next two weeks. A shrewd and warm young man with a very open mind under a pre-Raphaelite mane of black hair, he used his time wisely to win the musicians' trust. Although he spoke Arabic, this took longer than he'd expected. Some players sensed his British upbringing. He was somehow, 'not authentic Iraqi', but on the first rehearsal, when he sat down and strummed one chord on his oud, the players immediately responded. 'Aaaaah' went quietly round the room, as if they were back home again.

We gave *Blood Dance* our first run with Khyam. The most radical oud concerto ever written (out of the five we know of), we worked intensely to get it together. Khyam had never played with an orchestra before, and the modern accompaniment wasn't supporting him, so he and I had to work closely to keep it tight. The music was way too difficult and time consuming, but we had to see this through. I believed in Khyam and Gordon, while the players' enormous faith in each other and in me sustained us through laborious rehearsals. Without the Edinburgh players, it simply wouldn't have been possible. I remember Gordon coming in to listen, and after we'd run through, one of the players asked him what it meant. After a very pregnant pause, he explained it was about the pain and suffering that Iraq had gone through. Somebody in the winds retorted, 'Then why are you doing it to us again?' Not a bad line really.

It was partly inspired by Handel's 9th English song HWV 228, *From Scourging Rebellion* written in honour of the Duke of Cumberland, particularly the verse below. With Frand and Murtada on trumpets playing the Handel song, and all hell breaking loose around them, I wanted an apocalyptic sound: 'Terminator Two please!' They knew exactly what I meant.

'How hateful the tyrant, who lured by false fame,
To satiate his prade sets the world in flame!
How glorious the King, whose beneficent mind
Makes true grandeur in protecting mankind!'

Gordon's programme note concluded, 'When looking at the mess that we in the West have historically made to the social cohesion of the Middle East, it seemed particularly apt.' Later, when I put our recording of *Blood Dance* on the Internet, it became a viral hit in Egypt, on the wake of the Arab Spring uprisings. Perhaps this was where it made most sense.

However, the amount of new music was making everyone uncomfortable. One tutor's feedback read: 'The only thing which I felt could have been better was the programme itself. I understand the reasons for choosing the repertoire, but for me the balance would have been better with more classical repertoire, and fewer contemporary pieces. I think the orchestra would have learned even more about sensitivity to feeling and ensemble if this had been the case.'

It was hard not to agree. I'd designed our programme with the Fringe in mind, more offbeat and experimental than the International Festival, but this year's political balancing act had made it somewhat precarious. I hoped I knew how to calculate the risks, and still create the most innovative and Iraqi concert we'd done so far. On one hand, we had the British Council and Scottish Government doing cultural diplomacy with Iraq and each other, and on the other hand, we had the visit of Dr Abdulraman Dheyab.

It was Monday 13th August, and Dr Dheyab, Director of the Iraqi Cultural Centre in London, turned up to campus accompanied by British Council Scotland. As funding for his centre came directly from the Ministry of Culture in Baghdad, his impression of us influenced our future. We'd met recently, a week after the centre opened its doors in fact, and he came across as a warm, articulate guy, a journalist by profession. Today, he was dressed very sharply in suit and tie as representative of the Iraqi Government, and allowed himself to be escorted round.

As we were rehearsing chamber music, there were plenty of small ensembles to watch. First off, we visited Sheena Gordon coaching the Edinburgh strings with Waleed in a Vivaldi flute concerto. Waleed stood in the corner, flute held up at the ready, black eyes fixed in wonder at this small Scottish lady injecting her feisty intelligence into the music. A few moments later, a stout, elderly lady wearing a thick padded jacket and a hat with plastic flowers round the brim poked her head round the door. It was Mum. I nearly collapsed. She'd been threatening to turn up for a few days, but this was right at the start of Dr Dheyab's visit. I begged her to wait outside for a little while. Julia from the British Council found a chair for her and kept her chatting. I excused myself to Dr Dheyab. He fully understood. After all, he said, she *was* my mother!

We moved onto a mixed Iraqi and Edinburgh violin group. One of the Edinburgh players was teaching them a Scots fiddle tune, which they followed with a Kurdish melody that Hogar, the world's most cheerful second violin, had taught them in return. I was over the moon: true peer-to-peer learning. Dr Dheyab, through his smile, told me: 'This is an international orchestra'. I wasn't sure if this was good or bad. He'd mentioned to me in London the need for young Iraqis and Brits to work alongside each other, and here it was happening in front of him. But the reality of seeing Scottish players in the National Youth Orchestra of Iraq had made an impact.

When we arrived to watch our first violin tutor, David Juritz, coaching Beethoven's String Quartet Opus 18 no.1, Dr Dheyab's face genuinely lit up for the first time. There in the corner sat our Arab cellist, Hussam. Finally, someone from Baghdad. I knew from various sources that we were not a national youth orchestra in the Ministry's eyes, because the majority of people in Iraq are Arabs, and not proportionally represented by us. The Ministry didn't care that fewer Arabs applied to NYOI than other groups, and that the Kurds simply worked harder at their auditions to get in. Nor did they understand that I needed the best possible players across the whole of Iraq if we were to represent their country to a respectable international standard, and most of those players came from outside Baghdad. To hell with quality though, this was Iraqi politics.

Baghdad believed it *was* Iraq, and everyone else should bow to its superiority: a centric mindset that put London and New

York to shame. This partly explained why the Iraqi National Symphony Orchestra, mainly Arabs living in Baghdad, got Ministry funding, and we didn't. Many older musicians neither developed younger players for fear of losing out to them, nor tried to expose them to international culture, as they themselves had no idea.

The Iraqi National Symphony Orchestra quietly benefitted from the training and new instruments their younger players were getting from us, while their older players became uncomfortable. Majid, who played trumpet with them, found himself in an increasingly difficult political position. We exposed their weaknesses and undermined their authority.

We got their envy, we hurt their pride, they had no control over us and the only way to save face was to keep us away from them. To add insult to injury, everybody knew the Kurds wanted independence, and claimed their Iraqi passports in name only. Still, NYOI remained a national youth orchestra of Iraqis living across Iraq, a politically naive definition, but the only solution that actually worked. To be fair to Dr Dheyab, I could see his point of view. Imagine if the National Youth Orchestra of Great Britain were based in Edinburgh instead of London, and two thirds spoke only Gaelic. This was how we looked to Arab Iraqis.

Back to Mum. I took her to the campus restaurant while BBC Scotland filmed a report for the evening news. She certainly didn't hold back on the questions, referring to the orchestra as 'your boys.' After finally getting the medical care she deserved at the age of 70, she had miraculously rebuilt her life and, in spite of her humble existence, turned herself into a grand old lady of Edinburgh. She was the toughest person I knew: a real survivor. After a spot of free lunch, we agreed to meet again down town for Harry Ramsden's Fish 'n' Chips in Waverley Shopping Centre.

As the Iraqis' inadequate instruments came under pressure from intense rehearsing, we became deeply indebted to Neil Ertz, a local violin maker who repaired our instruments for free. Marjory Dougal's formidable network had swung into action, and the orchestra was receiving the best care imaginable.

Neil was faced with a sorry state of affairs: 'What's on my bench, well this week something quite different for me... Almost every instrument I saw had a very low flat bridges that where bent, very odd string spacings and often very thick, terrible top nuts, pegs that barely worked...very many had open seams and quite a few wide open cracks. I spent a couple of days this last week doing as much as possible, prioritising to do the most pressing jobs first.'

As Neil's workshop filled up with our wounded instruments, he shaved, drilled and glued away, putting the worst patients in metal braces to heal overnight. Here was the visible evidence of how instruments and their owners had suffered neglect in Iraq. All we could do was to carry on repairing broken musicians, and give everyone the chance to recover.

That evening's concert with the London Philharmonic Orchestra in the Usher Hall became another casualty of our stay. The audience was kept waiting on the pavement for 50 minutes until they were told that the power had failed in the hall, and the concert would have to be cancelled. Undefeatable, NYOI went on a ghost tour of Edinburgh, whose lame actors in *olde worlde* costumes failed to scare our battle-hardened players. In true Iraqi style, they ended the evening throwing a party on a street corner, accompanied by a busker on accordion.

If this were Baghdad, the Philharmonic would have memorised the music and played through the power cut anyway.

After two intensive weeks, the tutors said farewell with their own chamber music concert for the orchestra: Mozart's Clarinet Quintet, an arrangement of *Till Eulenspiegel*, Malcolm Arnold's Sea Shanties and John Corigliano's *Stomp*, with David Juritz. Out came the iPhones and iPads to capture this intimate gold. The comedy mounted when the two violin tutors, David Juritz and Claire Docherty, played out a little pantomime while trying to play one violin. Wrapped in an awkward embrace, David bowed while Claire fingered the strings like a human hurdy-gurdy. Majid leapt up out of his seat, and striking a rapturous pose, videoed the double act on his phone. 'Poetic' was how David later described it.

For NYOI to see and hear these outstanding musicians play together especially for them had an unbelievable impact. Chamber music encouraged musicians to visit each other informally and make music together. As mobility in Iraq was still severely compromised, the traditional Iraqi Maq'am along with other forms of music suffered almost to the point of extinction. Indeed, Tuqa, Waleed, Hellgurd and others had already created their own ensembles. Chamber music always began with mutual respect and awareness, the first building blocks in healing Iraqi humanity.

The tutors fed back on their fortnight with us: 'I found the transition from the first few days to a true ensemble with its own unique identity and character was quite moving.' 'The musical achievements alone were outstanding, given the background of these young people.' 'The efforts to bring everyone together were exceptional and everyone, tutors, management, Iraqi staff and students, felt part of a wonderful team. The translators were lovely, incredibly helpful and much appreciated by all.' Our project manager, Becca, summed it up for me in an off-the-cuff remark: 'How can you create such great results from so much shit?'

We began our third week together feeling a little vulnerable, a skeleton music staff of Sarah on horn, Dave on cello and myself. It was time to reach out to Edinburgh. And so, our chamber music course reached its culmination with a few of us going to Broughton High School to play for the students of the music department. As we prepared for our first step from the fringes of Edinburgh into its heart, I knew we were facing a very critical young audience.

In their beautiful recital room, all the music students, some of whom were playing in NYOI, assembled to hear a mixed programme from them and us. Though my players were a good five to ten years older, we performed to each other with mutual respect, mixing Kurdish, Scottish, Gaelic and Billie Holiday with Mozart and Boccherini. As I moderated, the various backgrounds of the players framed each performance with new meaning. This was never by way of apology, but rather to help these very privileged Edinburgh musicians understand the barriers my players faced in producing something as simple as a string quartet or a horn trio. Their Head of Music movingly suggested to his students that they try learning Kurdish music from YouTube.

That afternoon, Jewel and Esk College erected a tent in the grounds for a garden party. Here, Khyam Allami presented an oud piece accompanied by five players, and Waleed performed the Vivaldi flute concerto he'd been working on with Sheena and the Edinburgh players. This was our way of thanking Jewel and Esk's staff, who were slowly getting sozzled to our Gershwin on bassoon trio and Scottish fiddle music.

Saturday 18th August, a week before our Edinburgh performance. That afternoon, we attended Gergiev rehearsing Szymanowski's *Song of the Night* in the Usher Hall with the London Symphony Orchestra. Sitting in the balcony, surveying the mass of musicians and singers on stage, I spotted Ahmed Abbas, our third bassoon, who'd wangled permission to sit behind the bassoons on stage. I watched him stare intently over their shoulders at the notes on the stands, absorbing all that world-class musical heat pouring out of their instruments. On the other side of the stage, Ranya and Ali sat right up close to the horns, watching them breathe together, living the teamwork that we had been instilling into them. Sarah Maxwell, our horn tutor, arranged to bring them backstage to see her teacher, Jonathan Lipton, for one-to-one coaching. Through us, they had become the most educated horn players in Iraq.

A few days later, I'd fixed up with Kim Sargeant, Managing Director of the European Union Youth Orchestra, to attend their Usher Hall rehearsal and do a brief photo call with both orchestras. All National Youth Orchestras are Rolls Royces, but EUYO auditions across Europe are so competitive that many students call them 'E-U-Why-Bother?'

While our players looked down from the balcony in utter wonder at the rehearsal of Debussy's *Nuages*, Majid and Hassan got up and left. They knew this was exactly the kind of excellence Iraq could never offer, and it hurt like hell, but they had chosen to embrace Edinburgh regardless of how much it challenged them. When the two orchestras met at the break for group

Gudrun Euler, Karl-Walter Keppler, Will Frank and me at a board meeting of
the German Friends of the National Youth Orchestra of Iraq, Cologne 2011
(Georg Witteler)

Some of our players in the main square, Bonn 2011 (Beethovenfest)

Hellgurd Sultan and Dorothee Appelhans rehearsing in Beethovenhalle,
Bonn 2011 (Beethovenfest)

ABOVE: Shwan Aziz and Saman Hiwa at Beethovenfest, Bonn 2011 (Beethovenfest)

LEFT: Shwan Aziz and Saman Hiwa, Suleymaniyah 2013 (Will Frank)

Icebreaker with Bundesjugendorchester, Beethovenhalle, Bonn 2011
(Beethovenfest)

Kids concert, Beethovenhalle, Bonn 2011 (Beethovenfest)

Tuqa Alwaeli and Sabat Hameed
performing with Tannenbusch
School Orchestra, Bonn 2011

Arabella Steinbacher rehearsing with us in Beethovenhalle, Bonn 2011
(Barbara Frommann)

Rehearsing for the concert in Beethovenhalle, Bonn 2011 (Beethovenfest)

Beethovenfest's Ilona Schmiel, Deutsche Welle Intendant Erik Bettermann,
President and Frau Wulff, with Daroon Rasheed from our viola section and Iraqi
Ambassador Dr Hussein Alkhateeb backstage in Beethovenhalle, Bonn 2011
(Barbara Frommann)

Arabella Steinbacher and NYOI, triumphant after the Beethoven Violin
Concerto, Bonn 2011 (Barbara Frommann)

Me with the Iraqi Ambassador and
German President in Beethovenhalle,
Bonn 2011 (Barbara Frommann)

Waleed Assi partying after the concert in Beethovenhalle, Bonn 2011
(Barbara Frommann)

Ahmad Karim, Tariq Hassoon, a Scottish piper Chris Grieve and Bashdar Ahmad before the ceilidh with Edinburgh Youth Orchestra, Edinburgh 2012

Sarah Maxwell rehearses horns Ali Mahdi, Ranya Nashat and Mohammed Saad in Jewel & Esk College, Edinburgh 2012 (Tariq Hassoon)

ABOVE: Julian Lloyd Webber performing with us in the Queen Elisabeth Hall, London 2012 (Tariq Hassoon)

RIGHT: Julian Lloyd Webber with us at the Royal Conservatoire of Scotland, Glasgow 2012 (Tariq Hassoon)

Fiona Hyslop, Cabinet Secretary for Culture and International Affairs with us and British Council Scotland's Lloyd Anderson at the press launch, Edinburgh 2012 (Tariq Hassoon)

Samir Baseem leading the basses in Jewel & Esk College, Edinburgh 2012
(Tariq Hassoon)

Murad Saffar leads Ahmed Abbas on the bassoons, Edinburgh 2012
(Hassan Hassoon)

Waleed Assi leading the morning warm-up in the courtyard of the Darius Milhaud Music School, Aix en Provence 2013 (Hassan Hassoon)

Alan Kamil, Peshawa Mohammed and Sherwan Mohammed play Kurdish folk music in front of the town hall, Aix en Provence 2013 (Nina Kazourian)

Performing in Grand Theatre de Provence, 2013 (Hassan Hassoon)

Hussam Ezzat at the French Iraqi induction, Aix en Provence 2013
(Anna Soliman)

The Iraq Foundation distributes aid, Baghdad 2016
(Iraq Foundation)

Iraq Foundation's TABEIR project which taught Freedom of Expression
defenders how to protect themselves, Baghdad 2016 (Iraq Foundation)

Dobbs Harteshorne surrounded by his audience after playing bass and
storytelling in a refugee camp in Kurdistan, January 2016
(Kurdistan Save the Children)

Dobbs Harteshorne playing bass to children in a refugee camp in Kurdistan,
January 2016 (Kurdistan Save the Children)

Rachel Maley, our project manager from the Elgin Youth Symphony Orchestra, Elgin 2014

Aya Aiham and her German host, Bonn 2011 (Beethovenfest)

ABOVE: Arab concertmaster, Saad Wadi and Kurdish concertmaster, Rebaz Sdiq, Bonn 2011 (Beethovenfest)

LEFT: Sherwan Mohammed, Daroon Rasheed and me riffing with daffs, Bonn 2011 (Beethovenfest)

Samir Baseem and Hassan Hassoon, Grand Theatre de Provence, 2013

photos, Ahmed, who was out of his mind with joy, homed in on his European counterparts and got pictures taken with them. His passion paid off in ways he could never have foreseen. Marjory Dougal and his teacher, Heather, worked behind the scenes to donate a decent bassoon for him to take back home to Iraq, paid for by the Edinburgh Youth Orchestra.

With the end of Ramadan, Edinburgh Youth Orchestra brought its considerable folk talents to bear in a Ceilidh for us all at Jewel and Esk College, whose canteen also supplied halal haggis and Barr's Irn Bru. A Scottish institution, this came close to those radioactive soft drinks in Iraq, glowing violent orange and green.

Marjory booked a piper in full highland costume to welcome us, while NYOI players bopped to his jaunty tunes on the lawn. Zuhal and Samir vamped ceilidh music on piano and bass with the Edinburgh players. As the evening unfolded, the piper resurfaced in an impromptu Kurdish-Arab circle dance led by Bashdar and Tariq, our photographer, both in traditional Arab and Kurdish costumes. Soon came the Iraqi pop music, sending Waleed into a frenzy. When we finally returned to the more genteel Scottish tunes, taking to the floor for Scottish country dancing, our Edinburgh-Iraqi pairs looked utterly quaint in comparison. As in Germany, it had taken a while for both groups of players to really warm to each other, but we were now in flow, working and partying inexorably towards our first concert.

I took over from Zuhal, ploughing away at an electric piano on stage, so she could join in. Watching them from the keyboard, I could hardly believe how much fun these radically different young people were having together. I remembered going to Iraq for the first time, how alien it felt, how glad I was to leave after two weeks. Yet in the space of three weeks, NYOI had deeply embraced Scotland, music and the Edinburgh Festival in ways I couldn't have foreseen. Before we even stepped on stage, we had owned the experience and started repaying the Scottish people's unbelievable generosity and good will.

Every morning at 9.00 am, we held a management briefing. One morning in the week before the concert, a crisis of cosmic proportions materialised. I'd planned carefully for the concert to happen a week after Ramadan, but nobody had told me about Eid Al F'tr. Bashdar, who'd been playing cello with us since 2010, became the spokesperson on this matter. Over two years, he'd become very trustworthy, a gentle diplomat with charmingly dysfunctional English. He said he'd accept whatever decision I took.

'It's like our Christmas, Mr Paul. We really need to celebrate it.' he pleaded. So, their Christmas was right on the last week of the course, which they knew about months beforehand, and nobody had bothered to tell me. I was livid. Despite months of careful planning, it was typical of an Iraqi to expect everything to change for them at the last minute. The problem was, nobody could tell me when Eid actually was.

I asked Saman, who normally had a scientific mind. Well, he said, it's really down to the Imams in Mecca. After Ramadan, they looked up at the moon to decide the end of the lunar month, and the official start of Eid. So that wouldn't be difficult. The moon is the moon. We could be sure of that, couldn't we? Well, no not really, he said. If there was a little bit of cloud in the way, then they'd have to discuss it, and they might conclude that Eid is on this day, or that day. We just had to wait and see what they decided. Cloud, in Mecca, in August? I sighed, Eid in Edinburgh landing somewhere in the last week of our rehearsals.

I recalled the Iraqi response to all planned events: Insha'Allah, or 'If God wills so'. This was by far the best exit tactic they had for rejecting responsibility for anything. Normally, Insha'Allah is added to the end of a sentence to wish good luck on a plan or project, and is wholly positive. But in Iraq, after years of being ground down, it went something like this. If Allah wills it, we needn't do anything, because cosmic forces will manifest it anyway. If Allah doesn't will it, nothing we do can defeat his will, and we'd rather not annoy him. This was helplessness, dressed as fatalism, taken to an extreme.

So, we negotiated. They could have a free afternoon and evening on whichever day Mecca decided for Eid, and could go to a Kurdish restaurant in town. But *only* if we scheduled an extra evening rehearsal later on in the week. However, when Eid

Al F'tr did come round, our intrepid players did more than just eat. During the Edinburgh Festival, international artists vie for the attention of global punters in a continual street party throughout the old and new towns. Wearing NYOI T-shirts, playing Iraqi music and handing out our flyers, they proved much tamer than their competitors, but still enjoyed promoting our show, meeting punters face-to-face and being part of the festival buzz. They went way beyond what Iraqi culture deemed possible or acceptable, and I took immense pride in them.

On Monday, we were back on the bandwagon, rehearsing for next weekend. The Edinburgh players had settled down with us, and we with them. Players from all sides freely mingled. Our rehearsals flowed better, though we still faced a week of challenges.

When we reached the last day of rehearsal, Friday 24th August, we were as ready as possible. Zuhal, myself and Khyam with an intrepid band of NYOIers piled into a couple of taxis to do a live Radio 3 broadcast of the flagship 'In Tune' show with veteran presenter, Sean Rafferty. For the players, entering the BBC's festival compound with gaudy tent, fake lawn and makeshift bars was now just another day in their crazy festival experience. I made Rebaz promise to do maximum three minutes of Kurdish music, which he half promised with his teasing, wry charm. I do love Iraqi humour, at its best even blacker and more self-deprecating than Scots, crossed with German Schadenfreude but without the shame. I couldn't imagine anyone surviving Iraq without it.

Khyam's group rattled off the arrangement of one of his oud compositions. Rebaz and his buddies, all natural pros, hit three minutes of Kurdish music on the dot. Zuhal and I wove all the necessary sponsors' names into our interview, and Sean Rafferty manoeuvred us through the broadcast with slick warmth. A wonderful pinnacle to our superb media build-up.

We finally reached Saturday 25th, our first concert day. The first of the three concerts was at the Royal Conservatoire of Scotland in Glasgow. John Wallace, the Principal, welcomed us with open arms in our debut UK concert. Gill turned up, camera and all, with a sound guy positioning microphones in all the wrong places to record an orchestra. She tried to explain to me that each mic cost £2000. I tried to explain that it's the sound engineer, not the mic, just like the cameraman not the camera that makes the difference. I had no time to manage amateur sound technicians and just wanted to concentrate on the concert. Gill and I had already run out of patience with each other, and although I was feeling very nervous about the amount of rehearsing she'd filmed, after three courses with her, I just wanted her documentary to be over and done with. In fact, it was never to materialise.

That afternoon, Julian Lloyd Webber made his first appearance with us to rehearse the Fauré *Elegy*. Even after three weeks with Dave Edmonds filling in as our practice cellist, nothing prepared us for Julian's Stradivarius or his interpretation. He threw us for six, and the orchestra, having learnt everything by rote, couldn't just turn on a dime to accommodate him. The other boomerang was Osama Abdulrasol, just in from Belgium, who insisted the opening of his piece, *Habibu*, be faster. Based on the 10/8 Georgina rhythm from Iraqi tradition, we were doing well to get it as tight as we could, but now we had to perform a last-minute crank-up.

This is what the Glasgow preview performance was for. In the intimacy of the Stevenson Hall, we could iron out nerves, glitches and get a feel for the Scottish public. Indeed, when the concert got going, Murtada on second trumpet was so chilled that, when he wasn't playing, he was stretching his feet out under his music stand, hands behind his head, as if basking in the audience. Meanwhile, Frand, sitting next to him, was in meltdown over his trumpet; something had got caught in the tubing, and he couldn't get a sound out. After spending much of the first half fidgeting with various valves and pipes, the interval came and he dashed out to rinse the whole instrument out under a tap. We got through the second half, including Julian's solo, well enough, the critics stayed away and we headed back to Edinburgh for the night, tried, tested and tired.

The next afternoon the rehearsal for our big concert in Greyfriars Kirk, a few of the players started playing up. First, there was Frand, who'd turned up to the church without his trumpet and had to go back to campus to get it. This took him out of half the rehearsal. Both the Iraqi basses, Samir and Chia, decided to lie on a pew with headaches, leaving the two Edinburgh players to carry the rehearsal. A couple of violinists also opted out with dubious complaints. Somebody had to go to the toilet. Waleed just would not play in tune, and he wasn't the only one. I'd never seen such psychosomatic backlash on the day of a concert.

On the up side, Claire Docherty, our second violin tutor, came along specially to advise on the sound in the church acoustic, a much more resonant experience for the players than Glasgow. A professional sound engineer who Marjory used for recording the Edinburgh Youth Orchestra, set up a recognisably effective rig, and sounded like he knew what he was talking about.

The sold-out church began to fill up around 7.00 pm, and Fiona Hyslop arrived with Cathy Graham from British Council London, Dr Al Shaikhly from the British Iraqi Friendship Society and Lloyd Anderson from British Council Scotland. Representing the Iraqi Culture Center in London, Dr Dheyab was heard at the side of the church arguing with Zuhal and Majid about the number of Arabs in the orchestra, while Wasan Al Shaikhly from British Council Iraq sat in the front row with her Iraqi flag and a face beaming with pride. We'd brought the Edinburgh arts community along with a number of Iraqi Scots, perhaps experiencing their first orchestral concert, or even their first visit to a church.

The audience alone felt electrifying. When we put everything together, not even the dark and difficult tones of the programme could suppress the shared sense of joy and love glowing throughout the church. Paradoxically, audience and orchestra had turned darkness into light, and we had thoroughly initiated ourselves as artists in our own right.

The Scottish people had come closer to the Iraqi people, whose lives their taxes had destroyed, reconnecting with love instead of bullets. I'd put NYOI onto buses and planes out of harm's way to a haven of musical growth. Without intending to, I'd even managed to create a sense of family. And I'd conducted Schubert in Scotland. As our resident earth mother, Marjory Dougal, said to me: 'Nobody else could do it. Nobody else *would* do it.' Dougie Mitchell, our wind tutor, added: 'Everybody got it. This shouldn't be happening, but it did.'

Nine seats apart from each other on a forward row, sat my mother and father, completely unaware of each other's presence. They hadn't spoken in 25 years. Some things you just can't reconcile.

SIXTEEN
Breath and death

Directly after Edinburgh, we travelled down to London to repeat our success in the Queen Elizabeth Hall in London, our seventh public concert since 2009. Julian Lloyd Webber appeared on BBC Breakfast TV that morning to talk about our work, and ensure a sell-out concert. As the orchestra assembled to rehearse, I laid down the law: 'The only way any of you are leaving this stage before the break is lying on a stretcher, being taken out to an ambulance, because you're dying.' Saman sniggered through his Kurdish and Arabic translation as the orchestra looked back at me, nonplussed. Whose bladder wouldn't make it till the break? Our afternoon rehearsal went relatively smoothly, though it was clear to all that we'd peaked in Edinburgh two nights before.

By the time the concert was upon us, we were turning people away at the door. This time, all four composers, Sir Peter Maxwell Davies, Osama Abdulrasol, Karzan Mahmood and Gordon McPherson were present to take a bow. I was especially delighted that Max was in London for this, as he'd never heard *Reel of Spindrift, Sky*, which we'd premiered in Iraq the year before.

This time, we began the second half of the concert, not immediately with Julian and the Fauré *Elegy*, but with a short film from our Kickstarter crowdfunding campaign of 2011, which told our story in a nutshell, while having Max put the boot into the allied forces' desecration of Iraqi culture. Except, comically, the giant projector in the Queen Elizabeth Hall wouldn't work. The audience, plunged into darkness, heard the sound but saw no image, then saw the image and heard no sound, then total darkness. The Queen Elizabeth Hall had made Iraq proud, and the various Iraqi diplomats and listeners, who occupied over half the full house, felt quite at home. Dame Gillian Moore from the South Bank administration hurried backstage to the technicians' booth and huddled with them for a few moments, before returning to a fully functional video.

The orchestra came on afterwards to warm applause, minus Hersh, our leader of the second violins. Just as everyone settled down, on he rushed and gave a cheeky little bow, which the audience responded to with an equally cheeky burst of applause. Good to know not everyone had been infected by Western punctuality.

Afterwards, at the British Council reception on the balcony of the Royal Festival Hall, I talked to David Juritz, Dougie Mitchell and BBC's Iraq reporter, Hugh Sykes, about how far we'd come. Or rather they talked. I just stood there in autopilot, stupefied, sapped of energy. However life-enhancing the experience had been for the players and tutors, I was facing increasing disillusion at the prospect of jumping from one country to another to keep us going. What was I getting out of this? Where would it lead to?

The morning after the concert, everyone had a few hours to spare before going back to the airport, so I beseeched them from the steps of our residence, as though in front of the Roman Senate, to visit the Tate Modern Gallery, which stood right behind them. I had grasped that the sensory overload from Scotland and London had spun them onto a different plane from their towns and villages back in Iraq, and that they were blind to many of the opportunities around them. In the car park in front of our residence, players grabbed me for group iPhone photos. Through the departing upbeat atmosphere, I saw the questioning sadness in Waleed's eyes. He sensed I was already cut off from myself and from them.

After lunch, the orchestra boarded the coach on the South Bank and waved goodbye for another year. I was left waving back on the pavement, my fake smile lobotomised by burnout. I turned yet again to Alan and Mark, my friends in Leyton, for refuge. My passport had gone missing and I would have to go up to Glasgow to apply for a new one, as the London waiting list was three weeks long. I didn't know where I was. Nothing made sense any more.

After a couple of days, cleaners at the Queen Elizabeth Hall finally came across my jacket, with wallet and passport, hooked onto the back of my dressing room door. I collected it, said farewell to my two dearest friends in London, who had supported and nurtured me throughout this difficult journey, and headed back to Scotland.

I found bed and breakfast in Edinburgh and moved in for a week. Mum, who had last caught me with my trousers down showing Dr Dheyab around rehearsals, needed proper 'Mum' time. We met at Harry Ramsden's, the fish and chip outlet at the food court of Waverley Shopping Centre. Once the premium restaurant in a converted fish shed in the Leith Docks where Peter Maxwell Davies and I had many a lunch, the chandeliers, pink walls and Sauvignon Blanc had been replaced by food court utilitarianism. After years in health-obsessed Germany, Scots' eating habits appalled me. German salad, drowning in salad cream, was at least green and unfried. Mum and I sat together in the food court with our cups of tea and fish suppers, and said nothing. We were at peace.

'We've been through a lot, you and I.' 'Yes' she replied, with a little chuckle. This was as far as I could go with this orchestra, with myself.

I went back to London and reached out through Facebook for a place to stay. Tara Jaff, our Kurdish singer from 2010, took me straight in and gave me her own bedroom while she slept on the sofa. Tara understood the Iraqi madness I was fighting, a battle which had already become desperately personal. As a trained counsellor, she sensed I was in trouble, and began talking me through the recent experience of NYOI. The better the orchestra became, the worse I was becoming, but I couldn't bring myself to let on just how low I'd sunk.

Back in Cologne, I put out another call on Facebook to stay somewhere other than my own flat for a short time, close to friends, and Steve Nobles, my Texan pal, jumped into the breach with an offer of his spare room. There were no words for how I felt, as I had so little life force left to give. I asked Zuhal to start the audition process for me to pick up when the videos came in around January.

This year, due to the $25 audition fee, applications had fallen from 216 to 150, but the number of resulting videos was roughly the same, and the overall quality higher. People who paid, committed to the audition process. This was a very double-edged tactic in Iraq, as talented young people without self-confidence mightn't apply, and those with guts but lacking ability did sometimes get accepted, and began to improve. However, on the whole, word of mouth about the UK tour produced the incentive for regulars to practice harder and new faces to surface.

I was, however, sick of carrot-and-stick leadership. The amount of energy required to deliver on my promises was incalculable, but NYOI's spend wasn't. My ballpark figure was $1,400,000 since 2009, and what exactly did we have to show for it? What were they doing with their newfound self-confidence and skills on returning to Iraq? For sure, improved quality in the 2013 auditions was one measurement, with more people playing in tune, fewer mistakes and more sensitive musicianship, unrecognisable from those first joyless videos in 2009.

Zuhal's laptop went on the blink again so, as soon as the videos came in, I began organising them into our private YouTube account for the auditions, amassing 120 by the mid-January deadline. Volunteer professional musicians evaluated them over the following month. On 16th February, I showed the list to the Iraq team for Zuhal to inform everyone by e-mail the next day.

Frand, who had recorded his video the day before the deadline, produced the least strong trumpet audition and was excluded. He was the first 'regular' to fall. Ballen Aziz, last year's second clarinet, had, along with Bashdar Ahmed and Sabat Majeed on cello, who had been strong for us over the years, hit 30 and they were now too old. Much-loved faces were giving way to new players who would have to hold their own in Aix-en-Provence alongside the National Youth Orchestras of Spain, Italy and France. As e-mails and Facebook chats started popping up on my laptop, it was clear Zuhal still hadn't informed all the players of audition results.

Nor would she directly explain why. A couple of nebulous messages on Facebook betrayed her emotional turmoil when rejecting much loved friends, but that was nothing to the turmoil in Iraq caused by the interminable waiting.

In mid-February, Grand Theatre de Provence took me back to Aix to look around the music school where we would rehearse, have a PR meeting and agree on food, logistics and so on. We discussed reliable air conditioning in the Mediterranean summer, halal lunches, accommodating the tutors at arm's length from the orchestra and the ramifications of various flights from Iraq to France. I'd already prepared the orchestra's passport scans for the ticketing and visa process.

I wanted our PR strategy for this year to be dramatically different. First, lack of interest from the French Foreign Ministry allowed us to properly concentrate on music, the musicians and our French partners for the first time. No more political football to play, no tiptoeing round multiple diplomatic agendas, just a bunch of youngsters playing in an orchestra and partying. Previously, the Bundesjugendorchester and Edinburgh Youth Orchestra had taken back seat supporting roles, only sporadically in the limelight, but Orchestre Francais des Jeunes' long relationship with Aix-en-Provence and their deep impact on the community probably meant we would cross paths often. Dominique Blouzet, the Director of Grand Theatre de Provence, who clearly understood we were a fragile band on a strong mission, offered all the support he could muster, part of which meant juggling facilities between Orchestre Francais des Jeunes and us.

The most important piece of our PR strategy, brand new but vital to the orchestra's sustainability, was to highlight what our players were doing in Iraq. How would they take this nugget of networking, hope, and experience back home and use it to rebuild their communities? We had Waleed's Baba Goorgoor Chamber Orchestra, Tu'qa's piano trio in Baghdad, the horns' improved playing in the Iraqi National Symphony Orchestra, Bashdar's cello teaching in Suleymaniyah and Hellgurd's orchestra in Ranya, as proof of NYOI bringing people back together through music. Nevertheless, Iraqis utterly lacked generosity towards each other at a time when it was most needed. So, nobody else would rebuild musical culture and education for them. But for me, this still wasn't enough to justify NYOI.

One thing was clear; our honeymoon was over. No matter how kindly the cultivated international audience of Provence took to us, we would be mercilessly compared with world-class youth orchestras. What's worse, we would be invited to hear them perform Debussy's *Ibéria*, Stravinsky's *Rite of Spring* and Ravel's *Tombeau de Couperin*, and be plunged into a collective depression. Yet how else would they learn about the musical world around them? NYOI facing a Festival of National Youth Orchestras felt like David confronting Goliath.

My obsessive creativity, perfectly fuelled by frustration at Iraqi apathy, had built NYOI, but it was also our liability, replacing any motivation that the Iraqi team should be fostering for itself. Once again, I had to tell myself, 'Just stop.' What I really meant was, 'Stop rescuing Iraq and start rescuing yourself'. The German Friends, still the only organisation to represent NYOI, had ceased paying me a monthly fee. It bore no relation to the work at hand anyway, and they had done little fundraising since Beethovenfest in 2011. As the coffers dried up, so did our patience with each other.

Throughout April I felt acutely that time was running out for our potential trip to America in 2014. After I had met the National Youth Orchestra of the USA at the League of American Orchestras conference in 2012, this time in Dallas, they came on board as our partner, and it seemed that the Aaron Copland School of Music in New York would be our base. The Metropolitan Youth Orchestra of New York also generously gave me solutions for local service providers, while the League of American Orchestras provided leads for insurance, PR and tour organisers. By the end of April, with little inclination to keep going, I submitted an updated funding proposal to the US

Embassy in Baghdad, carrying on from where Majid had left off in January, complete with project partners and budget of around $500,000.

Meanwhile, the Regional Representatives were having kittens. Bashdar in particular, representing Suleymaniyah, explained that some players hadn't received a reply about their auditions yet. I went into our Gmail account and saw that Zuhal had indeed sent out all the accepts and rejects, but that some had bounced back. In the face of a reputational risk to NYOI whose applicants were now paying Majid $25 for the privilege of applying, Bashdar and I formulated a beautifully worded Kurdish rejection, which I sent out in my name, after double-checking the applicants' e-mails with him.

While the quality and integrity of NYOI depended on the fairness of auditions, our operational structure remained on a shoestring. For five years I had stood with a handful of diehards in the middle, carrying much of the risk, while many others sat on the edges pretending to participate at minimum inconvenience to them. Five years hadn't made it any less risky, complex or exhausting, and still, NYOI appeared to be the only national Iraqi organisation operating with any fairness and equality. If the players perceived that we were corrupt or incompetent, the trust we had built could collapse along with the orchestra.

In discussions with the Iraqi Ministry of Culture, Majid had secured the funding of NYOI to perform in Baghdad on returning from France, with me conducting, and the 14 French players supporting. That was a lot of visas to get through. Most of the Kurds had never visited Baghdad, so their fear and animosity towards the capital also had to be reckoned with.

Everything went well until Majid let slip that we would all be staying and performing in Baghdad's Red Zone. With that, all my red flags went up, and without much more prodding, I discovered the Kurds would be in a hotel in the Kurdish part of town and Majid was not clear about security or the schedule. Leaving ethnic divisions to one side, scattering the orchestra through town and trying to manage logistics didn't sound like a good idea. The whole visit, from 17th to 22nd September in the Red Zone meant one thing. With Baghdad suffering about 1000 deaths by terrorism in the month of May alone, and my players too scared to leave home to attend crucial exams and rehearsals, Baghdad had completely flipped.

I hurriedly organised a Skype call with Zuhal who said straight out that the Ministry would never get their act together under these circumstances. My heart went through the floor not only at the now extremely unlikely Baghdad concert, but also at the Ministry of Culture and our Baghdad team. They were ready to put our lives at risk to create the high profile delusion that Baghdad was safe. This was pure propaganda. Heartbreaking madness. As CNN and Al Jazeera were having their licences to report in Iraq revoked, I learnt a fundamental difference between the Western and Arab worlds. We attempted a free press, where the continuum between truth and lies could be tested by public information and investigative journalism from multiple sources. They censored journalists and issued propaganda to maintain personal pride, mitigate against shame, and save face.

Cologne awoke to a new month of June. Crystal blue skies, effulgent foliage and bronzed muscle gods stretched out taut in worship of the sun beating down on my local park. And yet, darkness fell across the laptop in my tiny flat.

As terrorism spun out of control in Iraq, Facebook became my CIA. Reverend Andrew White, the Anglican Bishop of Baghdad, posted a desperate message about being prepared to die with his flock rather than leave them, in the midst of pleas for him to give up and go home. Ali, one of our violins, told me he was dating a new girlfriend whom the violence had stopped him seeing since April. Koki, a young musician in Baghdad, had been killed by a car bomb outside his home. His innocent face appeared again and again in tributes from our players. Du'aa Al Azzawi had missed exams, terrified of leaving her front door. Hussam, our principal cellist, posted a picture of a 10-year-old boy he was teaching with a cello that was too big for him. Musicians tried to hang on to their humanity amid increasing despair and hopelessness, watching violence and corruption drain their futures away.

SEVENTEEN
Paradoxes

Of all the interviews I did after the UK tour, the American magazine *School Band and Orchestra* gave me the most pause for thought. Carried out by e-mail with editor Eliahu Sussmann, we went deep together into the heart of NYOI.

SBO: The 'orchestra is a paradox from top to bottom'? Could you expand on that?

PM: The first paradox is why a Scottish conductor based in Germany is doing this. I still don't really know, other than it still sounds like a great idea, and it's easy to fall for the young players and want to try and help them.

The second paradox is how a 17-year-old female pianist in Baghdad rallied considerable support in that first year to get NYOI off the ground. Zuhal has a magnetic charm and is furiously intelligent. We're lucky to have her.

Thirdly, how can a bunch of young people who can't even speak each other's language, and have been taught to hate each other, sit in front of the same music and play beautifully together? Because of the discipline of orchestral playing, we have a very secure and productive framework to come together. Having me and the other foreign tutors there also creates a neutral third space between the Kurds and Arabs through which we can mediate and pour our energy safely.

The fourth paradox is between Arab, Kurdish, and Western musical culture, but this is also a generation who globally switch between cultures more effortlessly and articulately than ever before. It's a real 'Generation Y' orchestra, with a high awareness of music outside Iraq through the Internet. Taking a very conservative format, the orchestra, and fitting it into a very conservative country within this globally aware context fits strangely well.

The final paradox is the most tragic and most important, and that is the suffering of the players themselves. Although there is little evidence on the surface of what they personally have been through, everyone's family has been affected by gas attacks, invasion, tribal tensions, and war. As young people, this is their normality. That comes out in the sound, which has been borne out of their determination to play through dangerous times, in order to shut out the world around them. It's a crazy, tense energy, but one which we could convert into joy together.

The deeper I thought about our existence, the more it struck me that this was not only the reason for our success, but that the central paradox was myself. Why was a gay conductor doing major cultural diplomacy for Iraq and Kurdistan, where my own people were being blackmailed, imprisoned and murdered? More to the point, why were we doing diplomacy at all for governments that neither grasped nor wanted our efforts, in a country that didn't believe in itself anyway?

I decided to wrestle with this and start to make some sense of what we were doing. Around mid-March, I threw myself into the preparation of a talk for the local TEDx event in Cologne. We fitted their theme perfectly: the Hero's Journey. Unaware of how I truly felt, some of the brightest voices in NYOI over the years helped me answer my own questions: Boran, Hassan, Samir, Shwan, Saman, Hellgurd and Khyam.

Q: How could a 17-year-old girl in Baghdad motivate so many people to help her create a National Youth Orchestra back in 2009?

Samir: Zuhal did it using the foreign contacts (British Gov. and Media) and the way it started (professional teachers and good organising) motivated the players to join this orchestra driven by their eagerness to learn more music, and this orchestra provided a place to run from bloody reality to a world of dreams created by music.

Q: Would this have happened if Zuhal had gone to the Iraqi National Symphony Orchestra or the Ministry of Culture in Baghdad?

Khyam: No chance, ever...

Boran: I do not believe so. In Iraq, people and the government are still not open to the fact the younger generation can actually make a difference, start something new, have a creative idea.

Samir: If she'd gone to Ministry of Culture at that time probably they would have listened but done nothing for a lot of reasons (her age, short-sightedness from the ministry, money, security, corruption etc.) but now the Ministry is more open to receiving ideas from artistic people and go with it.

Q: Was the fact that Zuhal was a teenager and a woman, an advantage or a disadvantage?

Samir: The fact that Zuhal is a woman it is an advantage as a lot of Iraqi females are taking leading roles through society, especially if they are determined to act creatively.

Khyam: With respect to Zuhal approaching the British Council, I'm certain it was an absolute advantage. If she had approached the Iraqi National Symphony Orchestra or the Ministry of Culture in Baghdad, it would have been an absolute disadvantage, even if, in my opinion, it wouldn't have made much difference if a teenage male approached them.

Hellgurd: I would say an advantage in some cases, but also it could be a disadvantage. That depends on whom she is asking for help. Does she have a strong religious background, and much more importantly whether she is Shia or Sunni?

Boran: I do not believe that Zuhal being a woman had an advantage or disadvantage. However, the fact that she was a teenager was a great advantage: She had a dream that she followed, giving her time and investing a lot of passion and love into it. It's something natural to the young spirit, she was fully dedicated and had the time and the mind set to do so.

Q: The organisation of NYOI was 100% online. Was this the only way?

Boran: Given the funding problems, and the lack of a reliable neutral local teachers, yes I believe it was the only way.

Hellgurd: Not really, it could have worked other ways as well, as most of its meetings, events and performances were in Kurdistan, which is the safest part of Iraq nowadays; I can certainly say that it could have worked, as neither Iraq nor Kurdistan are poor countries. Money can do everything. We could be the luckiest youth orchestra in this world.

Saman: I think yes, because, honestly you won't understand how things are going on inside Iraq unless you've lived in it for a while. However, the idea of online processing was not that easy as well, because Iraqis still prefer the hard way. They prefer doing things physically rather than completing the work through an email.

Q: How helpful are the Institutes of Fine Arts in Iraq?

Boran: Not very helpful. I studied and graduated from one yet I feel that I'm self-educated. 90% of the students graduate knowing literally nothing about music, and end up working in other fields (like working for the government or as elementary school teachers). The Institutes of Fine Arts in Iraq are suffering due the general situation of the country, unqualified teachers, short-sighted vision and corruption are the key to producing weak players but, after all, it is better than nothing.

Hellgurd: Of course they're very helpful. Institutes or colleges of fine arts are where you can certainly learn an instrument; you rarely have other chances to learn. The upside of institute or college of fine arts is that you can study for four or five years for free, even get paid, not a big amount of money, and more importantly you can get an instrument if you don't have one. In my view the down side is that they won't prepare you to be a musician as much as to be a teacher after your graduation in one of the Kindergartens or primary schools.

Hassan: Conservatories and governmental organizations in Baghdad have not produced good results, maybe one good player out of every 20.

Q: What is the quality of teaching after the war?

Boran: A lot of teachers fled, a lot of institutes were closed or ruined. The quality is much lower than it used to be.

Hellgurd: I can certainly say that teaching in Iraq (in general) after the war got worse, because of this high level of corruption.

Saman: I think that the quality of teaching has changed, but not much. You can't stop everything due to war issues. Obviously there is exaggeration in the media, for what is going on inside Iraq, but it is unlike that in reality. Life goes on and people continue to practice music.

Q: How can they teach themselves by Internet?

Boran: Well, you get the music scores, you watch videos of performances on YouTube, and you go to music forums. Most importantly, you have the passion to learn, no matter how bad the conditions are.

Khyam: Western classical instrument teaching has developed to incredible detail and standard, with hundreds of thousands of teaching materials and aids, from books and scores, to audio and video materials. Their accessibility through the Internet makes it very easy to use those materials and reach a reasonable level of musicianship without any direct help from anyone. With a little desire and dedication, anyone can learn to play any instrument they can get their hands on. The same does not apply to any Arabic instruments.

Q: Where do these instruments come from?

Boran: The grand piano and the two upright pianos in my institute in Erbil were a donation from the UN I believe.

Hassan: Instruments exist in the domestic market, but it is from poor quality Chinese factories and mostly cunning counterfeits of famous brands.

Khyam: When you've never had access to good quality instruments, how can you tell if something is of poor quality?

Q: Why do they prefer western to Iraqi classical music?

Boran: Because like any other country, we are living in globalisation. We see orchestras on TV playing beautiful cheerful music, and we feel how badly we lack that in our music. So we try to learn and relate to the 'better' music that comes from somewhere beautiful, magical, and very different from where we live.

Samir: Iraq was one of the first Arab countries to move to classical music in the 1950s, when they established the Iraqi National Symphony Orchestra, followed by Music and Ballet school. Foreign teachers started to teach, creating a professional generation of players. These great steps still to this day motivate a lot of people to keep going even through these difficult times and implant the love of classical music in society.

Khyam: Traditional Iraqi music is heavy, mostly very serious, with difficult intonation, a seemingly monotonous style and very difficult to appreciate until you can get into the depth of its details. Poor quality sound and video recordings of 'great artists' don't help young people break through the aesthetic barrier. It also doesn't contain the same type of virtuosity found in western classical music.

On the other hand, high quality videos with high quality sound, of world-class orchestras performing fantastical epic works by Mozart or Beethoven triumphantly to large audiences, are easily accessible and impressionable.

Add to this a complete dissatisfaction with your homeland and the desperation to escape from the day to day, coupled with the Arab-wide 'minority complex' with regard to 'the West'... and things start to make some sense.

Q: How can the National Youth Orchestra of Iraq sound so joyful after its players have been through so much conflict, between Kurds, Arabs, Sunni, Shi'ite, the invasion and war?

Hellgurd: Our love and eagerness to make music stopped us thinking about any differences. Music could even make us be such great friends as we are today. Even though we don't live close to each other, we can obviously realise a friendship on Facebook and Twitter.

Q: How important is the background of each person to the players in NYOI?

Hellgurd: It is very important, for each person and for the sake of NYOI, I really care how my Arab stand partner thinks of me and vice versa. If I don't accept him/her then I can't make the music sound so joyful, and I can't help NYOI to keep going.

Boran: In my first year at NYOI, it was extremely important to the point that someone wouldn't talk to another from another background. However after making music together, living the joy of a successful concert, I saw that in the second year, the atmosphere started to change, and the players started to feel more bonded through music.

Hassan: I imagine that all the musicians have less intention to know the background of each person than knowledge of music education and music playing.

Khyam: I think it's very important. In particular their social class, and which areas they have grown up in. Those who have grown up in Kurdistan for example, have led a far calmer and safer lifestyle, for example.

Saman: Every group of players come from different parts of Iraq. There were silly conflicts at the initial years, but it has improved year by year, as they understand that the aim of the organisation is music.

Samir: NYOI is a shelter for young musicians to forget what they were forced to live through the conflicts in their suffering country, where dignity, civic and human rights are just a dream. That is why we devote ourselves just to music and discovering who we are and where we can stand in the world. So background, gender and race do not matter when it comes to music!!!

Q: How do the women in the orchestra deal with being musicians in Iraq?

Saman: It is not easy at all, especially in Baghdad, it is really difficult, it is not related to religion, but it is related to the current circumstances, the conditions are not supportive and we need lots of effort to survive.

Khyam: I think the fact that they keep that aspect of their lifestyle relatively private is the only way for them to deal with it. Right now, it is still almost impossible for them to be able to present that aspect of their life in public without worry.

Boran: I'm not sure I can answer that since I'm not really an Iraqi, so I wouldn't understand the exact pressures that they might feel from society or family. I believe that eventually they learn to fight for what they love even if the society is not very happy with it.

Hellgurd: I have to say that it depends on which part of Iraq they live. If they live in the south, they might not feel so secure and they could also have social problems with being a musician, but women living in the north are luckier, as they don't have security problems. They could still have social problems and sometime they have to give up, especially for those who have got married.

Q: What role does music play in healing the lives of the players?

Boran: Music gives them hope. Gives them a feeling of accomplishment and satisfaction, that although there is war, bombs and killing outside, they can still produce something beautiful. It makes them survive, and keep on living.

Khyam: It would be very easy to make the usual romantic statement that music and arts can help heal anything. At the end of the day, I agree but... without the opportunities provided by a safe environment, freedom of movement (locally) and freedom of expression, that concept falls slightly flat on its face.

I think that the escapism when listening to or watching music is extremely important, but the real power comes when they are actually practicing and performing with others... which for the NYOI is difficult or at the very least infrequent.

Hellgurd: If I see others like myself, sometime music is the only thing that could make me stay and not leave the country, because of the bad situation. I can't imagine that I could live if I couldn't have the chance to be a musician.

Saman: It plays a very crucial role. The musicians are like prisoners. They get imprisoned during the whole year, and they are set free during the NYOI course, hungry for music to fulfil their needs.

Shwan: Those players live for their music. It's their only way to forget this world and live the dream of being peaceful.

Q: What are the risks today of being an orchestral musician in Iraq?

Boran: Orchestral musicians in the dangerous areas in Baghdad and Mosul for example would be threatened with death. This is why some musicians in the Iraqi National Symphony Orchestra hide their violins for example in suitcases rather than their original cases, so that no one would know that they are musicians while they're walking in the street.

Hellgurd: Being an orchestral player is really tough for us as Iraqis from many sides, because that does take most of your time, and if you do it right, you don't have other chances to do some other work. Nowadays the Iraqi National Symphony Orchestra is the only place where players can get paid monthly by being a member. Players from other orchestras such as Kurdish String Orchestra can only get paid per concert, that means you have to risk your life to be a orchestral player, it is much more difficult when you have your own family.

Shwan: I would say that the risk is merely the same as being a physician, dentist, mechanic etc. The risk is not related to the type of job you do. Terrorists are aiming to destroy as much as they can. As we said, things are much better now in Iraq, it's perfectly normal to be a musician here, but we do need the right education and good instruments to start the journey with.

Hassan: There's no danger as before now there is more openness from people inside Iraq, but there are those who live in the regions lagging behind the rest of the population, and apprehensive about carrying their instrument or practising in their homes and they are a very small minority.

Saman: I haven't tasted this as much as someone from Baghdad, where his/her life could be in danger by being a musician or an artist, but definitely their eagerness to play music makes them take the risk. Despite this, it is also tough to find someone who could teach classical music professionally, but all of these obstacles couldn't stop those young people and it is obvious that they've made a great progress so far.

Shwan: After the war it was so difficult to carry a musical instrument in the streets of Baghdad & even harder to practice your music in your own house because of the sound. Our eastern society would never accept this, but things now are much better. The people now understand what music means in a country full of misery & destruction.

Throughout April, the TEDxKoln event loomed. They'd offered me 9 minutes in their day-long forum to explain the past five years, and so I focused on one aspect, *Paradoxes of the National Youth Orchestra of Iraq*. Naturally, this would be in English, as I needed this talk to be online for the American visit in 2014. Still, talking to a German public on such a rarefied topic also required a careful choice of vocabulary. TED.com is a native English language ghetto, YouTube for intellectuals. Not everyone around the world understands the insane talking speed and idioms of slick executives from Silicone Valley. So, my talk would also have to make sense to intermediate listeners of English around the world, and especially in Iraq.

The agonising and editing regressed me into the nervous thespian of my childhood, where school plays allowed for my brilliant, if somewhat desperate talent for improvising forgotten script. But TED had to be precise. I felt as if the future of the orchestra hung on every word. Even though it likely wouldn't, I might risk the orchestra if someone in the Middle East took our message the wrong way.

The night before the conference, I turned up to the Alter Pfandhaus in Clodwigplatz for a sound check, miked up and got down on the stage. The small horseshoe arena suddenly bore down upon me as low theatre lights blasted my vision. Addressing 2000 people in a concert hall was easy, but knowing I would see the whites of this crowd's eyes, and hear my baritone voice booming around the claustrophobic auditorium, I froze, then stumbled through to the end. Damn. That was a sound-*chuck*.

The next day, dressed like veteran TED megastar Ken Robinson, I returned to the Alter Pfandhaus and was led backstage, to pace up and down murmuring the text to myself over and over again. When my turn came:

'If you're an Iraqi teenager, how do you create a National Youth Orchestra? Do you go to the Ministry of Culture and Defence? Well, following a war, they had other things to do than listen to a teenager. What about the Iraqi National Symphony Orchestra? Maybe, but the teachers who once worked there had already left Iraq.

'Back in 2008, a 17-year-old pianist, Zuhal Sultan, living in Baghdad, wanted a National Youth Orchestra of Iraq, bringing together musicians from across her deeply divided country, and the first thing she set about doing was finding a conductor. The British Council put her in touch with Raw Television, a reality TV company in London, who sent out a press release.

'And it was in the *Glasgow Herald* that I saw the headline; "Iraqi Teen Seeks Conductor for Orchestra" and what immediately struck me, after years of violent reporting, was why I knew nothing about Iraq? What was their culture? Who were their people? What did their music sound like? Where did they get instruments?

'And so we began an Odyssey that is now in its fifth year, with the National Youth Orchestra of Iraq performing in Aix-en-Provence this August with the National Youth Orchestras of France, Italy and Spain.

'But back in 2009, we had big problems. I needed to audition the players by YouTube, but internet was so bad that five minutes of video could take ten hours to upload, and only if a power cut didn't set you back to square one. But young musicians throughout Iraq had such faith in Zuhal that they made the videos and sent them to me, a complete stranger. And what I saw broke my heart. These young musicians were very serious, but with terrible instruments and musical problems. Worse than that, they were joyless, and their instruments were disconnected from their souls. Nevertheless, I went ahead and chose 33 of the best players from across Iraq's divided society.

'We also needed to find $50,000. Thanks to British Council again, an article in the London *Times* about Zuhal went online, and she sent the link, via Twitter, to the Deputy Prime Minister of Iraq, Dr Barham Salih. Two days later, she was standing in his office, and he offered her $50,000, which gave us the green light to proceed. Here, at least, money followed vision.

'But do you see what's happening here? The internet became the safe space that Zuhal, myself, the players, British Council, Raw TV, the London Times and the Deputy Prime Minister of Iraq were using to bypass the historical conflicts between the peoples of Iraq. So the National Youth Orchestra of Iraq was born online, leading us to our second paradox; if there are no teachers, how can you play?

'The war had destroyed Iraq's musical life, but ironically, Bach, Beethoven and Tchaikovsky survived because the players could teach themselves from CDs, DVDs, YouTube masterclasses, and downloading technique from the Internet. Zuhal used Skype to learn a Mozart piano concerto with a teacher in New York. Even though they were poor quality, instruments could be bought or borrowed. That same support is not available for traditional Iraqi music. Also, during the war, it was too dangerous to travel to other musicians, and so many young Iraqis stayed at home and used music to create a protective barrier against the world.

'What we do is come together once a year for an intensive orchestral boot camp. In the planning stage, our safe space is the Internet, and when we meet, that space is created again between teachers from Germany, Britain, America and the players, where all we care about is making music. My role as conductor is to sit the players down next to each other, help them lower that protective barrier that they've spent years building up, and become open to each other as musicians. That doesn't mean they have to like each other, but they do have to respect and listen.

'But seriously, how can you make any progress in two or three weeks of teaching a year?

'Well, they have a tremendous hunger that we in the West do not understand. We often have to teach till one in the morning to keep up with them. As Dobbs, our bass teacher said, 'I used to think that good music education was about nice schools and weekly lessons. I now know it's about highly motivated students.'

'So the most efficient, effective way to teach music to a large number of young people is through an orchestral rehearsal. The Internet can support music teaching, but it cannot replace it. Which leads us to the third and most tragic paradox; if you're going through hell, how can you make beautiful music?

'One terrible thing about war is that you become conditioned to be afraid, in survival mode, long after it's over, and the continued terrorist attacks ensure that Iraqis stay in this state of post-traumatic stress. And for young musicians, especially those from Baghdad, stepping over dead bodies to get to school, disguising their instrument case for fear it might be seen as a bomb, or worse, a musical instrument, was their childhood normality. What we do is give them back the childhood that they lost during the war. It's essential that the orchestra perform outside Iraq, so they can relearn normality.

'But with all this tension and history in the orchestra, how can anyone play with joy?

'I think the answer lies in the art of the artist. Diplomats seek harmony, ironing out tensions, smoothing out the way forward, but we artists need tension. We live in a state of paradox, using the energies found in conflict, anger, despair, because all energy can be recycled, transformed, and sometimes usefully, turned into something as useless as art. And so the conflict and history of Iraq in the bodies of the players comes out as this raw energy in their sound, and together we transform that into joy.

'One of our favourite composers is Beethoven, who knows a thing or two about triumph over adversity. In his Heiligenstadt Testament of 1802, he wrote to his brothers about his deafness:

"Someone heard the shepherd singing and again I heard nothing, such incidents brought me to the verge of despair, but little more and I would have put an end to my life – only art it was that withheld me, it seemed impossible to leave the world until I had produced all that I felt called upon me to produce, and so I endured this wretched existence."

'And so Beethoven broke through the barrier of his deafness, went on to write his joyful Second Symphony, and like the musicians of the National Youth Orchestra of Iraq, used hell as a springboard to get to heaven.'

EIGHTEEN
In a drought

Each year after returning home from NYOI to the small Kurdish town of Ranya, Hellgurd Sultan taught music at his local Institute of Fine Arts. He'd picked up some basics of conducting from me, and founded the Ranya Symphony Orchestra with his friends, a string band who presented themselves as comfortably on the street as at the local theatre. One of their first concerts commemorated Ranya's rebellion against Saddam Hussein, with players in traditional costumes performing Hellgurd's own arrangements of Kurdish music. While in Bonn, he'd also managed to meet with an arranger who specialised in school orchestra music, and procured some sheet music for the limited forces at his disposal.

After Beethovenfest, Deutsche Welle asked him to write several blogs on education in Iraq that so provoked his fellow citizens that he started receiving death threats wrapped round stones thrown through the windows of his home. The blogs stopped, but not before he'd exposed many uncomfortable truths.

Hellgurd's parents grew up in a small village near the Iranian border. His father never completed school, but was instead sucked into the Iran-Iraq war while Hellgurd was still a baby. The family eventually had to flee until it was safe enough to move to Ranya. As luck would have it, his father loved singing, painting, calligraphy and playing a wooden flute called the Shimshal. Though both parents came from a generation where education was rare for men, and forbidden for women, the young Hellgurd and his brother, Chia, found themselves in a supportive musical family. For many young musicians in Iraq, this was the only way to grow. Music was forbidden to most women, and many men were discouraged on religious grounds.

The tough people of Ranya resisted Saddam Hussein on many occasions, but most memorably in 1991, a rebellion that set their place in history as 'Darwâza-I Râparin,' the Gate of Uprising. Back then, the town had only 25,000 inhabitants. They erected a monument on the main road, a massive stone 'five' and 'three' to commemorate their uprising on 5th March. As Hellgurd grew up, Ranya experienced dramatic changes, increasing to some 61,000 citizens, opening new schools and further education colleges, and slowly addressing the role of women in society. The Kurdistan Regional Government legislated against the deeply embedded practices of honour killing and female genital mutilation, as well as setting up a safe-house there for victims of domestic violence.

Hellgurd's family had nurtured both him and his brother Chia through Kurdish music. When he reached 16, it made sense for him to register at Ranya's Institute of Fine Arts, where he received his first violin. His deeply held belief that he would become a musician put him at odds with his contemporaries. Many attended simply because they happened not to be good at anything else, and knew they'd get a job as a state primary school or kindergarten teacher at the end of it.

When he graduated and found a job as a kindergarten teacher, specialising in music, the next generation of children was already on a new path. Girls and boys ate, learnt and played together as friends but, as these children grow older, social order will separate them again, the boys getting more power and rights to break rules, while girls after the age of 14 will find themselves more oppressed. Today, women, whose ambitions and earnings are restricted by their husbands, parents and society, still find it hard to find jobs, let alone play music.

Hellgurd found it harder and harder to live with the world he'd grown up in. As NYOI fuelled his awareness and skills, his motivation to learn and grow as an individual increased to bursting point. When, after writing 11 education blogs for

Deutsche Welle's website, rocks came hurtling through his window, he knew something had to change.

As we gradually approached our 2013 course, the meetings in Cologne between the German Friends and Gürzenich-Orchester slowly progressed. Finally, in May, they confirmed a joint ten-day teaching tour in the Kurdistan region of Iraq. Gudrun Euler, who worked with the German Friends to realise the project, took Hellgurd on as an assistant project manager, and Ranya got put on our tour schedule.

From the outset, I found this project difficult. NYOI's issues around the impending France visit and then America for 2014 already troubled me deeply. While juggling with those projects, I felt torn between the two key cultures in this venture, Germany and Iraq, as though I were tied to horses bolting in opposite directions, while in reality I belonged to neither. A deeper blow came from the German Friends themselves, who decided to pay Gudrun, a former orchestral manager, ten times more to run this project than they had paid me for running NYOI. It wasn't even as if anyone had done any fundraising. The British Council in London had put up all the cash. I sat in our final board meeting before departure, staring out of the window and trying my best to hold onto my integrity in this emotional smorgasbord. I just wanted to be left alone, and walk away when it was over.

We arrived in Erbil on 14th July, met by Karda from the British Council, waiting by a minibus. Gudrun was surprised not to see a larger welcoming committee, and I noticed her virgin expectations shrivel up in the heat as mine had back in 2009. After settling down in our hotel, we arrived at the Institute of Fine Arts, just down the road, to be greeted by armed guards who had not known of our visit. Our contact, Daroon from our viola section, who at least held keys to the building, got us past the guards and let us in to start work in the filthy, empty rooms with impossible acoustic and no air conditioning. The temperature outside hit 45 Celsius, but word was out. Students began to arrive from across town, many unknown to me. Will Frank, our retired lawyer from the German Friends, put his observer role to good use, noticing the building's wall crumbling away to reveal the bare structure beneath. This perfectly symbolised Iraq, the country that saved face, ignoring substance or sustainability.

Ten players from Baghdad, led by Hassan Hassun, had come to stay with us in the hotel and take part, joined by a number of musicians from Erbil. A couple of teachers also arrived to observe, including an older violinist from the Iraqi National Symphony Orchestra, who asked me for help with his composition. Their Baghdad concert had been suddenly rescheduled by the Ministry of Culture, which clashed with our visit. But Mohammed Amin Ezzat, the orchestra's Music Director, had arranged that a few could attend our classes in the Kurdistan Region. We had, after all, set aside budget to get them here. I was deeply honoured someone had taken the trouble to come up at all.

So, we set out on our deliberate mission to train young current and future teachers, and it quickly became clear from those we'd met, that teaching practice in Erbil was nowhere. Although their regular lessons comprised of little more than scales and arpeggios, everyone still needed better basic technique. Whether self-taught or not, most were between 18 and 25, had started music around 16, and had already deeply drilled years of mistakes into themselves. We tried to bring out some creativity in their performance, using fantasy to create different timbres and feelings. Gerhard, who had changed career from tenor to viola, used much of his physical voice training to free up the bodies of the violas and cellos and let their sound flow.

My one piano student had started promisingly with a Russian method beginners' book, so I took him in the direction of improvisation, which he could already do well, and duet practice. When another guy came in for conducting lessons, I asked my piano student to improvise responses to his various gestures, giving him direct musical feedback to his body language. Seated some distance from me, music staff from the Institute looked on, judging the scale of the threat.

Every morning, over three days, we taught violin, viola, cello, flute, clarinet and piano, the most common instruments in the Kurdistan Region, with Gabriele, our oldest and pluckiest tutor, kicking every morning off with a group physical warm-up. Fadi, now a 19-year-old, who had played second flute with us in 2009, turned up with new, fresh faces from Baghdad. Hassan, his teacher over the years, watched as Gabriele took her class of Waleed, Fadi and one other flautist through solid German technique. Claire Docherty, our violin tutor from Edinburgh, also joined the team. She had found herself with a 16-year-old female violinist who could play Beethoven's *Spring* Sonata. Her motley class of young men looked on as Claire and the girl irrepressibly took Beethoven apart phrase by phrase, and soon got everyone playing the beginning by ear. I couldn't resist gathering them around me to emphasise that they alone must take responsibility for the future of Iraq's culture – spreading good practice by stealth against the backdrop of indifference and greed.

Three days in Erbil, a rocky start to our visit, became our journey's baptism. Every night, we found our way to the hotel roof, armed with cans of beer, and sat under the warm stars, or stared across the ruby and diamond studded carpet of Erbil's streets sprawling below. On the fourth day, we clambered back into the bus bound for the road to Ranya. Coursing along motorways turned into shuddering along dirt tracks of rock and dust, negotiating our way round sharp corners, squeezing past lorries and isolated armed checkpoints. The mountains of Kurdistan, baked onto the faces of soldiers and old men along the way, felt bleak and reassuring. I saw why Kurds were difficult to defeat in their own terrain. Claire and I entertained each other with bawdy Scottish blether along the way. Others sat in silence and reflected through the window.

En route, Hellgurd, our Regional Representative for Ranya, warned us about the only hotel in his home town. In charming tones, his lips twitching in irony, he referred to the communal cold showers, cockroaches and hammocks for beds to make us feel more grateful for the reality on our arrival. After a few hours, we passed the massive 5th of March monument and a solitary donkey, standing forlorn by the road into town. We pulled up to the hotel, this time to a welcoming reception of staff from the Ranya Institute of Fine Arts which Gudrun made sure Hellgurd had set up for us. Claire's 'luxury suite' became our breakfast room, a magnificent feast of fruit, cereal, bread, yoghurt, hard-boiled eggs, coffee, tea, and laughter.

The evening of our arrival, as I helped the team stock up on our beer supplies in the local off-licence, I heard a deep American voice from behind me: 'I thought I'd find a Scot here!' There stood Marc Thayer, Deputy Director of American Voices, taking time off from his own project in Suleymaniyah. They had completed a large ten-day course in performing arts, including their own string programme. I took him to be less solid and tattooed than he actually was. Maybe this was how American violinists needed to be to teach in Iraq?

Marc and I had never before met face to face. American Voices, the performance organisation in New York that the US State Department paid to spread soft diplomacy around the world, bred deep distrust in some NYOI musicians. After all, their primary interest was America, not Iraq, and they were highly competitive. But Marc and I had worked well together, making sure our annual activities with the same pool of players didn't clash. Both highly strategic, we saw that diplomacy and sustainable music education were two sides of the same coin, at least here. He was staying with the family of Chwaz, one of our violists, whom he later awarded an American Voices scholarship to study in St Louis. We both agreed that the lucrative oil city of Erbil was a weird music town. Little Ranya, alongside the thriving musicians of Suleymaniyah, always yielded Iraq's finest string players, more so than even Baghdad. Still, perhaps he was a little wary of our German invasion, all superb pedagogues and players who brought something that young players could compare to American Voices.

The next day, we pulled up in front of the Institute of Fine Arts and ascended the filthy staircase to the Director's office. They lacked qualified teachers, good quality instruments, clean, air-conditioned practice rooms and tuned upright pianos. There was one electric piano. A depressing building in disrepair, it lacked everything, that is, until we entered the Director's office.

Like the switch from black and white to colour in *The Wizard of Oz*, all one had to do was look at each side of his doorway to see exactly where the money stopped and the dirt, decay and dishevelment of his school started. A captain's chair stood behind his broad wooden desk. Pictures hung all around the office, including a map of old Kurdistan, presiding over carpets and lush sofas for the guests. A few floors underneath our feet lay the cellar, which had been used as a torture chamber during Saddam Hussein's regime, so fostering creativity here seemed extremely bizarre. Against these conditions, the students, both male and female, maintained an incredible optimism.

Our first day in Ranya brought us together with about 50 young musicians. These young people were turning up in BMWs and Range Rovers with poor quality or broken instruments. At the end of each day, as we sat in the pristine, beautifully furnished director's office to share our daily feedback, we began to get a clear picture of what was really going on here. Rose, our Gürzenich-Orchester violin tutor, having had enough of talking English all day, suggested we all give our feedback in German. Saman, back with us to translate, burst out laughing and said, 'If you give your feedback in German, we'll give our feedback in Kurdish.' Thank goodness for someone with a sense of humour. German culture was hard work, especially in a country with no interest in complying. I watched as we grew more and more tired. The familiar giving and giving of NYOI; soon, we'd be at each other's throats.

One of my students, Rawezh Qadir, who had physical and learning challenges, showed himself to be by far the most resilient of my piano class. He had been discouraged from playing piano by his teachers and fellow students, but showed enormous perseverance. He obviously had loving parents who gave him his own electric piano. It wasn't until we got away from the piano and into improvised clapping games that it became clear he had the strongest, most creative sense of rhythm in the whole group. As there was no standard for piano playing in the Institute, I saw every reason for him to continue enjoying his music. Nobody had the right to tell him to stop.

I attempted, in our little three-day window, to introduce the pianists to more collaboration and creativity with the European Piano School published by Schott. These three books, filled with children's songs and easy classical pieces, brought out creative listening, inventing accompaniments, duets and improvisations. None of the pianists had ever played duet with each other or accompanied anyone else. Like many players in NYOI, they lived in a self-made bubble of ignorance and protection, cut off from all the creative possibilities around them. A little modern teaching grated against their 1950s view of classical music, but fitted rather well with being a traditional Kurdish musician. If only this generation still had those instincts. Better to be a good folk musician than a bad classical one.

Out of the sorry state of Ranya came a very fine piano teacher, Hemn Hassan, who refused to teach at the Institute, along with a student of his to play Rachmaninov's C sharp minor Prelude. He produced wonderful technique and feeling, but copying a YouTube performance, had fallen way outside the composer's intentions. So, it was back to the printed page for everyone, watching him cope with playing the opening chords in perfect time while the rest of us mercilessly clapped the pulse to him. Iraqis love their relativism.

Nothing is ever exact or predictable, which is what makes teaching here so frustrating. Despite that, teaching was dictatorship. Clearly, nobody had ever asked these students intelligent questions before, let alone expected to be asked. I brought a little book for more advanced players, Josef Lhevinne's *Basic Principles in Pianoforte Playing*, pure pedagogical gold. I imagined all the books I'd brought being slapped mercilessly onto Iraq's weapons of mass dissemination, the photocopier.

In his beautifully furnished office, the Director stood uneasily next to Gudrun and Will, photographed holding a certificate of our appreciation of our visit to help his Institute. What a charade. He thanked us and asked for help with the Institute's other arts programmes, a familiar Iraqi mantra. Whatever we gave, they wanted more, as long as they could keep the money for themselves. We were subsidising their corruption and greed. I confronted the Assistant Director with our ridiculous presence; a German charity, funded by British money to deliver music education in Kurdistan. He nodded, smiling, comfortably unaccountable for his own Institute's growth.

Three days of intensive care per town couldn't replace real education, especially one intended to train music teachers for kids. Those students who determined to stay the whole three days, made more progress than in their entire year, but our leaving for the next town would return them to an environment that failed them at best and sabotaged them at worst. Making musical progress in Iraq took an iron will. NYOI players could take a handful of lessons and make unfathomable leaps. But for this pilot project, we could only plant seeds and hope that, in a drought, the roots would grow deep.

As tutors, we also determined to have an amazing time, working extremely hard while still taking time to make sense of the very foreign world we were in. As dusk set in and the air cooled, we fuelled our makeshift camaraderie with beer on the grotty hotel roof until the wee small hours. With us all sat comfortably on cushions, Will Frank stood on Gudrun's little finger. Saman and Zanyar immediately came to the rescue, being medical students as well as translators. Fortunately, their training had already covered fingers.

Under the Kurdish moon, Claire Docherty and I continued to bolster each other's Scottish lunacy. We found ourselves closer to the Kurds than the Germans, this small region landlocked by Middle Eastern madness. Kurdish humour, like ours, cast darkly ironic and self-deprecatory shadows, but also revelled in the shameless Schadenfreude of the Germans. Personal suffering and disaster were dealt with by macabre mockery, and Gudrun's unfortunate finger soon became the running joke of the visit. Under the crystal clear Bedouin canopy of stars, toddlers and their families brought a fairground across the way to life. We downed our beers into the night.

Off now to Suleymaniyah, and by far the strongest Institute of Fine Arts. By now, we knew how to organise the violin classes by ability, and pace ourselves as the exhaustion started to hit home. Our stomachs were adapting to the new food, and we looked forward to the considerably better quality of teaching rooms, but my temper was fraying. Hellgurd broke down in tears at Gudrun's demands. I lost it with Gudrun a few times, and in response, the gallant Gerhard lost it with me. Tired of the relentless pressure of NYOI on top of teaching, I began to think I shouldn't have come along, but through this valuable time I allowed Iraq to grow into my bones from under my feet as I smelled the air, absorbed the landscape by day, and gazed across at the oil flares by night.

We will never forget the mountains between Ranya and Suleymaniyah, frozen sheaths of rock and ancient mounds speckled with lone trees – a surreal landscape that powerfully painted the upheavals of Iraq's peoples. As with Scotland, these mountains acted as a double-edged sword; they both protected and divided. This time, as the bus took us along the road, European egos tired and unravelled to be swathed by the irrational drama of Iraq. We sat in awe.

On arriving at the Institute of Fine Arts, Gabriele, our plucky flute teacher, warmed up the 50 or so students with musicians' stretching exercises, and then off we went to class. This time, I had five students and a grand piano. Though my students were trying to play advanced Chopin and Mozart, they couldn't get through the first duet of the absolute beginners piano book, and so we ploughed through duet after duet, until everyone's sight-reading started pulling together.

Most Iraqi musicians were thwarted by lack of English language skills. Without this, much online learning remained a mystery or a dangerous game of hit and miss. They didn't do bank accounts and credit cards either, so ordering materials online became a non-starter, unless a good bookshop nearby could help. Without our star translators, Zanyar, Saman and Shwan, we would have been equally lost in communicating our lessons in Arabic and Kurdish.

I was dismayed to see how little people cared about their own culture in Kurdistan, a region clamouring for independence. Having a different language and genes doesn't add up to autonomy, and only about ten percent of the world's countries are monolingual and monocultural. Today's hope lies with digitally literate young Iraqis who learn online and take full responsibility for the future of their country, because it's obvious nobody else will.

It was 17th July, between the end of the masterclasses and the beginning of the summer course in France. I dragged myself along to another German Friends board meeting, to be my last, over coffee and cake. Out in the garden, Whisper, the Scottish terrier, teased me through the window with his antics. A vase of unopened lilies, tinged green in the crisp white living room, sang of summer. Gudrun had brought Georg some delicious nougat from the market in Suleymaniyah, which he shared with us. The ivory tower of the German Friends had crumbled away to reveal real experience, leaving Georg, our treasurer, as the only one uninitiated into the world of Iraq. The difference was clear. Karl-Walter and I sat smugly as Gudrun and Will reported back with real passion and insight, while Georg pondered his usefulness, interjecting only occasionally.

When it came to America, I had to report that the response to my proposal from the Embassy in Baghdad was lukewarm. They were fully aware of the institutional racism between the Baghdad and Erbil governments which blocked the interest of both in NYOI, but still wanted to know who supported us at that level. Oil contracts had been burnt over the tensions between those two, so any State Department involvement couldn't put American interests at risk. To the Embassy, culture mostly meant student exchanges and scholarships. Still, a few shared the sentiments of General Colin Powell as expressed to George W. Bush, 'If you break it, you pay for it, Mr President'. Iraq was not only broken, but falling rapidly beyond repair.

With days to go before flying to Aix-en-Provence for the fifth NYOI course, I put the master class photos online, the German Friends decided to explore their relationship with Gürzenich-Orchester further and I changed my Facebook status to: 'Now in NYOI lockdown...'

NINETEEN
The pinnacle of endeavour

Air France had managed to screw up my flight and lose my luggage. After talking to the useless check-in staff, I rerouted myself from Düsseldorf to Marseilles via Paris and arrived some 12 hours late on 24th July. Air France generously supplied a T-shirt, toothbrush and shaving kit to ease my inconvenience. I felt as badly handled as my lost luggage. Our trusty cello tutor and this year's soloist, Dave Edmonds, met me at Marseilles International Airport with Cécile Mièle, our project manager, who drove us to our campus accommodation in Aix-en-Provence. Here, I learnt that Air France, flying Angie Cho in from Boston, had also managed to lose her luggage. I'd planned our kick-off meeting for tomorrow morning. At least the orchestra and tutors were all here.

After a typically challenging preparation phase for the summer course, the Grand Theatre de Provence team had got much of it right. Almost everybody had arrived and was ready to start. Yes, some of the players might miss their mothers' cooking and complain about the single student rooms with *en-suite* bathrooms, but we'd been through this before. The tutors occupied larger rooms a couple of blocks away from the orchestra, to give us our own space after rehearsals.

The brand new building for the Darius Milhaud Music School wasn't ready in time for our arrival, so we occupied the old building, Hotel de Caumont in the Mazzarin quarter of Aix-en-Provence. Completed in 1742, this elegant hotel had been the music school's home since 1970. I sensed the occasion in the beautiful courtyard, the elegant staircase and 18th century rooms, as though we had arrived as guests of honour. We were the last occupants before its conversion into a cultural centre.

We walked through the elaborate network of rooms that lay at our disposal to adapt in any way we wished. Pierre Barrois, the Manager of Orchestre Francais des Jeunes, and I already knew which musicians should rehearse where, and Cécile provided electric fans to deal with the Provençale humidity. We found one big setback: the culture centre contractors. Closed windows meant we steam-cooked, open windows meant we competed against their pneumatic drills in the courtyard below. Still, it beat working through Iraqi chaos. The Mediterranean humidity opened our pores and expectations as the orchestra met the French project team for the first time.

We felt at ease, ready to search out our rehearsal rooms and start making music, but during the first three days, tensions arose between Cécile's team and the orchestra. They were surprised at how wealthy some of the players seemed, and felt they were being ordered round like servants. In very many ways, the south of France's culture was not so far from the Middle East, but some of our men didn't understand how to talk to French women. I was quite taken aback. The teams in Edinburgh and Bonn, all women, hadn't reported anything, and by now, most of our players had developed at least some intercultural competence. So, I talked to Bashdar and Hassan, our Kurdish and Arab orchestra managers, about making sure we always behaved respectfully towards Cécile and her colleagues. Now NYOI alumni, those two turned out to be a great can-do team. They learnt how to work well with Cécile's team, and got quietly on with the job.

Cécile put her finger on another point of conflict. Some of the players clearly came from wealthy families, and I strongly empathised with her task of raising €311,000 for the course. I also knew we were €30,000 short, peanuts in Iraqi terms. Both the Kurdistan Regional Government and Iraqi embassy in Paris had ignored us. Why were we killing ourselves to raise large amounts of money for their cultural diplomacy, when not one cent came from Iraq? I'd asked Majid this before. This helpless, selfish culture of blame was wearing thin on me. Majid wanted everyone to be treated equally, meaning everyone should take part for free, but this was no longer a solution. We, and Iraq, had evolved.

Summertime in Aix embalmed us with warmth and local rosé wine. However, it took very little time for Dougie Mitchell and John Holt, lifelong colleagues from the Royal Philharmonic Orchestra, to home in on the nearest Irish pub and overpriced pints of Guinness. Within a day, we'd found our home from home, a nod in the direction of the Edinburgh pubs from last year. Out of the whole tutor team, only John was a NYOI virgin; everyone else knew what challenges lay ahead. A bullish and hugely experienced bassist, he got straight down to the business of moulding Samir Basim into an effective bass section leader. Mysteriously, Samir resisted to begin with. We couldn't quite put our finger on why this was.

In full rehearsals, the orchestra had great fun with Mohammed Amin Ezzat's new work, *The Magic of the East,* which proved every bit as bombastic as I expected. In harsh contrast, Najat Amin's *Anfal* graphically commemorated the victims of Saddam Hussein's gas attacks against the Kurds in the 80s; more dark modernism coming straight from their shattered souls. Najat knew that Arab players were performing in this hugely loaded work. I knew they would play it because I wasn't Iraqi and we were outside Iraq. However, it was still a sore point. Some players from Baghdad believed the gas attacks came from Iran, and one even said to me: 'I think Saddam should have been hanged, but not for that.'

Our first Friday off gave everyone the chance to explore Aix-en-Provence properly. The restaurant chain, Flunch, offered a wide range of meals, and our daily €10 vouchers went quite far. One deep concern was Tuqa, starving herself of food and drink from sunrise to sunset; we were rehearsing in Ramadan. Her brother, Almujtaba, playing second trumpet, told me he was worried about her. We all were. Flunch stopped serving at 10.00

pm, while sunset came at around 9.30, giving her just half an hour to eat anything at all. We kept an eye on her over the coming days as she fought tiredness on the first desk of the cellos. She didn't put one note wrong. I often smiled back in concern. This was her spiritual cleansing, and at 19, she was old enough to take full responsibility for her religious duties. But still: seven hours a day rehearsing.

We'd reached 29th August, our last rehearsal before the French players joined us. I asked Hellgurd to write $1,400,000 in Arabic numbers on a sheet of flipchart paper and tape it up behind my podium for everyone to see. I'd thought about this speech for a long time and was ready to give it. They were adults, and they had to take responsibility. Pointing to the figure on the wall, with Shwan translating into Arabic and Kurdish, I explained that since 2009, we'd spent that much money on NYOI, and if we added the market value of all our voluntary work, it would easily exceed $2,000,000. This year, we hadn't received a single penny from Iraq.

I wanted players to set up their own ensembles, performing, teaching and writing music better and more often than ever before. I knew there were too many who came to our courses, returned to Iraq and put their instruments back in the cupboard until the next round of auditions. On this point, Rezhwan, the leader of the violas, sniggered. I knew that she knew it was true, and I felt cheated. If they didn't want to culturally engage back home, we were the wrong orchestra for them. This is what I told them, and in no uncertain terms.

There was silence in the room. Dougie Mitchell, back as our lead wind tutor, held his head in his hands. Samir stared at me in disbelief from behind his bass. In my exasperation, I was reclaiming my centre as musician and human being. I had behaved for too long like a charity, manager and diplomat. Everyone had lived off my generosity and I didn't owe Iraq a thing. After five years of NYOI, the players owed each other a proper Iraqi organisation, stronger culture and a sustainable future for music *in* Iraq, funded *by* Iraq. I mounted the podium, and began conducting.

At the same time in the next building, two Arabic experts from Paris took the 14 young musicians from Orchestre Français des Jeunes through Iraqi history, geopolitics and culture. For the last hour, I took some of the NYOI musicians with me after rehearsal to join in. There, transliterated on a whiteboard, stood Arabic text, which the experts coached us to sing to the tune of our old friend, *Che Mali Wali*. As the French students sang along, there, sitting under the open windows were Mohammed Adnan, Murad and Hassun playing the pained melody that had accompanied them though childhood. Totally in their bliss, a deep melancholy seeped out from within their Iraqi soul. This wasn't all. Naturally, the Kurds also needed to express their culture. Alan Kamil, our new concertmaster, struck up some traditional melodies on his violin with our wonderfully gifted new percussionist, Peshawa, imitating a zither accompaniment on the grand piano at the back of the room. Two intense musical traditions perfumed one small space filled with the finest of France and Iraq.

That evening, excitement filled the garden of Hotel de Caumont, where the orchestra met the 14 French support players for the first time. Pierre Barrois, here in Aix to manage the Orchestre Français des Jeunes summer course, looked on. With over 100 players, they were based on another campus, rehearsing Debussy's *Ibéria*, Bartok's *Concerto for Orchestra* and a vast tapestry of Wagner orchestral music with Dennis Russell Davies. Their challenge, albeit as mighty as ours, took them down a very different path.

I stood on the sidelines, watching, waiting. The garden party, fuelled with wine and snacks of French fruit and cheese, buzzed along in a typically genteel manner, till finally we hit our tipping point. Out came the daff and Sherwan struck up the call to party. The orchestra coagulated into its familiar ring of dance. Within moments, the French reacted by joining in with uninhibited gusto; no sitting apprehensively on the sidelines for them. I breathed deeply, relieved that our young guests had some Gallic spunk in them. It was looking good.

Who else should be there but Phia Welz, our 2010 manager from the South African National Youth Orchestras. Many of our players from that year delighted in seeing her again and we all noticed we'd moved on since. Phia was here at Pierre Barrois's invitation to observe Orchestre Français des Jeunes and help out with her assistant, Babalwa Tshula. More than that, we were preparing for a festival that would bring us into direct contact with the national youth orchestras of France, Italy and Spain. The Grand Theatre de Provence had organised the youth orchestra equivalent of planetary alignment, and we were Pluto.

Our orchestra now complete with French support, the routine flowed. Every morning, prompt at 9.30, in the sunny 18th century courtyard, before the pneumatic drills started work, Adam, our percussion tutor, led the orchestra through a physical warm-up. As well as being a freelancer with the London Symphony Orchestra and the Colin Currie Ensemble, he was also an actor, and so took it upon himself to activate our whole bodies every morning. The Iraqis, whose physical education had clearly never amounted to very much, badly needed to embrace this.

We hit 10.00 am, splitting off into sectionals and individual lessons, then reformed into chamber groups at noon. Dave, Ilona and Angie, our die-hard string tutors, organized the advanced Iraqi string players into three quartets coached by each of them. The other strings stayed with me and worked with the French players on the well-loved *Capriol Suite* by Peter Warlock. A modern interpretation of six renaissance dances, this hugely popular work found its way into the curriculum of music schools worldwide, and was ideal for our intermediate players.

After a few days' rehearsal on this, I instructed the French players to perform an excerpt alone, which they did flawlessly. Then I asked the Iraqi players to do the same, and they scratched their way through with little sense of sound or personal responsibility for the notes before them. To paraphrase one of the French players afterwards: 'I didn't really know why I was here, but when I heard the Iraqis playing alone, I immediately understood.' One of the Kurdish players came up to me afterwards to say: 'It was a very good idea to add the French players!'

Indeed, the plethora of Kurdish string players was causing some discontent amongst the Arabs. While the strings in total were by far the best we'd ever had, having all worked hard to pass their audition, the Baghdad players' pride had been affronted again. Despite the venerable institutions of the Iraqi National Symphony Orchestra and the Baghdad School of Music and Ballet, how could their players ever compete against the blossoming string culture in Kurdistan? Largely ignored by Baghdad, the annual American Voices string programme there gave the Kurds another edge. I knew what they were thinking. It simply wasn't fair that the Kurds had a safer, more open and liberal culture than the rest of Iraq.

They knew that the turmoil and growing sectarian rifts in Baghdad had drained its inhabitants of the will to practice, rehearse, and flourish; even of the will to live.

Over the course of the week, the French really came into their own. Even though I'd positioned them in supporting roles amid the strings, they still found themselves leading their Iraqi desk partners. When the Iraqi leaders of each string section forgot to lead, which was often, the French became responsible for leading from behind, often counting the bars rest and marking the music themselves. They became especially alert on realising that the Iraqi players next to them automatically copied every mistake they made. Although this was considerably more stressful than working with a French youth orchestra, through a long, patient process, they themselves learnt to become servant-leaders, and kept faith that I would get us all through in the end.

The orchestra took its second Friday off in Marseilles, while I stayed in Aix, alone and tired. Finding a pleasant corner cafe with wireless LAN, I ordered a coffee with croissant and started searching for foundations to apply for the USA visit next year. I'd been granted a month's free access to a professional funding search site and come up with some fascinating results, but I was still doing all the work. I couldn't see any of the Iraqis getting their heads around this, let alone writing a professional funding application to America, and the German Friends were mainly focussed on the orchestra's German relationship. Besides, an American success, while highly motivating the Iraqi team, would threaten their power. I also knew that, after 9/11, American foundations had become strictly regulated, though funding decisions were still political. After years of progress, it was hard to be back at square one again, just like 2009. I kept calm and carried on.

Meanwhile, the orchestra was having fun *sûr la plage* in Marseilles, playing on the beach, in the waves and shopping along the boulevard. Some new players had never seen the sea before, let alone topless French women showering in public, which made for good-natured hilarity. It seemed they were acclimatising to France, getting to know the French players better, and enjoying the humid Mediterranean climate. They had tried swimming for the first time and found the freedom to have fun.

Pierre Barrois came over from his rehearsals to check on us. In addition to his 14 supporting players, we planned a joint flash mob with Orchestre Français des Jeunes, playing *Ride of the Valkyries* in a local town square. Getting the orchestra out into the open felt like a great idea, in spite of our disastrous garden party in 2010! A flash mob in Iraq was impossible. I wanted to see my players enjoying themselves with Orchestre Français des Jeunes, out in the open, free of security and disapproval. Still, the two orchestras had to co-ordinate tightly on the choreography to pull their four-minute performance off.

While they were rehearsing that, Cécile and I had lunch, to update and chill-out. Mohammed Amin Ezzat, who'd composed *Desert Camel* for us in 2011 and now *The Magic of the East*, couldn't fly to France to hear its premiere. Hassan had explained that, as the Chief Conductor of the Iraqi National Symphony Orchestra, he'd lost his passport. The Ministry of Culture had paid an agent to fly his orchestra to another Arab country to perform, and this person had disappeared with all the money and all the orchestra's passports. Cécile smiled. I knew she didn't know what to believe from this and, frankly, neither did I. I just smiled back and repeated the same mantra my players had been using since 2009: 'It's Iraq.'

Sarah, our horn tutor since 2010, had quite a handful this year. First, a new horn player from Baghdad had decided simply not to turn up. His family had hastily scheduled his arranged marriage to happen at the same time as the course, possibly to make sure he stayed home. Ranya also didn't come this year. She was now married to Janaid, the concertmaster of the Iraqi National Symphony Orchestra, whose concerto audition Beethovenfest had rejected in 2011. We knew that Janaid was no fan of NYOI, and Ranya was now under his control. So, for a concert needing four horns, Sarah had just herself, Ali and then there was Mohammed, who hadn't touched his horn in three months. Fortunately, we were in France, not Iraq. Within a day, Cécile had found a local horn student, Johann, a 17-year-old rugby player built like a brick wall, who cheerfully spoke only French. He was brilliant.

John, our new bass tutor, wanted a word with me. He didn't understand why Samir was so unhappy. I put it down to his last year with NYOI, bitterness at not being able to reach his full potential in Iraq, and being a very beautiful, sensitive soul who couldn't deal anymore with the petty politics of the Iraqi National Symphony Orchestra. After analysing Samir this way and that, I finally told John right out that I didn't really care what his student's attitude was. Sixty-seven people had been murdered by terrorists the day before in Baghdad, and I was just glad he was out of there for three weeks. I knew Samir was resilient deep down, and would come round. Whatever John said after that, it worked. Samir's motivation rocketed, and he began firmly leading Chia and the two French basses through rehearsals.

It was 7th August already and, over the past two weeks, the orchestra had created several fine chamber ensembles, incomparable in confidence and musical sensitivity to previous years. Together, we were approaching a point on the youth orchestra barometer marked 'normal'. On this day, we visited the garden of a local psychiatric hospital to perform our chamber music programme. Their residential patients mixed with our players on wooden benches under the canopy of luscious green trees. A single cricket perched up in a branch, right on the middle tree, had decided that its music was every bit as important as ours, and began to start singing, though what that little creature produced came closer to heavy metal.

Bravely, we started competing, first with a movement of a Mozart quartet played by our best string players, whose delicate, schooled phrasing lost to the cricket. Then the wind quintet, led with tremendous verve by Waleed on flute, played a Brahms Hungarian Dance that still wouldn't shut the little critter up. However, when the Arab and Kurdish ensembles performed their traditional music, the cricket finally decided to stop and listen.

We'd not only had a lovely time, but given one too, and were invited into the care centre for a buffet and soft drinks. One of the residential minders, a tall, muscular guy in a staff T-shirt who I guessed had a North African background, towered over me, talking warmly in French. I wasn't quite sure if he was coming onto me, but there was always hope. He was, in fact, thanking me for bringing the orchestra together to France, and how incredibly important this was to his Muslim community. Of course, the South of France has a difficult relationship with its Muslim communities. I didn't immediately register – his biceps were quite distracting – but later cherished this honest moment from a French citizen.

TWENTY
Crossroads at Aix

That evening, we all walked along to the Grand Theatre de Provence to hear the first in the series of National Youth Orchestra concerts, Joven Orquesta Nacional de España. This huge ensemble, conducted by George Pehlivanian, began harmlessly enough with Chabrier's *España* and de Falla's *El Amor Brujo*, sung by husky flamenco diva Carmen Linares. The warmth and passion of the Spaniards, the sensual melodies snaking through the hall, deeply rooted in Moorish history, captivated us all. I waited for my players' hurt pride to take them out of their seats and leave, but they simply sat there, chin on hands, elbows on the edge of the balcony, staring down in wonder.

At the interval, Du'aa asked me what I thought. I began: 'It's really great to hear the Spanish orchestra compared to us because...'

'Aha' she retorted, spirits drooping at impending comparison. 'Wait a minute,' I retorted: 'because I can hear the Arabic influence in the Spanish music that we have in our own repertoire'.

Somewhat forlorn, she replied, 'Oh well, if we had been given the same opportunities that they had, we'd probably be better than them.' Eyes cast downwards. I smiled in sympathy, but I'd discussed this point at length with the tutors. Though we all loved coaching NYOI, many players' problems had so deeply set in over years of self-teaching, they could only be marginally improved in an annual course. A balance needed to be struck between over-provision, which could kill motivation by being too soft, and under-provision, which could do irreversible damage by being too hard. What made the difference was a supportive family, and most of NYOI had at least that. Most of NYOI *was* that.

If the first half had made some of us gloomy, the second half reduced others to tears. Stravinsky's *Rite of Spring*, gleaming perfection, ripped through us with animal ferocity, easily one of the best live *Rites* I've ever heard. I so felt for my players. For five years, they'd got away with thinking they weren't bad as national youth orchestras go, and now this. To top it all, the Spanish encored with a couple of light pieces, their percussion section comically dancing along as they played. It all looked so effortless.

Samir cornered me after the concert and insisted I give him my opinion of their basses.

'Well, they were in tune', I said pointedly. 'They were together, they all made the same sound with the same amount of bow. They watched the conductor and knew what to do with him'. He kept insisting on more feedback. Great that he was motivated, but I had other things on my mind. I grabbed our leader and soloist, Alan Kamil and Dave Edmonds, and took them into the deserted upstairs bar.

'What can we do to give everyone a final push over the next few days?'

Tonight had seriously crushed the players' spirits, and we had to lead strongly together through the final few days to help everyone do their best. Alan suggested he would be tougher on tuning the orchestra before rehearsals, making sure the lazier strings sitting at the back actually took the time to get it right. Dave, our sole remaining string tutor, offered more tips for the strings to polish the ensemble. As we discussed our options, a few of the theatre staff appeared casually in the bar, sitting close by, listening in. They were as concerned as we were about the effect of the evening, and wanted to know what was going down. As the three of us got up and left, I managed a half-reassuring smile to the Head of Marketing.

After the concert, the three youth orchestras in town, Joven Orquesta Nacional de España, Orchestre Français des Jeunes and NYOI all walked along to a conference centre not far from the theatre. On arrival, the huge hall had been set up for a disco with free beer, wine and canapés. Roughly 300 young musicians from Spain, France and Iraq took the dance floor over and within half an hour, a mass of sweaty young bodies were pulsating in jubilation. The beat kicked in and Orchestre Français des Jeunes locked itself scarily into co-ordinated blocks of 70s disco steps. But they were happy. Mine were not. Across the hall, I could see some of them hacking into the conference laptop with their own USB sticks, and as if by magic, up started the Iraqi pop music. Squares broke down helplessly into whooping circles, with selfies being flashed through the irresistible mayhem. I could smell the testosterone building up.

'POL POL POL POL' chanted the players; they were incanting me, their Dionysian dictator, to bop and bounce amid the fervour. I had a mortal duty to accept this role of virgin sacrifice, especially pertinent after the last dance of *Rite of Spring*. I knew to give into their power. They needed their little revenge after rehearsing for three weeks in three languages for one single concert; a single concert that, in Baghdad would take only three days to rehearse and sound awful. At least tonight though, they realised what this was all ultimately about. At least tonight, they were having fun.

The revelry intensified as I entered the ritual circle. 'YAAAAAY,' they hollered. No going back now. I loved them for their Middle Eastern bromance, open hearts and fiery temperaments. They loved me because they got to do something together that made them feel a new sense of normal and safe, not the 'normal and safe' of Iraq. Dave took countless group selfies from amid the tribal beat, their resilient faces beaming back tightly into the frame. They deserved my love, patience and compassion, but most of all, I'd sacrificed a lot to get us this far, and they knew it. In an unexpected way, we loved each other.

After extricating myself from the dance floor, I stood apart, observing from a cocktail table. Bashdar came over to me: 'We're sorry.' he said. Was he really apologising for the orchestra, knowing we could never be like other national youth orchestras? I was lost for words. 'And thanks for this.'

'Bashdar, I'm only a small part of this. Lots of people made this happen.'

Iraqi resilience is astounding. After shattering their illusions, and showing them what the 'competition' sounded like, NYOI had bounced back in a matter of hours. I looked on as our second trumpet, Almujtaba, danced like a liberated prisoner. In a way, they all were. When we talked later, he told me this was his first ever disco. He was 21.

Walking slowly back to our residence, Phia and I talked. We both felt what my players were feeling. I thought of poor Dave Edmonds, who'd really put his neck on the line for us by playing the Saint-Saëns 2nd Cello Concerto. I toyed with how to create a face-saving gimmick. Walking ponderously up the street, I turned to Phia. 'Right, I've decided. We're putting Dave on stage in a burqa.' The next morning, as I walked through the courtyard of the hotel, a new kind of music came from the open windows. I wound up the staircase to the first floor rehearsal room. They were all practising like devils.

We'd reached Friday 9th August, our first day rehearsing on stage in the Grand Theatre de Provence. Pierre and I had agreed that NYOI would work during the mornings in The Big One, a huge room that simulated the stage for opera rehearsals, while they worked in the theatre. After lunch, we'd swap round. Logistically, OFJ had a much bigger orchestra than us, with enormous percussion requirements, which had to be moved from one space to the other over lunch. This we left in the capable hands of the stage crew. It was, after all, one of the best equipped and most hi-tech theatres in Europe. After our first afternoon rehearsing on stage, Sarah, who was playing fourth horn, sat in the auditorium to check balance in the Beethoven symphony, and came back to me to say the woodwind had to be raised up to help them project their sound better. No worries, I thought.

Later that afternoon, in front of the 17th century Italianate town hall, we captured more tourists and townies with a repeat of our chamber music concert in the hospital garden. I knew what Pierre Barrois had planned with Orchestre Français des Jeunes throughout their residency. This included not only two concerts, but also workshops on the music business, open air chamber music, comedy concert presentations and special performances for the local hospice. His brilliant young players faced an uncertain future in classical music and Pierre, along with other national youth orchestras in Europe, threw everything he could at preparing them for a tough life ahead. So, through TV, press and performances, we worked with the project team to raise our visibility in town.

That evening, Orchestra Giovanile Italiana, conducted by Pascale Rophé, took to the stage. A long programme that started with Ravel's *Tombeau de Couperin* and finished with the 1945 suite from Stravinsky's *Firebird*, this concert, though incredibly fine musically, threatened my players less. Bombastically, it was a notch down from Spain. They were somewhat relieved.

Next morning, at the rehearsal break, I talked to the stagehand about getting risers for the woodwind and, in that very special French way, he answered: 'It's impossible.'

'What's impossible? A couple of risers for the wind?'

'Well, the staging is for Orchestre Francais des Jeunes. It's one staging for all the youth orchestras.'

'Well, we're not OFJ. We're different.'

'Yes, I know. It's very difficult, you know.'

'So, it was impossible a moment ago, and now it's just very difficult. Which is it, difficult or impossible?'

'It's impossible to get the risers in time. We have to reset the stage over lunch.'

'Impossible? IMPOSSIBLE?? That's all I've been hearing for the past three weeks! C'est *difficile*. C'est *impossible*. C'est *difficile*. C'est *impossible*! I'll tell you what's IMPOSSIBLE! This ORCHESTRA is impossible. This CONCERT is impossible. But we DO it. If we can do this orchestra, you can find a couple of risers.'

'You'll have to talk to my boss.'

'I will. Where is he?'

'She's not here. She's here on Monday.'

I was now talking to his back. He didn't need me to tell him. The door was the square thing in the wall. I set my tongue from

stun to kill for the next time somebody said to me: 'C'est *difficile*.
C'est *impossible.*'

That afternoon, we got the risers.

That Sunday evening, Gudrun from the German Friends, Najat
Amin, our Kurdish composer and all the key players and staff
from NYOI met Zuhal and me at a café across from the theatre
to talk about our future. I gave them the update on NYOI in
America. Our cards were good. We had some support from
Carnegie Hall and the newly formed National Youth Orchestra
of the USA. Queens College New York also opened their doors
to us for next year's summer residency. But we still needed a
huge amount of money, a project banker, project management
and a tour organiser. We still had no organisation in Baghdad,
there was little that the German Friends could do to raise money
for an American tour, and I couldn't keep going like this. Frankly,
I should have given up years ago. Life would be so much better
if I had.

We sat. We talked. We brainstormed. In a couple of hours, we
came up with a list of things to do back in Iraq to get money.
We knew how futile this was, but America was such a pinnacle
to our achievements so far, it was worth pulling together in one
mammoth effort to break through. I hoped this would be the
project to forge our organisational ability once and for all. As
Shwan translated everything for the Kurds, Waleed nodded.
NYOI, forever complex, had to grow up and take charge of its
destiny.

The day of the concert, 13th August, arrived. The German
Friends came along to the afternoon rehearsal with Georg's
Scottish terrier, Whisper. With them, they brought glad tidings
of a bassoon. This had been donated from a guy who'd e-mailed
me from Newcastle, and delivered it to me via a mate of his,
who I met in McDonald's, across the road from Kings Cross
Station, London. Back in Cologne, the German Bassoon
Association paid for its renovation, and seemed enthusiastic to
further support Iraqi bassoonists as an endangered species. In a
little ceremony that painted a thousand words, Gudrun and

Georg from the German Friends asked Ahmed Abbas, our zealous second bassoon, to take it home and teach someone in Baghdad. Ahmed may not be as good as Murad, but his hunger to learn certainly drove him forward, and we felt sure he was the right one to trust. Someone tipped off Murad. He appeared frozen, standing a few feet away. Samir explained the terms of the donation to Ahmed in Arabic, while I kept an eye on Murad, fixated on the gleaming instrument in its blue satin-lined case. His subordinate was getting a free bassoon, so he could teach someone in Baghdad. In his mind, this clearly didn't add up.

The orchestra and I rehearsed calmly and responsively that afternoon. There were no mishaps, no people disappearing, nobody was late. We rehearsed walking on and off smoothly, smiling to the public, changing the violin seating to make space for Dave's cello next to the podium. We'd adjusted to the sound of the hall, and everything came across well. For the first time in five years, I enjoyed the rhythm of a normal general rehearsal.

We waited in relaxed readiness backstage, shared warmth between us. Standing in white tie and tails, checking my hair one last time, the artist in me overtook the fighter. Alan and the other section leaders tuned everybody meticulously in preparation for the show.

We walked confidently, smiling, onto the stage, had a quick double check for tuning and began with Mohammed Amin Ezzat's *The Magic of the East*. Our lead clarinettist, Balen Qader, coaxed melancholic cries from his solos, the strings haunting in the shadows, then intensely penetrating the auditorium with elaborate melodies. A Bedouin kaleidoscope of colours swirled through the music to the end, a tapestry of interwoven themes reaching a dizzy climax and a defiant last chord. We'd kicked off well. I put Ahmed, who normally played second bassoon, on first to give him experience in leading and soloing. He clearly had no problem being the alpha.

Then, as contrasting as one could get, we performed Najat Amin's *Anfal*, evoking gas creeping through the streets of Hallabjah, the town where our deputy concertmaster, Rebaz, had grown up. The sickening pallor of the strings built into screaming panic and Saddam's military might blazed from brass through the full orchestra. Zuhal gently tried soothing the pain as raindrops fell from her piano playing, before the music built up to another military attack. Our concertmaster, Alan, broke into a solo on his violin, improvising Kurdish music in all its microtonal bitterness, a lone grandmother's tears pouring out as the percussion thumped bombs out of the bass drum. The fury built up once more and died slowly, gas dispersing, blasts fading into the distance. A shattered public sat in silence. After ten minutes of intense emotion, I was soaked in sweat.

Then came Dave for the Saint-Saëns. He had already left our reality as we struck up the introduction. He strode deftly through the first movement, striding out to the romance of French royal ballrooms, elaborate baroque corridors and proud courtly dances. We were, in fact, performing a major romantic work for the first time ever.

The delicate second movement, our personal triumph, proved that NYOI could produce a warm sound. Dave's syrupy tones trickled through the filigree texture of the orchestra as the players melded into a giant chamber ensemble, listening intently to every inflection, every change in timbre. Ali, our first horn, took the challenging solos in his stride, and closed his dialogue with Dave on a gently muted siren call.

The diabolic third movement galloped along at a terrifying pace, Dave furiously fiddling away at the intricate cello chords. Knotty French harmonies fell remarkably well into place: as foreign a musical language as any the players had encountered before. Murad nailed his mellifluous bassoon solos time and time again. He was on brilliant form. After a coquettish finale, we reprieved the courtly beginning in shiny D major and reached the end, The Sun King triumphant.

After the interval, the orchestra came back on for Beethoven's 8th Symphony, our biggest challenge ever. As we began, a rich, affirmative sound flowed from the orchestra. The energy tearing out of the players took the audience aback; a visceral sound balanced to be as clear as possible so that Beethoven's music could shine out. We could have been giving the first performance.

My charisma burst forth in ways I could never before have allowed as we locked ourselves into a fatalistic groove. Only by getting to the end together could we be released from Beethoven's power.

In the tricky second movement, the winds weren't as supple as I would have liked, but they still courted the strings, nodding to each other like two turtle doves, a beguiling ritual forming out of Beethoven's simplicity. Tuqa and the cellos inflected the chord changes gently enough not to be absurd, but clearly enough to lead the listeners through this romantic little dance.

The third movement, the Minuet and Trio, took us further into courtly dances of the 18th century. The Minuet proved no problem at all for us, but the trio, with Johann on second horn and Ali on first, proved too scary, and after a few notes, Ali stopped playing. Balen Qader, taking the tricky clarinet counterpoint, nailed that top note time and time again: a note Dougie had shown him how to get and which his teacher in Kurdistan said didn't exist. We were all immensely proud of him for taking the risk and making it work.

We took the mercurial fourth movement at a good lick, but I soon started fighting the resistance of the trumpets and timpani, who just sat unresponsively like meat pies in the middle of the sound. My job simply became to keep the momentum up and stop us from slacking into a mediocre gallop. We did manage to keep that up all the way through to the end and, in the last few notes, with the basses led by Samir rising triumphantly to a pinnacle, the symphony ended. We got a huge cheer, and the audience rose to its feet.

I had played as cool and in control as I dared throughout. More impactful than the concert itself came the realisation among the players that they were a generational movement. They knew they would never attain the standard of the other orchestras, but they could prepare the way for their children to grow up in a more positive musical world, if their country were ever left in peace. Together, we had changed France's view of Iraq, and France had changed the players' view of themselves for good.

TWENTY ONE
Mission to Mars

If bringing NYOI to Europe was like a mission to the moon, bringing it to America was a mission to Mars. The god of war had brought death and destruction to Iraq, and now we were ready to take on our biggest and most controversial diplomatic mission on the back of five unimaginably successful years.

2013 had been a landmark year for us, with a wonderful course in Aix-en-Provence, the German Friends organising masterclasses with German tutors around the Kurdish region and the Morgenland Festival from Osnabrück adding the first ever NYOI Chamber Orchestra to their events in Erbil. Sadly, the Iraqi Ministry of Culture, who co-ordinated Baghdad as 'Cultural Capital of the Middle East,' had cancelled NYOI's performances, scheduled directly after France, due to the risk of terrorism. That they wanted the concert in Baghdad's Red Zone raised many red flags. Dave, Sarah, the French players, and myself as foreigners in a high profile performance, considerably upped the risk of being targeted.

Back home in Cologne, I felt abandoned, crawling on all fours like a dog on its last legs. The NYOI team understood how tired I was and I believed they were doing everything they could to keep the orchestra alive in a political environment toxic with divisions, corruption and incompetence. The Baghdad players also had to reckon with daily bombings that killed 30 to 60 people a day. We were all, for various reasons, suffering from 'learned helplessness'.

I first came across learned helplessness in Martin Seligman's book, *Flourish*, about research into resilience. He and his colleagues showed that putting subjects in situations where, over time, no matter what they did, they had no control over negative outcomes, taught them to go into a mild state of shock, give up and take whatever was coming. Those subjects who had been offered the chance to escape did not learn helplessness later on. While Seligman later expanded this into his work with the US military, the book helped me gain insights into NYOI.

From this standpoint, I saw an orchestra full of young people whose dreams were being continually thwarted by war and terrorism. I couldn't blame anybody for feeling helpless. Even the Kurdish players, who'd been less affected by the Iraq war, were living the victim and minority complexes of their elders during the time of Saddam Hussein. While they existed, many thousands of other young Kurds had died or remained unborn from Saddam's sustained genocide. But the real killer was corruption. Wars came and went, but those with the wrong name, background or religion were doomed to become living ghosts from the word go, never fulfilling their dreams.

Most of all, I sympathised with Majid in Baghdad. Born in 1965, he was a child during the second Kurdish-Iraq war, a young man during the Iran-Iraq and Gulf wars and then a father during international sanctions and the Iraq war of 2003. I could see the tremendous sadness and frustration in his eyes, his passionate will to do everything he could for Du'aa and his family, his love of the young musicians in Baghdad and the decades of cynicism and resignation he was fighting to stay alive inside. Through music, a core of him had survived.

The lights behind the eyes of younger musicians like Samir and Murad had already gone out and their hearts flooded with cynicism. Most of our guys started giving up hope around 25 years old, but not our women. They were making music in NYOI because, by their very nature, they could defy and suffer their deeply misogynistic culture.

Then, on 29th September, a miracle occurred. Majid e-mailed the certificate confirming us as a non-governmental organisation in Baghdad, registration IR76544. After four years of fighting the system, he'd finally done it. We rejoiced in our victory, as he now had authority to go to the Ministry of Culture and ask for government funding as well as donations and sponsorship. I immediately forwarded the certificate to Cathy Graham at British Council London. Our very patient strategy to reach this vital point had been successful and I felt a huge weight lift off my shoulders. Five years on, we had an international reputation, good internal processes, the German Friends and our own NGO in Baghdad. The good feeling wasn't to last for long.

After years of trying to inspire impetus, I felt myself crumbling as they improved. I'd driven hard down this road and could see little hope for myself. Everyone was full of praise, but NYOI was a tough calling card for a professional musician: too difficult to comprehend, imperfect, off-the-radar. Indeed, I felt more like an international social worker.

Added to this, the cultural chasm between Majid and the German Friends had shut down all communication between them. Majid's world centred on Iraqi relationships, history and business. Generally speaking, what we called corruption and nepotism were simply regarded as the informal distribution of wealth and securing the family's future. When a percentage of dealings didn't go into the back pockets of business partners down the line, *that* was regarded in Iraq as selfish, corrupt. Only 4% of Iraqis had a bank account, and of those, only 1% had a credit card. Many banks had only a handful of cash machines in the whole of Iraq.

Family rooted itself deep in ways we could not grasp in the West and group oriented, informal relationships flowed through the arteries to nourish their bloodlines. Ironically, Cologne, home of the German Friends, had a reputation as Germany's most corrupt city, for not dissimilar reasons. Nevertheless, Karl-Walter and friends valued individual responsibility, reliability, thoroughness, fiscal transparency and risk aversion. I was deeply sick of being the only person either side would talk to; hardly a good basis for organisational success.

After five years of sacrificing my career, finances and friendships for the orchestra, there was nothing left but to go for NYOI in the USA. The German Friends couldn't help much. Not that they wanted to. No American would donate to them for an American visit, partly because they had no tax exemption status in the US, and partly because American foundations were required by law to give only to registered American charities. Besides, if this high-risk venture went wrong, standing on the sidelines could protect them and the orchestra in future.

A great many of my American friends in Cologne rallied round to support me through this difficult time. I was fed, loved and kept an eye on. Even through my most miserable moods, they held onto me. The five-year strategy I'd started in 2009 may well have come to a hugely successful end in France, but I found myself yet again running on fumes while fostering my US contacts and doing much of the project alone.

After cranking the laptop into action for another year of hell, I began by delegating certain duties to Zuhal. She knew how to run the auditions well. Then, I needed a visa lawyer, the one I'd met at the League of American Orchestras conference in Atlanta back in 2010. We needed a base for our summer camp, so after a year of probing, I ended up talking to the Aaron Copland Music School in Queen's, New York. This proved to be a great solution for our youth orchestra partners, the National Youth Orchestra of the USA at Carnegie Hall. The school wasn't far from them as well as being a known quantity. I also needed a project manager to set up the course and a US banker to pay bills and accept income. Though the Iraq Foundation in Washington DC was not in a position to offer much help, I found them by far the most responsive. But where to get the necessary half a million dollars?

Acutely aware of how foreign American culture had become to me, I took online courses from the League of American Orchestras on writing a funding proposal, American style, and hit every foundation I could: Carnegie, Rockefeller, Clinton, Presser, the US Institute of Peace, you name it. I also dug deep into US companies working in Iraq and Arab or Iraqi foundations working in the US. If there was even a remote chance they might fund us, I applied. This hit a number of barriers very quickly.

First, I needed a US-based charity as the project's banker. Without somewhere to put money in America, the project was paralysed. Heroically, British Council stepped in to let me use the Friends of British Council USA, based in Washington DC. They'd played a similar role in the US tour of the European Union Youth Orchestra in 2012. I could now write applications under their auspices.

Second, when I started filling out the Bank of America Foundation application and reached the page which asked me which of the following minorities would be in the audience, I saw no mention of Middle Eastern or Arab peoples at all. I couldn't even tick a box called 'other'. They weren't the only foundation to ignore this group. Were Arab Americans undesirable or just plain invisible to the needs of corporate socially responsible America? Those foundations that supported Middle Eastern communities in the US had small operations, showed no interest in music and, like many, didn't accept unsolicited approaches.

Third, and this was my big problem with the US Institute of Peace, foundations happily funded cultural diplomacy abroad as long as the artists stayed there, and America looked good while doing good. During the slap-down phone call with my contact, she insisted that everybody she'd talked to in Kurdistan could speak Arabic, thus music wasn't necessary for reconciliation. In fact, reconciliation wasn't necessary at all: a not uncommon American perspective towards the Kurds. I held back from asking which five-star hotels she'd been staying in. Every line of her argument twisted the facts and ignored the clear points I'd made for the visit. 'I'm just doing my job,' she added, without even drawing breath before ploughing on through her dismissive missive. They worked in Palestine, of course. Perhaps, if I were to create a project between Iraqi and Palestinian musicians, they would be interested? Oh, for God's sake! Neither they nor anyone else wanted to fund an orchestra of some 55 Iraqi musicians coming to America.

Finally, America was blighted by an increase in hate crimes against Middle Eastern citizens. These communities had neither the muscle nor the media appeal to fight back. Our visit to the

USA threatened the paradigm of paranoia; talented young Iraqis who'd grown out of nothing into a tangible force of reconciliation, using Beethoven no less, challenged the domestic view of Muslims.

I started to question my belief in America. NYOI was innovative, pioneering, meritocratic, hard-working, culturally diverse, resilient, positive and risk taking. These values might once have underpinned the home of the brave, but wherever I turned, I could no longer see it. No matter how much care I took, every word I spoke or wrote to US foundations sounded like a round peg in a square hole. Even my Scottish accent on the telephone from Germany couldn't charm its way through the wall of resistance built by administrators who ate broken glass for breakfast.

The most telling answer came from the US Embassy in Baghdad. Cultural diplomacy from Iraq should be paid for by Iraq. They would only get involved if the Ministry of Culture did so too. Five years of selling this expensive venture to foreign supporters had worn thin. I completely agreed, but also knew that relying on the Baghdad-centric Ministry of Culture to support a truly nationwide youth orchestra was a high-end poker game.

So, Majid visited the Iraqi Ministry of Culture and secured a verbal commitment. On 25th November he wrote: 'Today, after meeting for three hours with the General Director of the Department of Cultural Relations at the Ministry of Culture, Mr Aqeel Al-Mindelawi, I've got an approval from Ministry of Culture to support the NYOI project 2014 USA. And the support will be to the Iraqi National Orchestra Organization for youth, the official representative for NYOI. The amount of support will be between $15,000 and $50,000.'

'... between $15,000 and $50,000'? What on earth could we do with such a pledge? What did that actually mean? It probably meant they hadn't yet decided how much to cream off for themselves. I bit my tongue and fed this result through to our point of contact at the US Embassy in Baghdad, Denyse Kirkpatrick, who was prepared to match the Ministry dollar for dollar. Crucially, the RMVD Foundation in Holland had already donated

$9,000 to kick the project off. They needed to support musicians in conflict zones. I needed to pay a visa lawyer up front.

In those desperately lonely months from September to December, the auditions, led by Zuhal in Glasgow until her laptop packed in, and then by me until I packed in, went remarkably smoothly. She was on form, chatting away with me on Facebook and Skype, studying law and politics at Glasgow University. Through the painful transition of living in Scotland, she'd blossomed into a radiant young woman. Divested of her teenage frumpiness, the streamline figure of Iraq's future Prime Minister adorned Facebook in various fashionable guises, intellectually toying with her friends. Finally out of her brother's flat, she could taste freedom as a young Scot.

She wasn't the only one flourishing. As the audition videos flooded in, I felt elation at those players who just kept getting stronger and stronger. Competition without corruption, real fairness and the promise of a great summer course abroad kept pushing the players to do better each year. This year, I had every video evaluated by an NYOI tutor plus someone completely independent, to be sure we had the right people. I even insisted that all YouTube applications be set to public viewing so that applicants could see and hear why successful players had been accepted.

Going to the US required our highest efforts, so I used the same audition music as the National Youth Orchestra of the USA. Just like us, their course targeted only the very best young players nationwide and paid the course fees for them in full. Players across social divides could afford to apply. We also delighted in being two of the few youth orchestras using video audition. On what the auditions achieved we could fill ourselves with pride but, as with previous years, mountainous problems still cast a shadow over January, with no glint of a solution in the darkness. Much more sinister than before, a new terrorist organisation called ISIL had invaded the town of Fallujah, just 70 kilometres west of Baghdad, and declared itself an Islamic State.

Carnegie Hall and Queens College stayed upbeat and constructive with me. They both offered excellent support, but

I desperately needed somebody to take this baby over and make it work in America. NYO USA, facing a mammoth first year in New York, St Petersburg, Moscow and the London Proms under Gergiev, had very little extra capacity to offer, and the 14 players I needed from them were all they could reasonably offer. Queens College on the other hand, had everything and everyone we needed. Their prime New York base would maximise national publicity, put us on the doorstep of an East Coast tour and minimise flight costs from Iraq.

I stretched my virtual management and leadership skills, as well as my laptop, to breaking point. Every morning, audition issues came in from Iraq two hours ahead of Cologne time, and every afternoon to evening, course issues came in from the East coast five hours behind. But it was now 2014, fundraising was going nowhere, and I couldn't waste anybody's time any more.

TWENTY TWO
The Elgin solution

As joyless January lumbered on, I wandered the streets of Cologne, beyond the point of despair. Then, on the 11th, quite out of the ether, a fairy godmother sprinkled digital dust into my e-mail account.

'Hi Paul,

I've been reading about your NYOI tour, and I realize that what is planned is essentially an East Coast tour. Should your plans change or be expanded, I wanted to let you know that we would be very interested in hosting the NYOI in Chicago, with the Elgin Youth Symphony Orchestra (of Chicago) as a hosting partner.

We could provide homestays or work with you on other accommodations and we would work with you to give your students some fantastic performance venues and, of course, rich cultural experiences in Chicago. Chicago is an amazing American city with a vibrant artistic life and offers a lot.

This hosting would be very much in line with the mission of our orchestra and our Board, so let me know if you are interested. We also could discuss approaches to fundraising for your tour and would be willing to help with that.

We are a large organization of five orchestras and over 350 families, with deep ties in the Chicago community, and a diverse roster of student musicians.

Let me know if this is of interest to you, or how we may be of help.

Randal Swiggum
Artistic Director
Elgin Youth Symphony Orchestra'

Mamma Mia! In a few days, Zuhal would have to e-mail everyone with the results of their auditions, and I now had a new glimmer of hope to meet the players' expectations.

It took me one phone call with Randal to reach the decision to let go of Queens College and try to switch the entire course to Elgin. Randal and his team agreed. They'd heard my Scottish accent, seen me reciting Robert Burns' *To a Haggis* on YouTube, and been sold. NYO USA felt that this changed the complexion of the project dramatically, which it did, and we agreed to let go of each other and move on. Possibly they didn't feel the same way about my accent. Elgin became our new partner. We set our premiere US performances for the Elgin Arts Centre.

From the word go, I felt good about this small town solution, which I'd already seen work in Bonn, Edinburgh and Aix. Elgin, with some 110,000 people, lay about 70 kilometres west of Chicago, Illinois. Talking to the Elgin Youth Symphony Orchestra team, I felt the warmth and generosity that we needed to carry the orchestra to America and look after us. I also heard the same clear-headed problem-crunching and local connectivity I'd experienced in previous years. Most importantly, I heard women with passion and *nous*. Elgin presented itself as a solution I could believe in, and my relentlessness began to reboot. Elgin had found the pioneering spirit the big cities had lost.

Randal assigned me a Power-Frau as my point of contact: Director of Digital Media, Rachel Elizabeth Maley. Rachel, a horn player and pianist, took over co-ordination between me and the Elgin Youth Symphony Orchestra team, as well as a great deal of the American project management. On the one hand, her sunny, fresh temperament and utter belief in the visit more than compensated for my accumulated burnout and inexperience with current American culture. On the other, my input gave her everything she needed to move forward. Our combined social media savvy allowed us to bridge six time zones and feed each other with a virtual cycle of energy, ideas and answers. In every sense, we were virtually on the same wavelength.

Meanwhile, as audition results became known in Iraq, the predictable wailing and accusations of unfairness rippled through the musical community. Baghdad was relatively happy, because five of the six cello places were theirs. Fadi, our 14-year-old flautist from 2009 and our only Assyrian, much taller now at 19 years old, had done such a good job of his audition, he'd got back in. The Kurds won hands down yet again on violin and viola. Frand had got back in, and with some relief, I put him on first trumpet.

We lost Samir, now too old to apply, and I decided to let go of Murad. Ahmed had beaten him squarely in the audition. I also felt very strongly that he'd learnt all he could from us and since he'd never taught bassoon in Baghdad, I had no further case for investing in him. Bashdar had evolved tremendously over the years, and found himself a place studying Masters in cello at Western Michigan University, supported by the Kurdistan Regional Government. This precluded him from joining us. I had to target all our resources at Iraqis living in Iraq.

By February, our new project management was successfully underway. EYSO secured us the use of a local school in July and August from the Mayor of Elgin. This fitted perfectly with his State of the City speech in December, outlining greater involvement of minorities. I prepared to travel to Suleymaniyah, where NYOI had started in 2009, and work with their local orchestra, a good portion of whom were NYOI alumni, for two weeks.

In Suley, my friends from the orchestra treated me like royalty. Shwan and Saman, our loyal translators, along with Alan Kamil, our concertmaster, and other players from the orchestra, took me out to dinner night after night. Some evenings, we'd be in exclusive clubs and hotels, while others we'd be driving down the back streets of Suley to sample the best turkey and beans in town. I felt honoured by their love and attention and got a nostalgic kick out of eating pizza in Costellos, our 'stomach-safe' restaurant from 2009.

One evening, in a food court over pizza, Alan Kamil sat me down and asked: 'Soooo. Is it really happening?' Yes, I was as sure that everything was as much on track this February as in past years. Elgin Youth Symphony Orchestra and I were moving mountain after mountain on a daily basis. Conversations kept moving forward and the spirit and substance of our project felt right.

The following evening, I called a meeting of all the local players for the American visit in the hotel foyer. After a quick update, I asked if, on their free days in the US, they could cover their own meals. We always incurred horrendous catering costs for a whole orchestra over two or three weeks, and if they didn't like it, we ended up throwing good money and food away each day. We all agreed the players would carry some costs, for each other if need be, whenever necessary. The relief I felt that they could agree to this not only came from keeping our budget down, but also bringing them into the process of taking responsibility for the orchestra. They'd driven me round Suley in cars and used smartphones I couldn't afford. While the Kurdish economy functioned in ways the west could never fully grasp, the irony stung.

When Waleed came up from Kirkuk, we were overjoyed to see each other again. We went out with the guys for dinner and sat across from each other. As ever, his dark eyes were bright with passion, his face radiating self-belief. He told me he'd been looking at some books and teaching himself English. He could speak slowly but accurately, and understood everything I said. I can't remember what we said, but the feeling of now communicating directly with someone I'd helped develop since 2010 was indescribable. No matter what fate threw at him and his friends, their indomitable spirit kept fighting, learning, living on.

After a couple of weeks rehearsing, I walked out on the stage of Telary Huner for the first time since 2009 to conduct the Suleymaniyah Orchestra in Fauré's *Pavane*, a new work by local composer Kawan Mahmood, the brother of our 2012 composer Karzan, and Schubert's Fifth Symphony. In this shortish programme, we focused on quality rather than quantity, and the public loved it. So many friends and strangers came up to me to say hello and congratulate me. It felt like a homecoming. After all this time, I still found it hard to grasp that I was the culture Iraq sought to have.

Come March, the US project had built up a good head of steam. I still needed to hunt down a visa lawyer who would take us on and navigate those troubled waters, with way too great a risk of 55 Iraqis arriving at the border on tourist visas and being turned back.

Then, on 18th March, we hit another roadblock, this time from Elgin Youth Symphony Orchestra itself. Two board members had flagged security concerns around the visit, and their President had run these past a consultant. The inflammatory tone pressed all the wrong buttons in me. Whoever this guy was, he sounded more like an insurance salesman than a security expert.

He started by stating that we needed our own security, something we'd never required abroad before, even in Britain, which had also gone to war with Iraq. While Elgin did indeed need to do due diligence, his recommendation that we prepare for an international incident was completely over the top, in my opinion.

According to this consultant, Elgin faced perception risks from Americans and Iraqis in the States who may take issue with one or other 'faction' travelling together. Then there could be protests of any kind, meaning he had no idea why anybody would waste their time protesting against an Iraqi youth orchestra. Most dramatically, he suggested someone could make a political statement by invoking violence. I seriously began wondering which country was more paranoid and violent, America or Iraq?

Then he tied in his mates, who ran 'executive protection services', with someone in each 'jurisdiction' rather than someone travelling with us throughout the entire tour. These people would evaluate transport routes, scout out the housing sites and venues, and ideally speak the language of the students, such as a retired police officer or FBI agent doing this work on the side. He could make recommendations. I bet he could, though I was curious as to whom they would recommend with knowledge of Iraqi Arabic and Sorani Kurdish.

The President proposed a reasonable step forward, to contact past promoters of NYOI and ask how they'd dealt with security. Gladly, I supplied them with names from Beethovenfest, Grand Theatre de Provence and Edinburgh, knowing that this would neutralise the hysteria.

I fed back to Rachel by e-mail:

Having talked a lot to security personnel in Iraq over the years, if you ask them if you need security, they'll say yes, because it's their job to, and then recommend their mates for the contract.

Since Iraqi Americans already presumably travel with other Americans, I'm not sure what their objection would be to us travelling together. However, every culture contains dangerous individuals. To date, we've never come across any. The orchestra travelling and playing together would be unavoidable, so I need to know if your board members believe their reputation would be damaged by this.

I didn't find the word 'factions' particularly helpful here. They're musicians, not warring tribes. I take the safety of NYOI very seriously, and giving them a safe environment is key to the success of an orchestral course, which is why I take them out of Iraq.

Tellingly, the key question wasn't being answered by anyone. Who was protecting whom from what, and how? Were we seriously discussing Americans posing a further threat to Iraqis after they'd already wrecked the country? I didn't see Saddam Hussein ordering an invasion of the US and losing 4,815 Iraqi soldiers while inflicting well over 120,000 American civilian casualties. Nope. It was definitely the other way round. And did Elgin really contemplate somebody 'riding shotgun' on campus and in the buses?

There appeared to be no clarity to these concerns. Smelling the sulphur from America's love affair with guns, I argued:

My players grew up in a war with armed Americans, and I'm not terribly interested in triggering post-traumatic anxieties by adding such individuals to my rehearsals and their free time. If someone with a weapon wants to sit in on our rehearsals, I will tell them to leave.

Can you supply more information on the brief? I should also mention that my players have daily interaction with security, and they can sniff out inappropriate use of it a mile off.

Rachel was also taken aback by this development. She e-mailed me:

The string players we select to join your students, since they must be over the age of 18, will be our alumni and friends, not current students. Though I've expressed this multiple times, board members still come to me and say, 'Well, I wonder if I would feel safe having my children in that environment,' to which I say, 'Then keep them at home.'

Tara from the Iraq Foundation swung into action to bring perspective and experience to the e-mail thread:

It sounds like the fears that are being expressed about the safety of the Iraqi students and the American students travelling together on the music exchange are born out of inexperience and ignorance in regards to the peoples and culture of Iraq, as well as a misconception that our two countries are unable to strengthen ties safely via exchange of our peoples.

In our experience of running the Iraqi Young Leaders Exchange Program... for the past 60 years, Americans have not targeted our incoming visitors to make any political statements, whether through peaceful protests or violent attacks.

By 19th March, I'd finally sourced our visa lawyer in New York and signed the contract to prepare and present Elgin Youth Symphony Orchestra's application to the US Citizenship and Immigration Services, with the fast track 'Premium Processing'.

But I also knew I was ahead of myself, because without the full support of EYSO, this application, made in their name, wouldn't happen. Over the coming weeks, Rachel worked towards getting the board's backing for the visa process. She, Majid and I prepared as much of the paperwork as we could. Having developed good instincts, I became increasingly uneasy about the visa time frame, and March was pushing it for a course starting late July. We added $10,000 for security to the budget to put everyone's mind at rest. Elgin Youth Symphony Orchestra had indeed generated a lot of in-kind sponsorship, and this seemed fair.

All of this seemed so small in comparison to what Iraq was going through. ISIL had wreaked enough havoc to drive some 300,000 people from their homes, mainly in the Anbar province. The Iraqi army fought back by recapturing Ramali and parts of Fallujah, while the Iraqi Prime Minister accused Saudi Arabia of funding the terrorist army. We soldiered on.

We reached the next roadblock on 1st April, when Elgin City Council delayed the motion that allowed NYOI to use the school which Mayor Kaptein had committed to us. Rachel assured me we were collateral damage for an entirely different issue. Whatever, EYSO went into overdrive to find another solution. The answer came quickly and brilliantly; Northern Illinois University agreed without hesitation to take us in and donate their facilities. Although this put us out in the countryside, and I could hear a sigh of relief from some in Elgin, NIU gave us everything we needed in one location: accommodation, campus security, catering facilities and the necessary solitude to rehearse in their music department with Elgin Youth Symphony Orchestra tutors.

Meanwhile, in Washington, the Iraq Foundation kept pressuring the Iraqi Culture Center to release the Ministry of Culture's funding to our banker. We needed to pay for flights. The Iraq Foundation committed $10,000 of their own funds to our DC visit and proved to be great partners who understood Iraqi and American mentality. Tara and her boss, Rend, accepted the Iraqi Culture Center's invitation to help them with the online transfer of funds to the Friends of British Council USA. But no:

Subject: More bureaucratic drama from the ICC

We went over there under the impression we would be assisting them in the transaction as discussed. Instead, they brought in three other staff members and said the Ministry is demanding the following before they make the transfer: a full budget with line items, a description of what they will be paying for and the names and origins of all the youth.

I thought the first two requests in her e-mail to be perfectly reasonable, but 'the origins of all the youth'? A familiar chill ran through me. They wanted to know if the orchestra's ethnic balance was to their liking, and given the number of Kurds in the orchestra, it probably wouldn't be. Majid and I bit the bullet and complied immediately. We sensed where this was going.

Next, we paid the flight deposit with Royal Jordanian. I had to make sure everyone was on one plane in Erbil, flying first to Amman in Jordan, then directly to Chicago. A familiar cry came from Baghdad. In order for this to happen, the 20 Baghdad members had to take the bus up to Erbil, a 5½ hour journey that was still, at this time, possible. But they wanted instead to fly from Baghdad to Amman and rendezvous with the 35 Kurds there. We looked into the cost and timing of this, but given our constant fight to stretch funding as far as it could go, I didn't see this working.

Another cry came from the Kurdish region. The American Embassy insisted the Kurds come to Baghdad for their visa interviews, rather than using the Erbil Consulate. While the British, French and Germans had let us use their consular services in Erbil, America only had one visa officer in place, booked out months in advance. Apart from obvious cost control, the American Embassy was happy to motivate Kurds to come to Baghdad and acknowledge the safety and authority of 'their' capital city, ignoring the 509 people who'd been killed there by terrorists since the beginning of the year. Honestly, the reason they called Baghdad's international district the Green Zone had as much to do with naivety as security. However, this uncomfortable tactic did fit the international community's strategy of preventing Iraq from breaking up in order, among other things, to maintain a geopolitical balance in the region. How much this cost, in lives, carried no weight with any politician. The Kurds, who had achieved virtual autonomy, still had to stay married to Baghdad.

Majid appeared quite robust in his position as head of our new charity. It was about time, he thought, that the Kurds made the same effort to visit Baghdad as the Arabs had done to visit Kurdistan in past years. Otherwise, why were they playing in a national youth orchestra of Iraq? Meanwhile, the war between Iraq and ISIL was simmering away: the quiet before the storm.

In May, the stand-off with the Iraqi Culture Center in Washington DC continued. Nothing from Baghdad or the Iraq Foundation would budge them to release funds, so Elgin Youth Symphony Orchestra responded by authorising an emergency loan to make sure we could pay for the flights on time. Erin, the President of the Friends of British Council USA, turned up at the Iraqi Culture Center on the 21st to find out what was going on. A new list of demands thumped into my inbox:

Hi Paul and Tara –

I met with a delegation (7 people) from the Iraqi Cultural Centre today. They are happy to be supporting the NYOI tour. They said they are ready to transfer the funds as soon as they have the following information:

1. *Full day-by-day itinerary for the NYOI group during their entire stay in the US*
2. *Names of all members of the party – they would like copies of their passports as well – they also want to know where in Iraq each one is from*
3. *They want the details about costs such as the hotel in Washington DC and bus transportation*
4. *They want copy of the plane reservations for everyone and the prices – eventually they will need copies of all of the plane tickets*

5. *They want to see copies of the VISAs for the group*
6. *They want to ensure that their logo will be on all of the materials promoting the NYOI – even in Illinois*
7. *They want to have the Iraqi Ambassador at the reception and performances in Washington DC*
8. *They might assign a representative to travel with the group during their entire stay in the US*
9. *They also asked for the contact details for the British Council Iraq country director (I will send through to them)*
10. *I reassured them that their money would go to the FOBC and that we are a registered 501c3 charity here in the US and offered to send copies of our audited financials and 990 form if necessary*

I reiterated 5+ times about how important it is that we receive the $50,000 as soon as possible so that we don't lose the flights – they said that if they have this information tomorrow they should be able to release the funds.

They asked for Paul's cell phone and email, which I gave to them. They also took lots of photos and spent a lot of time debating with one another about what they needed and how they needed it.

Erin had walked into a very loaded situation and handled it well. Whereas the majority of their team were not introduced to her and most of their discussions happened in Arabic, she had at least found out what they wanted. We were one step further on. The next day, we sent them everything we could. We waited.

And waited.

Meanwhile, the tour was taking shape. Zuhal had been working with Nancy Hunt, President of the We Are Family Foundation in New York. Although the foundation couldn't directly help, Nancy believed she could rally enough individual support to get the orchestra to New York City. Through Carnegie Hall, we got in touch with the LaGuardia Culture Centre in Queens, who, as it happened, were planning a season of Middle

Eastern culture. Much to their delight, we appeared out of the blue as their perfect inaugural act.

In DC, Tara had booked us into the Lisner Auditorium at the university. Performing in August, when most people were on vacation, we simply lacked the resources to hire and fill the vast Kennedy Centre, whereas Lisner had about 600 seats and many students would already be back. The Iraq Foundation had never done this before, and we needed to deeply understand local promotion and pricing structure to sell seats. So, trusting my instincts, I contacted the most powerful social network in town, the Gay Men's Chorus of Washington DC. They were fabulous. Their President gave me the complete low-down on performing there. The National Youth Orchestra of Iraq faced yet another ludicrous irony of receiving more support from them than from the Iraqi Culture Center. Meanwhile, utterly undeterred, Tara and I worked on satellite events: a concert in the US Chamber of Commerce as well as a public discussion on being a musician in Iraq and working in NYOI.

Next, I worked with Elgin on communicating the visit. I felt it important to keep the trust up over our vast distance, and happily shared control over NYOI's social media with Rachel. We openly discussed the sticky issue of reconciliation. Obviously, by bringing players from across Iraq together, NYOI had become a role model, but we knew the media would pick up on the broader dimension, reconciling Iraq with America. I already knew from talking to foundations that this idea stuck in some people's throats. Reconciliation implied liability. Liability challenged American exceptionalism, and not everyone was ready to go there. I felt strongly that we should concentrate on making music and let folk draw their own meaning from the visit.

On 21st May, our visa lawyer informed us that the US Citizenship and Immigration Services had issued a 'Request for Evidence'. Over the past 15 years, USCIS had been happy to know which year the performers had started working with a group. Now, from us, they wanted the exact dates. They also required a union letter from the American Federation of Musicians or the American Guild of Musical Artists stating they had no objection to our support staff, the translators and production managers, coming to America. This appeared anachronistic, as neither union covered these jobs. So, for a fee of $500, I authorised a letter of no objection to be requested from one of the above unions just to keep us on track. We were running out of time.

Additionally, US Consulates in the Middle East usually allowed large groups' visa interviews to take place before the visa petition had been approved by USCIS. This prevented them from being swamped at the last minute and allowed local security clearance to begin in good time. In our case, the US Embassy in Baghdad denied us this option. We had to sit and wait to make a move. Something began to smell.

The rape of Iraq continued. ISIL published its notorious crucifixion pictures. The Iraqi army managed to recapture Ramali and parts of Fallujah, but the worst was yet to come. By June, reports were coming in that ISIL had captured most of the northern city of Mosul where Louis, one of our violinists, lived. They also moved swiftly south to overrun Tikrit. Further down the road, they clearly had Baghdad in their sights. Original estimates of two to three thousand fighters had clearly undershot, and more Sunni groups in Iraq, sick of the Shia government in Baghdad, were siding with ISIL.

On 2nd June, the Embassy contacted Majid to prepare the visa interviews. All the players and support staff had completed the online application process, and were on standby. On the 5th, ISIL invaded the city of Samarra but were forced back by Iraqi military air strikes. Two days later, they stormed the University of Anbar in Ramadi, taking 1300 students hostage, again to be ousted by the Iraqi military. On the following day, the 8th, they pushed towards Kirkuk, where Waleed lived, taking over surrounding villages. That same day, Majid visited the Ministry of Culture again to try to move the Iraqi Culture Center to release funds to us for the flights. Randal at the Elgin Youth Symphony Orchestra had already begun to consider upping their contribution to $100,000 if this didn't work. Majid opened up his laptop and reported back to Rachel and me:

I'm sorry I did not write to you directly after my meeting with Mr Aqeel Al-Mindelawi and the law accountant in Ministry of Culture today, because when I went out after the meeting, I had an accident. A car bomb exploded twenty meters in front of me. I had a drop in blood pressure.

'Today and after long meeting with Mr Aqeel Al-Mindelawi and the law accountant in ministry of culture, who made me take look on the systems and rules of the ministry about sponsoring culture projects, and through supporting it financially. One of these rules is the ministry can never give finance to flights tickets, that are the first bad news.

Second, the culture relations department can't give finance over 45,000$, and if it's more than that, we would need the agreement of the minister himself exclusively, which we might get in 2015. After long discussions, we reached this solution, the 45,000$ we can get it & use it for flights, but it's like we're going to use the money for the following:

1- 30,000 $ as part of the accommodation,& we must give a receipt to the ICC.

2- 10,000 $ as a part of the insurance & also give a receipt to the ICC.

3- 5,000 $ as part of food money, also we need to give a receipt to ICC too.

I felt so sorry for him, and us, that they were saying this now. They reckoned we could spend $45,000 up front and be reimbursed by the Iraqi Culture Center on presentation of receipts. Our hotel costs in DC didn't remotely approach $30,000. Obviously, food and hotel receipts wouldn't be given till after we landed anyway.

Normally, this is what a typical Iraqi deal looks like. Someone else carries 100% of the risk, paying everything up front and they withhold any reimbursement until the very last minute in a verbal agreement. This acts as a control mechanism to make sure they get what they want and the necessary bribes are paid before the amount is settled. But this was sabotage, pure and simple. I spent five years avoiding the Ministry of Culture like the plague and operating NYOI online from Germany, precisely to avoid this. They'd had their chance with me and blown it.

On 9th June, Mosul fell to ISIL. Louis, who had led the orchestra in Edinburgh, fled along with 400 other Christian families and about half a million residents, seeking sanctuary in the Kurdish region. On the 10th, our lawyer received a second 'Request for Evidence' from USCIS. They really didn't want to grant us visas, but we would not let them win. Clearly, they were putting the brakes on their so-called fast track procedure as firmly as they could, to time out the window for interviews in Baghdad. We knocked that request back at them within three hours.

On the 11th, ISIL seized the Turkish Consulate in Mosul, kidnapping its staff, and took over Baiji, without yet being able to seize its oil refinery. Two days after that, Kurdish Peshmurga forces took over Kirkuk after the Iraqi army had abandoned it. This was good news for Waleed and his family. For the moment, they were safe. As the perfect storm built, everyone stayed optimistic. We all determined to keep going. Randal's church prayed for us. Interviews and broadcasts started coming in. Zuhal's media brilliance shone out.

On 14th June, I left a message on the voicemail of Nicholas Papp, Head of Culture at the US Embassy in Baghdad, asking to talk about visas and the Embassy's contribution. By now, I was begging him to help us through. Never before had our battle to establish normality become so relevant in the face of ISIL. Next day, ISIL captured the city of Tal Afar along with its air base, while the Iraqi army reclaimed the town of Ishaqi.

Nicholas replied on Monday 16th June by email, after feeling fully rested from leave, with an application form for State Department funding that I knew would take weeks to process. He still insisted the Kurds come to Baghdad for visa interviews, knowing full well the roads between Kurdistan and Baghdad were now controlled by ISIL. I couldn't believe it.

The next day, he and his staff evacuated the Embassy. In a perverse leap of faith, I considered that, just maybe, there would now be enough visa officers in Erbil to create the capacity for the Kurds to do their interviews there.

On Wednesday 18th June, Majid wrote to us again:

Dear All

A few minutes ago I called Aseel in the US Embassy in Baghdad, and she officially told me that visa issuing from Baghdad is stopped and also the embassy apology for sponsoring due to the situation in Iraq, which means that the project has reached its end.

On Thursday, our lawyer received a second 'Intent to Deny' from USCIS, this time ten pages long. USCIS was utterly determined to keep us out of America. Following one Intent to Deny with another was extremely rare, and told us they'd kept the second one in reserve in case we could answer the first. They were clearly hoping to delay the process for as long as possible and run out the clock. They were also snooping around various websites, including Elgin Youth Symphony Orchestra, an extremely rare step to find something they could use against us. They invented arguments that held no water. For example, the fact that we were engaging in a summer course somehow made our performances irrelevant.

The crux of their paranoia lay in the fact that our orchestra's membership was not constant, and we performed only once a year. So in their minds, a potential terrorist could have been added to the list by pretending to be a violinist. I didn't know whether to laugh or cry. Anyone who'd bought into such extremist ideologies would have either given music up or been executed by his comrades for playing a violin long ago. They were also concerned that, in the face of ISIL, some players would enter and not leave, though this was an issue for the State Department in Baghdad, not them.

Their final *coup de grace*, which they came back to repeatedly, was ample evidence that the orchestra was more noted for its determination in the face of adversity, rather than its musicianship. So, at the end of the day, we were deemed not good enough for America.

We continued to monitor the well-being of our players as closely as possible, focusing particularly on Louis, who had fled

Mosul, and Waleed in Kirkuk. The shops in Baghdad were shut. Waiting to see what ISIL would do next, it had become a ghost town. The players all over Iraq continued their daily lives as much as possible, numb and helpless as the country fell apart for the second time in their young lives. Except for Majid. His brother had just been kidnapped, and he was channelling all his energy into finding him before he was too late. It turned out, sadly, that he was.

The battle hardened between ISIL's apocalyptic fundamentalism and the Kurds' immense will to protect and expand their region to towns such as Kobani. The Iraqi army, regardless of their numbers or American weapons, had no such fight in them because Iraq as a national identity, as a pulse in the hearts of its people, had already been destroyed.

The Kurdish Army calls itself the Peshmurga. This means: 'Those who face death'. Having survived five years, the National Youth Orchestra of Iraq faced death with them.

TWENTY THREE
Reconciling Iraq

There are many paths to reconciliation. We can simply ignore it, as many Iraqis do. We can punish offenders such as Saddam Hussein, or set up a Truth and Reconciliation Commission, as with South Africa. We can try to create a situation where everyone sees each other as equal, and many argue that there can be no reconciliation without that precondition. We can try to be fair and just, both legally and personally. Victims can be supported through aid from local and international aid agencies. Society can be reformed, as both the Kurdish and Iraqi governments are trying to do, to build a more stable future.

Whichever path to reconciliation is chosen, it is often endless, messy, inefficient and demotivating. If we ignore the problem, we fall into racism, sectarianism and fundamentalism, because they are simpler to deal with. War is easy. Peace and reconciliation are very difficult. As Canon Andrew White, the former Anglican vicar of St George's Church, Baghdad, illustrates, one day a week he worships God, the other six he's doing reconciliation.

For NYOI, the first step towards reconciliation was restitution; restoring people's childhood lost to war, improving a broken education system and building a healthier link between the peoples of Iraq and the wider world. Scotland, which demonstrated overwhelming opposition to Britain's role in the Iraq war, turned the penalty of a Glasgow-based engineering company for its crime against the people of Iraq, into support for the orchestra's visit to Edinburgh; an act of justice.

Our YouTube auditions were about fairness. People with an instrument, access to a video camera and the Internet could apply from home, anywhere in Iraq. Unlike live auditions, they could record and check their submissions over and over again before submitting them. But even online, this was a tough environment to control. People with poorer instruments, less support from their families and peers, religious pressure or even just poor video quality did less well than others. There were miracle workers, exceptional outsiders like Waleed who could, through sheer grit and talent, break through their circumstances to pass the audition to play with us.

Staying fair about our upper age limit of 30 sometimes became tricky. Our only musician from Mosul played violin wonderfully. It seemed unfeasible that he should be so good in a city without music. Though he looked considerably older than the birth date on his passport, nobody asked questions. One of our Baghdad players, aside from carrying bass drums and playing trumpet, also wrestled for the Iraqi Olympic Team. His passport had also been 'made younger' to ensure he got into lower age class competitions, where his testosterone-fuelled physique made easy meat of his opponents. The Kurds, whose birth records either never existed, or had been destroyed during Saddam Hussein's regime, often had a default birthday of 1st January on their passports to compensate.

We clearly had musicians from wealthy backgrounds, whose family name put them on the right side of privilege and access to the meagre musical support available. But by passing the audition, players from poorer backgrounds had all their course costs covered by the project. Some privileged players also became complacent and lost their place in the orchestra, not anticipating the increasing ferocity of competition each year.

Every so often, an Iraqi from Sweden, Holland or Jordan would apply. They were usually wonderful musicians, but by forcing myself to limit membership to Iraqis living in Iraq, we kept resources targeted where they mattered. I only accepted foreign players, such as Burju from Turkey on second bassoon, if there was no other way to fill a seat. We also based orchestral seating purely on ability. The better players, often women, led their sections, whereas the weaker players would sit next to a stronger Iraqi player or one from Germany, Britain or France for support.

The issue of equality versus justice transformed itself over time. During the orchestra's lifespan, the Kurdistan Region became safer, more diverse and internationalist, while Baghdad became more violent, fundamentalist and disrupted. On the other hand, the Baghdad players all had a network through the Iraqi National Symphony Orchestra, while the Kurds relied on their diaspora and foreign tutors who could visit them due to the unique visa rules in Kurdistan. The tutors and I couldn't gain access to Baghdad due to different visa regulations and the security situation. So, although in 2009 the Arabs dominated NYOI, by 2013, the Kurds had the upper hand, simply because they were able to flourish in peace, make more connections and work harder; the wisdom of the minority.

Within this context, the auditions were fair, but were they just? I believe they were a sliver of fairness in a deeply unjust society. Despite evaluating YouTube auditions with international teachers, there was no way to completely insulate players from their toxic environments. In the end, audition results had to come down to raw talent and hard work, regardless of privilege. So, in the end, I believe we did everything possible to meet the precondition of equality, so that reconciliation through music could happen.

Auditions also created diversity through merit in a way that existed nowhere else in Iraq.

More than once, Iraqi officials suggested I should include a quota of players from this or that town, unaware that none had applied because there were literally no musicians there, or they weren't good enough to compete with the rest. Our auditions did breed a natural diversity that managed to get men, women, Kurds, Arabs, Assyrians and Armenians into the orchestra.

Once, I was asked if we should only include 'the nice people', excluding those high quality players who tended to provoke tensions in the orchestra. My argument, partly fuelled by the need to keep good players in, was that we had no measure of who really believed what about each other, and it defeated the purpose of reconciliation to only let in people who'd already reconciled. Tensions did exist behind my back, and were sometimes reported to me, but it seemed the players could be trusted to solve their own differences, and what I did see had as much to do with normal personality clashes and lack of a common tongue as anything else. Cooperation was possibly the most powerful part of the course.

Even individuals with deeply racist or misogynistic beliefs, and there were a few, couldn't escape the reality that, in this orchestra, the only way to their seat was if all the people around them, regardless of background, were sitting in theirs. As every place was free to players and based purely on merit, we were able to get the most out of our musical utopia. And utopia it was.

Our tutor team focused on musical teamwork and putting everyone on the equal footing necessary for mutual respect and good listening. In practice, this meant laborious work on playing chords in tune, playing loud and soft together, getting the rhythms right together, and so on. Here, normal music education took on a new meaning. Sometimes, to break the daily slog, tutors would throw in an exercise in pure musical fun and teamwork, such as Terry Riley's *In C* or a Scottish fiddle tune. These moments inspired everyone, as much for the players' openness as for the teachers' need to develop learning.

Our translators, particularly Shwan and Saman, made sure that neither Kurdish nor Arabic were dominant languages, and that the art of communication stayed at the forefront of learning and therefore, reconciling. As an air conditioning engineer and medical student, they themselves had to learn a great deal about music in order to work with us, and are now among the most knowledgeable music lovers in Iraq. When they weren't there, the players themselves filled in to make sure everyone understood what the tutor had said. So we underscored the basis of survival in an orchestra: listening and collaborating.

In truth, I also needed players who wouldn't fall apart in a concert and were of similar standard, so I could choose from our limited range of repertoire. Somewhat usefully, they had no idea about the musical standards being applied to them, as there was little in Iraq to tell them what was right and wrong. They did what they did because nobody had ever told them they couldn't. Their motivation and faith remained unbounded throughout the five years.

When we took this one step further to mix with German, French and Scottish players, our players became experts in reaching out, communicating by all means available and growing through their international colleagues to create new, remarkable synergies for the final concert. As well as that, they experienced a different world of music, education and friendship. By 2013, the cultural isolation they had grown up with had well and truly ended.

Aside from the obvious benefits of having Shwan, Saman and the other translators for reconciliation, two other forces were culture based, without being about language. First, the tutors and I acted as neutral third parties in the course. Because we only cared about music and weren't Iraqi, everyone found it easier to work together. An Iraqi conductor with this orchestra would be unthinkable. Unlike the forming of the Iraqi Constitution in 2005, where various sides mistrusted the motives of the mediators, my team and I worked like crazy to build trust and stay fair over the course of the five years. This foundation for hope came back to us from the players, slowly at first, in hard work, discipline and respect.

Second, and this harks back to the very first course, we had a shared strategy from those little pieces of coloured paper we posted around the wall of the rehearsal room. Instead of just co-existing in peace, these gave us all a vision for our shared future together. How many players saw it that way I'm not sure, but they all knew it existed, and I had promised to make it happen.

Through Najat Amin's composition, *Anfal*, pressure was put on the Arab players to acknowledge 'their' dictator's genocide of the Kurds. It also became our strongest statement of reconciliation through a truth that some players still chose to deny. By performing this work, a kind of justice was served in bringing Kurdish, Arab and French players together in France to internationally recognize the gas attacks.

Unlike Daniel Barenboim's West/East Divan Orchestra, which filmed discussions among the players about Middle Eastern peace in perfect English, we had neither the time nor resources. Our players did not study in European conservatories, and we used three course-languages out of necessity. So we focused hard on education and communication through music. Given only two or three weeks per year, our goals were extremely limited. I feel that the shared kinship of being classical musicians in Iraq, the ultimate minority, bound everyone to very powerful emotions. Regardless of how divided home may be, they all carry the experience of a fully functioning national youth orchestra in them. One day, as Iraq's finest young musicians, they will be the people in power.

The British Council, which is the culture and education arm of the Foreign and Commonwealth Office of Great Britain, helped develop the orchestra as a way of rebooting Iraqi music education after a war in which Britain participated. From their point of view, the orchestra players were also victims who had lost their childhood, especially in Baghdad and Hallabjah. The orchestra was giving it back to them.

The money given by the Scottish Government for the UK visit was precisely meant as an act of justice for the Iraqi people against the crime of the Glasgow-based Weir Group, who used bribery to win contracts under the 1990s Oil for Food Programme to Iraq. The High Court in Edinburgh fined the Weir Group £3 million and ordered them to repay £13.9 million in profits from Iraqi deals. The undertones of this judgement involved the righting of a Scottish wrong to the peoples of Iraq, but also carried an oblique sense of restitution for the damage done during the war. On this basis, we were awarded the £100,000 to come to Scotland.

Overall, our actions were an attempt to make sure students learnt what good and fair music making meant without corruption, religion and politics. From a teaching point of view, this was simple, but frustrating. We just did the same jobs that we did in the West, but with musicians who faced different problems than usual. To the students, our foundation of professionalism, technique, creativity and compassion were a revelation. I think, of all these qualities, we have all learnt that compassion is the most transformative for music and reconciliation. After all, this comes out of a mutual understanding when we see suffering in each other. If there was a healing process, it was based on that.

We also concentrated on rebuilding Iraq by showing the way for players to form their own ensembles, passing their skills onto other musicians in peer-to-peer teaching, building friendships between each other across Iraq's divides, and through their international pals. This became especially powerful for the English–speaking players, who communicated easily with each other and their hosts in Germany, France and Britain. Many of the most fluent English speakers, Zuhal, Boran, Samir, Hellgurd, Bashdar and Murad made the leap to leave Iraq and build families, qualifications and careers in safety abroad.

We worked with some of the finest young people in Iraq, who one day will be elders in their own towns and villages, or working in ministries and making decisions about the future. They will never forget the hard work, camaraderie, international diplomacy and success of the National Youth Orchestra of Iraq.

TWENTY-FOUR
Zeal

By now, it should be clear that the National Youth Orchestra of Iraq was the result of enormous amounts of entrepreneurial zeal from myself and countless others. The question I ask here is whether NYOI really could have a sustainable business model, or simply remain a merry band of activists.

That first step, taken by Zuhal Sultan in 2008, to envisage a national youth orchestra in her war-torn country, didn't come out of the blue. Zuhal had already participated in the American Voices music project with Allegra Klein, and played piano for UNESCO in Paris. She was also the regular pianist for the Iraqi National Symphony Orchestra in Baghdad, often playing harp music, as the orchestra had no harpist. The British Council selected her for their Global Changemaker programme for young social entrepreneurs and activists. This led her to the world of reality TV in London, and the Channel 4 series, Battlefront. From there, a press release landed next to my fish and chips in the Barony Bar in Broughton Street, Edinburgh.

Back in 2002, I helped moderate a British Council conference in Brussels, *The Journeys in Between*, on artistic provision for asylum seekers in Europe. I'd followed this up from 2003-07 with my own small project in Cologne, *Musicians in Exile*, providing instruments and rehearsal space for musical asylum seekers locally. Through this, I'd built up friendships with many musicians from the Middle East, including a Persian death metal guitarist who'd claimed asylum in Germany after being caught performing underground in Tehran. All of us understood the power of music in society, and how the simple bringing together of musicians could continue to reap benefits into the future.

The idea of a national youth orchestra for Iraq struck an enormously powerful chord in me and many others back in 2008. By unifying disparate groups of youngsters throughout Iraq and delivering music education where there was none, we had created the beginnings of a solution that we hoped could reverberate throughout the country. Moreover, the ambition to create a full symphony orchestra and perform in public shifted everyone's perceptions of what was possible in the name of Iraq. The audition process, as stringent as it could be under the circumstances, ensured fairness and built trust in a land filled with disappointment and cynicism. It appeared that Zuhal and I were approaching the same clear, ethical framework from two different directions.

Our partners, the British Council, Scottish Government, Beethovenfest and countless others, understood the social impact of the project, responding with courage and generosity. I took the enormous risk of not charging anyone for my year-round project work in the first two years, to ensure it would survive, and also because my failure rate in this extreme environment, especially when seeking funding, was so high. Experience had taught me that the only way to find the one percent of solutions that worked was to plough through the ninety-nine percent that didn't. I was project managing by pure, blind faith, but doing so sent the right signals to stakeholders that I was doing everything possible to keep NYOI alive. More often than not, solutions appeared obliquely and unexpectedly, but only because we'd tried all the common sense routes.

I felt strongly about the players because we shared the experience of developing as young musicians under tumultuous circumstances. That these were utterly different didn't matter. They all needed help. We had reckoned with a childhood surrounded by madness, and learnt to tolerate it as normal. We all had to relearn normality in order to grow as responsible adult artists. I was lucky enough to be a few decades further along than they, and guided them to as healthy a place as I could. As musicians and minorities, we shared this unspoken empathy.

Culturally, the frictions we all experienced between Iraq and Europe became the grist in the mill that we used to help the orchestra grow. That they had taken themselves so far with the barest of teaching tools showed me their resilience and determination to succeed amid a culture deep in crisis. All we did was bring them together into a bigger, better, safer constellation. So, while we could sell the outward story of courage and communication to the world, we shared a backbone of tenacity to make NYOI work in ways nobody had ever seen before.

Of course, while living in Iraq, the players were impervious to what was happening on the orchestra's behalf elsewhere. Life as a freelance conductor had helped me to cope with barren as well as bountiful times, so there was never, in my mind, a question of giving up before we had established an organisation to protect and sustain the orchestra. When our charity in Baghdad became recognised, after our fifth year, I felt I could finally start letting go. Still, it says rather too much about me, and social entrepreneurs in general, that I never really gave up until the perfect storm, in the combined forces of ISIL and the US Citizenship and Immigration Service, brought us down.

NYOI became dangerous to me for two obvious reasons. First, I was putting my life not only on hold, but also on the line by keeping this highly controversial and high profile orchestra going. Second, I was manifesting Helper's Syndrome. This began logically enough, and the music business had prepared me well. I became very adept at seeing problems round corners and implementing solutions for other team members who either didn't see the risks ahead, or weren't doing their jobs properly. As the Iraqi team was inexperienced I felt they couldn't see trouble coming, and it became easy at first to cut them slack, then to completely take over the tasks they couldn't, or wouldn't, do. I ended up involved in processes that any other national youth orchestra would have a team of full time staff to manage.

That so much depended on me alone clearly put the project at risk. Zuhal, who had been so instrumental in 2009 as our founder, proved difficult to work with as she faced her new life in Glasgow, and remained relatively uninvolved. So, as the stakes for each year increased, I felt strongly obliged to see each course through for the sake of my own reputation, and that of our high profile partners. We had to deliver generously on their huge investment of money and trust. At no point did I even consider that anything but our absolute best was good enough. When the American tour collapsed, my reserves of time and energy had been so often depleted that, this time, I could find no way back. I have to admit, my Helper's Syndrome and the orchestra's Learned Helplessness turned out to be a perfect match.

The reality of helping others is that many people really don't want to be helped, even when they say they do. So, in the initial two years, many players returned home to resume their culture of apathy and disillusion. Fear of change, even for the better, is powerful. Nevertheless, going to Beethovenfest reframed everything. Through sustained effort, many players did eventually rise to their musical, cultural and purely personal challenges that led them into uncharted territory, and changed their lives forever.

You don't need to be mad to be a conductor, but it helps, and this project was perfect for my tremendous love of orchestras. Hitting 40, I was clear this chance, and the energy for the required devotion, wouldn't come again. Did I do a good job of taking care of my own interests over these six years? No. NYOI was pure sacrifice from start to finish, but I knew from experience what risks I could take with my existence, and that I would always get through the dark times and lead everyone out the other side. As a performer, I knew how to ride my personal edge, and pull the energy out from nowhere when it was needed.

Even with that experience behind me, given the sheer unpredictability of this project and the immense hurdles that changed each year, I learnt to place a deep trust in blind faith that the concerts would happen. As a conductor, these were the targets I obsessed at reaching. However, democracy in Iraq was far from mature, and I quickly found Iraqis casting me in the role of benevolent dictator. For the most part, though, the players fulfilled their side of the bargain with loyal and dedicated teamwork. In a world where your best ideas are freely copied before you know it, there is a certain advantage to going way out on a limb. Nobody else thinks you can do it, so opposition is quite low and, when you do, it's such a feat that nobody dares copy you. Though I found myself in a very privileged position of power and responsibility, I was also reminded that Charles de Gaulle once said, 'The graveyards are full of indispensable men'.

France, my first course without burn-out, was a joy. By then, we had established a good working rhythm, and I could simply take on the role of consultant to the French team before arriving at the summer course. Conductors, of course, cannot do their jobs without standing in front of other willing musicians, and so the musical motivation to get everyone together each summer became something like an Olympic training programme for a single sprint.

Along with Helper's Syndrome came Sacrifice Syndrome, when leaders burn out without renewing their energy. As we became more international, our need for higher quality increased the already intense pressure on the project. With such opportunities abroad, we hungered to learn as much as possible in our short time together, knowing every year we might never meet again. We also knew a couple of weeks' summer course would not correct years of neglect. Exhaustion crept up on us, we could lose perspective and often made bad decisions just when the project was reaching its climax. So, by the UK visit all of us, tutors and students, had learnt to spread our workload better, while our project manager, Becca, heavily pregnant, took the middle week of the course off, to recover and return refreshed. That the pubs and the beach in Portobello were just down the road provided ample relief.

How we handled failure unlocked our success. Without our willingness to experiment on all levels of the orchestra, and get regular feedback on what could be improved, we would never have kept our hope and renewal in place over so many years. Indeed, our reputation depended on how well we could learn and move on. The freedom to experiment, rather than blindly copy other national youth orchestras, was key to learning and improving.

So, did we succeed? Strategically, yes, we delivered everything we promised back in 2009 and a great deal more. At the very beginning, I promised Zuhal I would stay for five years, which turned out to be exactly the window of opportunity between the end of the Iraq war and the invasion of ISIL.

The deeper question is whether NYOI was a sustainable business model. It was not. It was an act of sheer bloody-minded determination. Without regular and reliable funding from Iraq, jumping from country to country running multi-annual projects to survive, was eventually doomed to failure. NYOI now has an organisational structure of charities in Baghdad and Cologne, but what they can achieve remains to be seen. Back in 2009, NYOI brilliantly solved multiple problems, but without any subsequent improvement in formal music education throughout Iraq, the orchestra would always be a makeshift solution. We could not replace the music education of an entire country. Our friends in American Voices knew with me that our annual summer courses were the only lifeline for young Iraqi musicians. We also knew it could never be enough to match the talent and potential of the people there.

As for the media, we generated ever more publicity wherever we went, and recycled that to attract the next sponsor. Again, I ended up organising all the videos, radio reports, podcasts and newspaper cuttings into social media, and kept people interested in our Facebook page between our annual courses, largely because the Iraqi team was contributing nothing. Alone, I built up some of the most successful social media of any youth orchestra. Most interest came from Iraqis living in Iraq who would never see the orchestra live, but had hope in what we stood for.

I won't say anything about our documentary makers, other than, to this date, no film has come to light. In future, I will refuse to work with any film-maker who doesn't produce written evidence of a producer and a distribution channel at the outset. Anything else is like a fly without a fly swatter. Given that most film-makers are highly visual people, and are quite happy to ruin the quality of your hard musical work with low budget or thoughtless recording solutions, it's also important to get the quality and competence of sound recording agreed in writing beforehand. In this sense, I was very lucky to have Mark Edwards on board as our recording engineer.

From the point of view of the players, we were a huge success. Though each summer course was profoundly important in itself, the after effects on players over the longer term are what really matter. To round this story off, let's look at the social impact of NYOI from three angles: personal effectiveness, intercultural learning and working with others. Everyone reported that their playing had improved through our rehearsals, performances and individual lessons. But how did players develop beyond that?

> Bashdar: 'When NYOI made its first journey to Germany and I came back home, after I got our concert recording on CD, I told myself "now Bashdar, even if you die, be happy because you have done something in the music world." Simply NYOI changed my life and made my dream true.'

Attracting the best young players in Iraq also meant we discovered Iraq's future cultural leaders. People like Bashdar had a vision for themselves which NYOI supported, and used us as a ladder for their ambitions. He's now studying for a Masters in Cello at the University of West Michigan.

> Annie: 'The online lessons about Mozart and Bach were so helpful. One of the pieces I recorded was Mozart's Fifth Violin Concerto. I had a lesson with Joanne (Quigley, from our 2010 course). I remember how she made me imagine characters. Lots of Mozart music is like opera. I find playing Mozart is so interesting and fun. I do apply this technique while teaching. One of the sentences I keep repeating to my students is "on the string". Angelia (Cho) was the first to introduce it to us in NYOI. I recorded the first movement of the Mendelssohn Violin Concerto that same summer. Angelia's performance with NYOI was so inspiring. Her notes, as well as yours, were really useful.'

Annie, another NYOI star, went on to win a Fulbright scholarship to study for a Masters in String Development in the University of Wisconsin, Madison. Early on, she piloted our programme for online teaching through Skype and YouTube, to try and provide support for players all year round. For cultural and technological reasons, this had limited impact. She now transfers the power of imagination to her own violin students in Baghdad. Most powerfully of all, tutors like Joanne, Angelia, Ilona and Claire became strong role models for Annie and the other female players.

> Louis: 'I practised a lot for the audition because I want to succeed and get the information that you shared with the Iraqi musicians. I loved sharing the music making and training after the last day of the course.'

Possibly the most isolated player in NYOI, Louis came from Mosul, about as musically arid as a city could get, even before ISIL invaded. He already possessed great self-belief and talent, while remaining one of the humblest people in the orchestra. NYOI was his only chance to evolve as a leader and teacher among other musicians, which he took back home and shared in the classroom.

> Alan Rasheed: 'My participation with NYOI was an important experiment in my life, because it was the first time I played with musicians my own age in such a large orchestra. It was really difficult for me, but totally advantageous. Another benefit for me was leading an orchestra for the first time in my life. What can be more interesting? It was a totally tough year to go through, though.'

Alan, who was with us in 2010 and 2011, went on to win an American Voices Scholarship to study with the St Louis Youth Symphony. He, among others, pushed through his boundaries and led a full orchestra of his peers in Iraq and Germany. He now teaches violin in Erbil.

> Daroon Rasheed: 'I've been lucky that I got to know many famous people in my life. I've come to love music more and more every year because of NYOI. It's encouraged me to work hard in order to improve my skills, and taught me how to teach music in the best way.'

Daroon is one of the few players who stayed with us every year. At first, he had little idea about playing viola, but with Sheila and Ilona's firm and loving guidance, he built up his technique and discipline, and is now teaching viola in Erbil. Importantly, NYOI also built up his feeling and motivation for music, which he now gives to others.

> Rezhwan: 'For the first time, we could go to a music shop to buy original materials such as books, CDs and good instruments.'

Our viola leader from 2010 to 2013, Rezhwan benefitted from having Ilona Bondar as a teacher and female role model. When NYOI finally left Iraq, a whole range of services and supplies opened up for them in Germany, Britain and France that the very few poor quality music stores in Iraq simply couldn't provide. Many players have the cash, but lack the access or knowledge of the market to make good choices. By changing the environment, NYOI showed players how to take better care of their instruments, make more intelligent purchases and find better resources for teaching and performing in Iraq.

> Tuqa: 'Actually, NYOI was a real change, challenge and adventure in my life. Since the first season of NYOI, everything has changed, in all aspects not only in music. I became more accurate in doing everything.'

Tuqa, another NYOI regular who loves her cello as much as her hijab, became much photographed for NYOI. She remained true to her religious upbringing, maintaining humility, hard work ethic and compassion throughout her five years with NYOI. She also brought with her a terrific sense of humour. There is nothing fundamentally wrong with a culture that places feelings and relativism over accuracy and objectivity. It's just different. Orchestral music, however, needs a skilful understanding of both polarities to make it work. Tuqa, like many NYOI players, can now integrate these values into her own culture and teaching practice in ways that I can't.

Ali Alghabban: 'The whole experience gave me the courage to play without fear, to enjoy the music I played and project these feelings to the audience. I learnt that music is all about giving. I have to give with all my passion, time and effort until my music can reach the audience's feelings. From time to time, I try to play (for free) in churches, United Nations conferences or public places (where possible), such as my university and pupils' groups.'

Ali played violin with us from 2011 to 2013. A civil engineer who designs high voltage towers and plays with the Iraqi National Symphony Orchestra, he was one of only a handful of violinists who auditioned from Baghdad. NYOI set out to create a loving, supportive and professional environment for players, precisely to help them develop an attitude like Ali's. As is the norm in all national youth orchestras, performing without a fee shifted players' attitudes, because it taught them how to simply give with love and, in doing so, reconnect them with the reason why they were making music.

Hassan: 'NYOI made me more advanced in the area of my work as a flute player and composer in the Iraqi National Symphony Orchestra and increased my experience to teach a new generation how to play the flute with new techniques.'

Hassan also stayed with us over the whole five years, first as a flautist, then as an orchestral manager. As principal flute in the Iraqi National Symphony Orchestra, he was an influential support in Baghdad. Over time, his confidence and professionalism grew. He now works for an American organisation in Erbil.

Frand: 'It takes a lot of time to prepare and accomplish what we've done in a month or less, showing each and every one of us that limits are only a mental thing. After every tour, I don't feel exhausted, and I'm not kidding! I feel replenished and get motivated to practice more, and my musical abilities grow. Even my playing becomes super enjoyable. The orchestra led the way for my leadership persona and I delivered everything I got from my tours to my friends, in an attempt to help music making in Iraq.'

Balen Qader: 'When playing in an orchestra, I feel much more confident; for instance, I learnt how to communicate with fellow musicians. I can also criticise them without hurting their feelings, by letting them know their mistakes and informing them of how to correct them. The things I've learnt from NYOI have enabled me to pass my knowledge on to the community. NYOI has given me a confidence boost and now I'm not scared or shy when playing in front of an audience.'

Waleed: 'I have learned a lot from you, Paul, about how to control the orchestra and how to speak with musicians, and how they didn't forget one day with NYOI.'

Frand, Ballen and Waleed all learnt a style of leadership based on compassion, quality of learning and good communication, to take home and into their communities. They exemplify individuals who have learnt to share music with their peers based on knowledge and analysis, rather than judgement and fear. A born leader and teacher, who founded the Baba Goorgoor Chamber Orchestra in Kirkuk, Waleed seems to have taken the most from me, which is the greatest honour I can ask for.

Du'aa: 'I have been proud of NYOI on many occasions. One particular time was in a wind sectional. While working on some of the repertoire, the tutors decided to try some new techniques that were out of the musicians' comfort zones. Where European music students might have been reluctant to try this, the NYOI members jumped straight in and the end results for their playing were fantastic.'

Du'aa still plays oboe in the Iraqi National Symphony Orchestra in Baghdad.

Hellgurd: 'Getting to know western professional musicians and getting individual lessons from them were also great opportunities to improve my musical abilities and also to practice and improve my English. More importantly, becoming one of the Regional Representatives and working beside Paul gave me a way to enter the management field in a professional way. This even led to becoming one of the bloggers to write about music in Iraq for Deutsche Welle, which was one of my dream organisations to working for.

'Working for the annual summer courses beside cultural institutions like Beethovenfest, Edinburgh Festival Fringe, Grand Theatre de Provence and the German Friends gave me so much experience to manage my own projects, for example founding and conducting my own orchestra at the institute of Fine Arts in Ranya (as I also had the chance to get the first conducting lessons from Paul MacAlindin in Iraq and Barry Roshtoe in Bonn, I was very glad to conduct the orchestra and to use what I have been taught), managing Dobbs Hartshorne's 'Bach with Verse' project twice, being assistant manager and translator for the project of Master Classes for Iraqi musicians, etc' Hellgurd is now studying music education for children in Germany on a scholarship from the Deutscher Akademischer Austauschdienst.

But what about the impact of going abroad on the orchestra? Having grown up in isolation and hostility, our journeys to Germany, France and Britain, where orchestral life is normal, transformed everyone.

Firman: 'It showed me that other players were amazing at playing their instruments. This helped me a lot. I thought that these other nations lived on another planet, not Earth, when I saw the way they performed!'

Frand: 'The first time on tour to Europe in Germany, I received a cultural shock, even though I'd read and watched TV about Europe and the US, but going there was another thing.'

Hassan: 'It made me see the world differently in terms of community and convergence of different peoples in the name of humanity. I loved working with NYOI. It was an example of the interdependence of all individuals regardless of their religious belief or nationality.'

Ali Alghabban: 'It gave me the chance to meet wonderful new people, make new friends and discover new cultures.'

Daroon Rasheed: 'NYOI has simply taught me how to understand people from different backgrounds and get to know more about their culture. Now I have friends around the world. NYOI showed me things that my country doesn't have. I will do whatever I can to make this happen in my country too.'

Tuqa: 'I believe that NYOI was able to unite different cultures and different religions through music, so it was an unforgettable experience for me.'

Rezhwan: 'First, meeting many intelligent musicians from different countries, especially the teachers, and being friends with them on social media, meant we could ask them any questions about music, and get new information. Second, we don't have any summer festivals. NYOI gave us a great experience of what's going on during the summer in other countries. We created good relationships between Arab and Kurdish people. NYOI was the first opportunity for us to get closer to each other. Third, we got out of Iraq or Kurdistan. It's really difficult to get a visa from any country, especially those we've been to.'

Alan Rasheed: 'This orchestra had its own mission to promote another side of Kurdistan and Iraq, and letting people all over the world know that there is life, art, music and many talented adults who need to be encouraged and promoted globally.'

Annie: 'Learning Irish music was so much fun, as well as supporting events for the British Council in Baghdad.'

Hellgurd: 'NYOI gave me the first opportunity in my life to travel abroad as a musician. I took the chance to get to know other people and I had the hope that one day I could come back on my own to realise my ideas and dreams. Suddenly I realised that I had made very good contacts abroad and it made feel like I am not only a musician who could do their music, but I had the feeling that I could be more than that and do better things for myself and for my community. NYOI made me dream bigger and all of the experience that I collected during these four years led me to be granted a scholarship from DAAD to further my study in Germany, which was very competitive.'

So, NYOI opened up a whole new world to everyone, and they grew stronger for themselves and Iraq. The impact on NYOI's women, which the final chapter elaborates, cannot be underestimated. Everyone played their role as cultural diplomats brilliantly and won over thousands of hearts and minds, through the supporting youth orchestras, performances and international media. Determined to bring isolation to an end, the players forged international friendships and learnt to communicate not just with each other, but with the music world. Inevitably, a handful grew beyond all expectations to create a new vision for themselves and others, who will carry NYOI's energy forward in new and different ways.

The final question is, how did they share this experience back home?

Bashdar: 'I encouraged all my friends to apply, because NYOI is the group that has given best service and help to young musicians. I was honoured to be part of the NYOI team because, through my hard work, I deserved it. Many of my friends didn't believe in NYOI in the beginning, but then I became a good example for my city and they knew that this orchestra had changed many things.'

Louis: 'I've done a lot of musical activities including training in the churches and giving lectures and lessons on violin and piano, and some leadership lessons. I am now a school teacher, giving music and voice lessons for pupils in my village.'

Daroon: 'One of the most influential tasks of NYOI is that it encourages the players and the staff to engage with their daily lives. This has created a strong relationship with my family and friends so I can be inspired to perform at my best, and most beautiful. NYOI has inspired me to serve my community in the best way, because NYOI's service to Iraq has been very influential, compared to what we had in the past. Now, I'm teaching viola in the College and

Institute of Fine Arts in Erbil. I teach my students everything I've learnt from NYOI, and last year, I had 18 viola students. I have participated in several orchestras and also established a string quartet in Erbil. I believe this is the best thing NYOI players can do for their communities. Two people have inspired me to love music: Paul MacAlindin and Zuhal Sultan. They are my role models and inspiration to succeed more in my life. I'm happy I worked with NYOI, because it has introduced me to many people in my community.'

Annie: 'I'm busy preparing a library and music room for a refugee camp in Baghdad. I wanted to do an all girls' quartet, and switched to viola. We practiced for a bit, but unfortunately stopped. I hope we will resume soon, but there's no room to practice, and their parents find it hard to bring them to my place when there isn't a set date for a concert.'

Tuqa: 'I had the chance to experience more cultures during my visit to many countries and I began to understand the real meaning of teamwork. Here in Baghdad, I began to teach some beginner students the basics of choir in the music and ballet school, and also in the PTA centre I taught homeless students the basics of cello and the music theory, and tried to transport my experience to them.'

Alan Rasheed: 'In my opinion, the things that the politicians didn't do were finally done by NYOI.'

They may not be cultural leaders in their communities yet, but they will be one day, and when that day comes, they will remember what we did together, and how it changed everyone.

This chapter completes our current mission. While I threw everything into achieving what we'd set out to do in 2009, I have no regrets, or hesitation in passing on what I've learnt. However, I cannot fully close this chapter of my life with the National Youth Orchestra of Iraq without properly addressing the question I asked myself in front of a plate of fish and chips in the Barony Bar back in 2008.

TWENTY-FIVE
Who are the Iraqis?

By 2015, the culture of Iraq was being brought down around the world's ears by ISIL in a calculated strategy not only to defile any iconography that disagreed with their religious extremism, but also to render a once proud region even more helpless amid its already shattered post-war identity. Irena Bokova, Director General of UNESCO, remarked: 'Extremists don't destroy heritage as a collateral damage, they target it systematically to strike societies at their core'.

The commonly quoted Iraqi proverb, 'May the books be a sacrifice for the people' tells us that a living Iraqi is of more value than a destroyed artefact or one of the rare books ISIL burnt in their raid of the Mosul public library. They are both right and wrong.

The physical history of Iraq has outlasted hundreds of generations, and stands for an entire civilisation, a way of life. Now, people are rapidly becoming the only cultural capital Iraq has left, which is why daily music making is a vital building block to bolster Iraqi pride. When Tuqa or Annie teach music in Baghdad's School of Music and Ballet, or at a school for Iraq's many internally displaced refugees, these simple individual acts guarantee that culture continues. Or when Karim Wasfi, one of the conductors of the Iraqi National Symphony Orchestra, takes his cello into a recently bombed site in Baghdad's Red Zone, to reclaim the space for decent people, he rebuilds not with bricks and mortar, which anyone can do, but with soul and hope.

When the iconic sculpture of Baghdad poet, Abu Nuaz, who died in 814 CE, is vandalised by sawing off the wine cup in his hand, many Iraqi intellectuals keenly feel the vengeance of religious authorities who regard him as immoral. Meanwhile, professional Arabic poets decry the rise of folk poetry in Iraqi dialect. Some young people have taken this ghettoised poetry slam to heart and become populist troubadours, spreading bitter irony and caricature as a form of dissent.

Young film makers still gather at Baghdad's Iraqi Independent Film Centre to discuss the latest techniques. The House of Iraqi Poetry organises events in the upper middle class Karrada district of Baghdad. They sit in cafes, defiant of the next blast that could claim their lives. Young Iraqi film maker, Mouhannad Hayyal, told the Arab news agency, *Al-Monitor*: 'Death is everywhere in the country, but being scared of sitting in a coffee shop won't make life here any safer.'

Activists build informal book clubs on street corners under the banner 'I read – I am Iraqi' to expand reading beyond the elite classes and reconcile a disenfranchised young generation with their own cultural heritage. Everyone is well past the point of fear. Life, however numb, must somehow go on.

The cultural battle isn't just between ISIL and Iraqis, but in the hearts and minds of the silent majority, decent citizens who, after 30 years of war and violence, still resist totally giving up on their lives. Part of that battle is reinstating discipline and technique into people's lives. Without that, nothing gets done. One doesn't misquote Shakespeare by saying: 'To be or not to be: that is the discussion...' In classical music, a note or rhythm is either right or wrong, in a fairly restricted context.

In NYOI, we were permanently engaged in the battle for accuracy. The universal principles that make orchestral music a part of the world's cultural DNA were treated relative to Iraq's culture. Not only is Iraqi culture ambiguous, it's also broken. In the cycle of endless correcting of mistakes, we nailed down one, and another popped up. We thought this had something to do with pushing the players' concentration to the limits. However, it was often difficult for them to come from a small group rehearsal and hold onto the learning when they sat down in the next room with the full orchestra. The context, and how closely they felt they were being watched, changed the way they retained learning.

All the players are incredibly individual, and our international partners fell in love with them for this. Compared to the Germans, Scots and French, we were a strongly mixed bag of characters. You can raze entire cities to the ground, but all you need is one survivor to rebuild a culture, and these resilient, personable young people are, to me, the harbingers of Iraq's future identity.

It would be gauche to suggest that war had made them stronger. Compared to the thwarted dreams of many other Iraqis, they are the lucky ones. I compare Iraq with the aftermath of the Second World War, where European music experienced unparalleled innovation through musicians such as Peter Maxwell Davies, the Beatles, Pink Floyd. The big difference is, post-war Iraq completely lacks the hopefulness and idealism of post-war Europe. It remains in a state of violent living death. There is no Marshall plan as there was for Germany, no wise nation builder like Germany's first post-war Chancellor, Konrad Adenauer. The intellectual class, whose ideas and cultural exchange once held considerable unifying power in Iraq, have largely fled the country or been killed in the Iraq war, leaving a huge vacuum in Iraq's common identity.

Significantly, the world's first national youth orchestra, in Wales, gave its first concert in 1947. This youthful impulse, working together to represent a new sense of national pride and future hope, is precisely what we wanted to foster, but Iraq spent precious little resource on it. Why? Because culture doesn't make anybody any money. Also, true competition as the West understands it is a joke, because a level playing field of any kind is impossible when corruption and nepotism are like eating and breathing. So, people teeter on the edge of giving up completely. From this perspective, we were extremely fortunate to have Dr Barham Salih on our side at the beginning, not only as funder, but as patron for our message of fairness and equality.

From this point of view, NYOI's auditions forced people to reassess themselves. Some of our players from Baghdad understood that NYOI's dramatic growth in quality came through fair competition, while others simply believed that their seat in the Iraqi National Symphony Orchestra sufficiently proved their excellence. This is the fine line between saving face through arrogance and admitting one's weaknesses, seeking growth. Our tutors and visits abroad provided many with a harsh but necessary reality check.

I believe many of the conflicts in the orchestra were as much personality driven as anything. The Arab guys looked strong and masculine and did compete readily against each other for status. The Arab women, though clearly feminine, were intrinsically stronger for being able to put male colleagues in their place and hold their own as musicians and section leaders. The Kurds, more group oriented, had a somewhat gentler, less physical presence. Overall, just to get into NYOI required all of the players, especially those living in Baghdad, to be inherently resilient. Nobody was a quitter. Quite rightly, those with the vision, talent and command of English used their new-found awareness garnered through NYOI to join the brain drain and escape Iraq completely.

The role of women in the orchestra had a profound effect on everyone. Female players such as Du'aa, Annie, Tuqa and Rezhwan, took on leading roles based on their ability. Although Annie had completed her Masters in String Development at the University of Wisconsin, Madison, when she returned to the Iraqi National Symphony Orchestra she was placed at the back of the second violins. Predictably, she was seen as a threat. In contrast, our rehearsals led by excellent tutors such as Angelia Cho or Ilona Bondar, as well as our visits abroad, empowered our female players to understand the prominent role of women in other cultures, and encouraged them to take a more leading role, where possible, in Iraq.

Our courses abroad opened musicians' minds up to a vast range of diversity, especially for the more isolated Baghdad players. They saw that our workshops were largely run by women to a standard unimaginable in Iraq, and sat next to outstanding female players from our supporting orchestras. Most critically, the necessary breadth of people required for NYOI to happen each year promoted quality and ability over identity.

Whether Iraqis or tutors, we shared a desire to grow through our experience with each other. The composers we performed all had strong individual voices. While players learnt about Schubert, Beethoven, Mendelssohn and Haydn through the tutor team, we learnt from them about the nostalgic Bedouin heart of the Arabs, the sense of tragedy underlining all Kurdish music, and insane levels of motivation and learning. We also grew enormously as teachers, creating solutions on the hoof for our myriad technical, musical and communication issues.

Where Iraq and I diverged was over the culture of rancid selfishness. Post-war Iraqis were scrambling for power and money in an already broken system of corruption and incompetence. Altruism in this environment led to being trampled upon, unless you were very careful or had enough privilege to absorb the exploitation.

Over the years, I gradually grew a thicker skin, though detachment through the Internet and my German home helped less and less as I became more deeply embroiled in the project we had created together. Those who were already privileged, the politicians and the ruling class, showed little inclination to rebuild Iraq's culture or spirit, instead creaming off massive bribes from multi-billion-dollar oil, reconstruction and communication contracts. Meanwhile, religious parties used politics to gain power over people's lives. Baghdad had been carved and walled up into sectarian strongholds. 'Divide and conquer' was never more evident than in modern Iraq. Just how were they supposed to rebuild a nation under these circumstances?

On the flipside of this, an orchestra is, of course, a community of musicians, and ours were ready to work together. Between courses, our Regional Representatives helped the players master the online application process, making and uploading video auditions, applying for visas, distributing audition and course music throughout Iraq. This was crucial in Kurdistan, where the players were spread throughout the region. The incentive still existed to get on an NYOI course – carrot and stick leadership, but at least young musicians were working together for the common good.

Back in Baghdad, Majid was the focus of all of those applicants. He set up the NGO for the orchestra after years of sabotaging bureaucracy. He and his team ensured all the Baghdad audition videos and applications were sorted in good time. Sarah, our horn tutor, also noticed that the horn players, Ranya, Ali and Mohammed had all supported each other's practice for the auditions, as they'd accidentally all learnt the same mistakes.

Our work with chamber music was the hardest. Just getting these headstrong young individuals to listen, count and play as a chamber group together, without a conductor dictating to them, took all our effort. Yet, that was the most vital part of the course, hopefully spreading collaboration and group learning throughout Iraq, while creating a shared social activity, concerts for the whole family that had nothing to do with religion. So, NYOI played its part in fostering community throughout Iraq.

Our auditions, a powerful way to focus players on achieving, were also contentious. Some losers in this process really didn't want to accept that we knew how to judge everybody fairly. Since standards at home were non-existent, or at best highly skewed, they couldn't grasp our concept of quality. We hurt their pride with the very notion that, for that year at least, they weren't as good as the rest. Inevitably, as the orchestra evolved, more and more players applied, and worked harder to compete in an Iraq that was slowly settling down to some kind of normality, and allowing people to grow again. The goal of an orchestral project and a trip abroad motivated players to learn the rules of fairness and hard work. Those who really understood the power of achievement could also become artistic leaders back home. Many also opened the gateway for others, helping them prepare auditions and supporting them during the orchestra course. We fought judgemental, closed minds with the seeds of generosity from which Iraqi culture could rebuild itself.

Nevertheless, payback was always important, and with that came titles: Majid as Director of Operations, Project Manager and later Chair of the NGO, Waleed, Hellgurd, Bashdar, Daroon and Alan as Regional Representatives, Hassan and Bashdar as Orchestral Managers, Zuhal as Founder, me as Music Director. Yes, we ascribed ourselves status to garner authority and respect. In reality, this only worked when we earned that respect by achieving results. Thus, we delivered another countercultural kick in the teeth to Iraq.

The core strength of the players, which fed their resilience, was the ability to channel their survival instincts into music, and shut out the war outside. When it was too dangerous to go outside, they would stay at home and play music by themselves. By the same token, the rise of religion during the war, which provides received wisdom to live by, became another way for peaceful people to shield themselves. Of course, religion also became a tool for violent people to create violence. Religious leaders ascribed themselves political status to impose their interpretation of law on people, dividing government, cities, provinces and eventually the Iraqi army. It's no wonder that many of the young people I met in Iraq were atheists.

Who wouldn't be sick of religion's role in destroying life and home? This position can't be openly expressed in Iraq, where questioning the existence of God is unacceptable.

In the face of this, the National Youth Orchestra of Iraq was an affront, an anachronism, a paradox. To this day, I still have little idea who in the orchestra was Sunni, Shia or Christian. It was a total non-issue. Our very real issue of Kurdish versus Arab had, in reality, much to do with language barriers. Because we stayed hard-wired to making music together, as often as possible, we could lower that barrier somewhat.

In addition to religion, the geopolitical war by proxy being waged in Syria and Iraq has prevented people in Iraq from returning to any kind of stable life. So, any form of post-traumatic stress from the Iraq war has been sustained. This had huge effects on some players' mental health, with symptoms including narcissism, eating disorders and depression. Learned helplessness, which I mentioned earlier, conditioned Iraqis over years into self-sabotage, resignation and continual mild shock, beaten down by years of war, genocide and stupid old men. Add to this the prevalence of suicidality, on which religion places a huge taboo, and the psychosomatic symptoms of men who have experienced violence or displacement, such as anxiety, headaches, dizziness and poor concentration. Iraqi mental health is a seeping, infected wound in a country desperate for healing. The orchestra attempted to put people back in control, leading them away from self-sabotage and towards success, but learned helplessness is everywhere.

Cam Matheson, who came to Iraq to film us in 2011, saw what was going on and told me about a film he'd made with Aboriginal Australians. This particular community received support from people wanting to help improve their situation. This did indeed happen but when all the resources of these well-meaning individuals dried up their 'helper's syndrome' kicked in, leaving them shattered and empty. As they left, the Aboriginals just waited for the next helpful person to come along. Even though we took great trouble to empower as many young musicians as possible, I identify with this in Iraq. In a strange way, keeping the orchestra alive became a zero sum game. The more they improved, the deeper my life sank.

This is the vicious cycle of aid, in any form. The questions are, where is it all going and when do you stop? I was completely aware that some individuals, both in Iraq and internationally, were sitting on the sidelines of the project doing very little, while being perfectly happy for me and the real partners to carry most of the work and risk. The absolute bottom line is that, even if the project had been done differently by someone else, work like this has no place for lazy, risk-averse people. It needs real givers with real talent and grit, who know how to learn fast enough to adapt to changing circumstances. I don't pretend I'm that person, but there was no manual, no case study for working on a project like this.

Venezuela's El Sistema and Barenboim's West/East Divan Orchestra were completely different animals in many ways and, though inspirational, didn't have much to do with us.

Another aspect of learned helplessness is the culture of complaint. Iraqis can be utterly unconscious of how much they whine and apportion blame, rather than taking charge of a problem. This huge part of Iraqi culture became particularly painful in the first couple of courses. The tutors and I often stood in stunned silence as we heard barefaced lies shamelessly directed at us. Epic face-saving was called for to cover up the shame of a society that had been brought to its knees. You can tell a great deal from a culture's proverbs, and a particularly popular one in Iraq goes: 'Life is like a cucumber: you get one in your hand, and ten up your ass.' Luck is bad; expect it.

The Iraqi National Symphony Orchestra in Baghdad, an institution since the 1950s, has the good fortune to be supported by the Ministry of Culture. However, religious influence on government can render music making in different parts of Iraq difficult or impossible. The complex rules for singing can best be summed up as similar to the Free Presbyterian Church in Scotland; one can glorify God with the human voice, unaccompanied, as this is an instrument of God. In Islam, Instrumental music can glorify Allah and his Messenger, but cannot be used for dancing, entertainment or as a hobby. Music that brings inner peace to help one remember Allah and religious responsibilities is more contentious. However, the daff as a powerful Sufi call to spirit can be used, along with other drums, in religious festivals, weddings and times of celebration. This useful caveat allowed NYOI to express its spontaneous sense of spirit whenever we needed to fill a dark or uncertain space with joy.

Music is expression through time, and time itself became a powerful cultural force. The constant need for Arab Iraq to hark back to its ancient Mesopotamian past, rich in cultural heritage, is understandable. But it won't lead Iraqis out of their current crisis. It's another way of ignoring the present and the future. The Arab music we played strongly evoked ancient and Bedouin traditions which, like the extended family, is a powerful force in the Arab heart. This is one reason why ISIL needs to destroy Iraqi heritage to break the last threads of Iraqi will. It's a calculated war of culture.

The Arab music that Mohammed Amin Ezzat, Osama Abdulrasol, Lance Conway and Ali Khassaf wrote for us all harked back to the old Baghdad before Saddam Hussein. The 1950s, 60s and 70s were a heyday of Iraqi culture and identity. Cafés, concerts, theatre, literature and art all flourished. Even Saddam understood the need to court intellectuals for their influence on society. Our composers sought to relive this golden era of Iraq. All of our Arab Iraqi compositions may have sounded kitsch to Western ears, but they also clearly expressed a gloriously upbeat Arab soul.

For the Kurds, the future is also a hopelessly romantic ideal. While independence for the Kurdistan Region of Iraq is not unrealistic, the whole lost country expanding through Syria, Turkey, Armenia, Iran and Iraq will never be reunited. Even if it were geopolitically possible, the Kurds are too divided amongst themselves. For Kurds to hang onto the big romantic ideal of uniting old Kurdistan, rather than concentrating on the very real possibility of independence for the Iraqi Kurdistan, is equally self-sabotaging. However, that they have so far managed to resist and win against ISIL speaks of an experienced and culturally driven fighting force, determined not only to preserve, but also to win back their language, traditions and territory. If you say you're a Kurd, you're a radical.

Kurdish identity through the compositions of Dr Mohammed Zaza, Ali Authman, Karzan Mahmood and Najat Amin pointed to their future through a modernist European language that we in the West have already abandoned. These composers are constantly surrounded by traditional Kurdish music, not only inside Iraq, but from the stronger Kurdish traditions in Iran and Turkey. I guess they saw the chance to write for an orchestra, especially abroad, as an opportunity to compose in a more modern, individual style with a complexity and sophistication that reacted against the apparent simplicity of Kurdish folk music. In doing so, they may have thwarted what we in the West expected from them, a quaint folk medley, but at least they had the opportunity for decent public performances that showed their real voices.

However, when it came to classical music and Kurdish soul, both players and composers often failed to make the connection.

While checking out their technical prowess was easy, it was also clear that many just didn't understand Western music. This is based on chords and works with a precise tuning system, whereas Middle Eastern music is linear, improvised and rhythmically complex, with several tuning systems. For many, making music is a way to earn money or get access to a free summer course, not just to celebrate and give of itself. NYOI sought to change that perception.

The archetypal Kurdish drum, the Daff, breathtakingly mastered by Daroon and Sherwan, is also a mystical Sufi instrument that awakes the soul. In our own way, NYOI tried to emulate this power, and stellar individuals like Hellgurd, Walleed, Bashdar, Tuqa, Annie and Zuhal went on to do great things. Without a doubt, NYOI awakened their lives. Less ambitious players worked quietly in the background, teaching and performing with greater authority and discipline in their local communities. Others just put their instrument in a cupboard and waited for the next round of auditions. To this last group, NYOI was more a travel agent than an educator, but with such a small pool of players to choose from, we needed to fill places in the orchestra.

When a sense of soul did break through, all the Kurdish composers wrote with a deep sense of sorrow, clearly on a mission to get that sound out into the world and remind people of Kurdish suffering. On one hand, the desire to impress guilt and retribution not only on the public, especially when Najat Amin wrote *Anfal* knowing Arab players were in the orchestra, comes from the deep-seated victim culture in Kurdistan. On the other, the relative safety of the Kurdistan region could also allow the Kurds to finally express mourning together for their tragic history. In comparison, Baghdad still needs to nostalgically hark back to lost eras to protect itself from daily violence and chaos. The mourning process, followed by a new future, hasn't even begun there.

If I'm right, then both artistic reactions are completely understandable. But how will Arab Iraq move on if nostalgia for ancient history, which ISIL is publicly destroying or selling off on the black market, is all they feel? And how will the minority Kurds ever attain independence if they romanticise their future, a reunification of old Kurdistan's six dialects and divided peoples? The Kurdistan Region of Iraq is as landlocked by potential aggressors as the Kurdish soul is trapped by the illusion of inferiority. Whether self-sabotage or self-preservation prevails, the Kurdish mentality is likely to avoid full independence.

As an orchestra, perceptions of time and history affected us all. But on a daily level, just getting everyone to sit down punctually and tune up together before the start of a rehearsal proved a long- term battle which we eventually won by taking the orchestra out of Iraq altogether. Most significantly, no matter how hard I tried to make the rehearsals work in a linear, orderly fashion, the orchestra would turn them into cyclic events; a groundhog day for musicians. One run through of a passage had mistakes in it, so we went back and corrected them. The next run though of the same passage had different mistakes, so we had to go back and correct those too. And so on.

How they felt about time and music counted for much more than what little black dots told them to do. Dougie, our wind tutor, cottoned onto this and often ended his work by asking, 'So, for the last time, can you hear the difference?' They nodded obligingly. 'Are you better than before?' A bit dubiously, they nodded again. Amid the grafting of self reflection, we all got caught in vicious cycles of tiredness and lack of concentration, which increased the mistakes. If we were tackling modern music, it became infuriating to them and me that musical rapport and context just couldn't be grasped with their educational level and experience. In 2011, we were rehearsing Ali Authman's *Invocation*. I said to a very grumpy Samir on double bass: 'Look, if you don't like the music, then the thing to do is get it right first time, so we don't have to keep going over it!'

In spite of all of this, with endless patience and faith, we somehow managed to make dramatic progress. As our UK project manager, Becca, wrote in her 2012 report:

'This is a truly remarkable orchestra. What you read in the press about this orchestra is 100% true. When they first played together at the start of the summer school I was genuinely worried about the concerts – they sounded like a rough school band. I honestly could not have anticipated the transformation over the next three weeks. The concerts were utterly gobsmacking, especially knowing the journey the orchestra had made. The summer school and what that brings in terms of high quality tuition and musical expertise in a concentrated time clearly has a profound and lasting impact on the young players. It is a lifeline to them.'

This ability to ride a steep learning curve may be one reason why immigrant workers and refugees are feared in the West.

In spite of our changing membership and differences over the years, the orchestra managed to develop a family-like feel with me at its head. Family lies at the heart of Iraq, while the need for family lay at the heart of my musical direction. Indeed, as so much infrastructure had been decimated, it was all that Iraqis could rely upon.

Modern Iraqi families are relatively small, with parents having only a few children, though the extended family can find itself living under one roof and sharing responsibilities. As there is no concept of insurance in Iraq, children of more traditional families often find themselves becoming the pension scheme. It makes total sense to have as many as one can afford and ensure that they too have good jobs and ample families of their own. Partly because of this, and partly due to religious pressure, the notion of being openly gay has no place in this world and the reality of same-sex intimacy behind closed doors remains a safely hidden taboo. In Iraq, there's a way round everything.

Religious power over family is profound. By nailing the role of sex to procreation in wedlock, religion ensures that young men and women cannot even physically touch each other where they might be seen. So the powerfully public culture of men being physically close to men, which may or may not lead to sex, is all that young men have. Heterosexual men in the West have lost this physical intimacy with each other, for fear of being labelled gay.

Family is also mafia. Since the rule of law completely collapsed after the 2003 invasion, never to recover, ethnic, religious and family disputes have often resolved themselves by hiring hit men for the price of a bottle of alcohol or some petty cash. This tightly woven net of community tensions breeds incredible self-preservation. In the event of a neighbourhood assassination or honour killing, everyone turns a blind eye. If they speak up, they too will be on someone's hit list. This is how to survive war and terrorism.

Oil is Iraq's 'resource curse', or as Bashdar so eloquently put it, 'The problem is, we're lazy.' War and peace will cycle through Iraq for as long as companies continue to drill there, but corruption and self-sabotage are a constant. When technology renders oil redundant, Iraq will be left helpless and shattered with little capacity for production, innovation or an educated, globally mobile workforce, most of whom have already left. But what is corruption? Transparency International suggests:

'Corruption is the abuse of entrusted power for private gain. It can be classified as grand, petty and political, depending on the amounts of money lost and the sector where it occurs.'

In 2014, they listed Iraq as the sixth most corrupt country in the world, and in the bottom 17% of all countries when it came to accountability. This is as vital as transparency, because in a culture as shamelessly corrupt as Iraq, people don't even bother to hide it. They know they will never be held to account. Iraqi people's confidence in the rule of law was measured in 2010 at the bottom 2% of all countries. There is zero governmental openness about budgets. Indeed, it's seen as corrupt to keep all the money from a deal for yourself. Your partners down the line expect their share of the cash, like unofficial taxation.

So, NYOI could only ever have existed internationally, and online. Iraqi banks took a long time to credibly re-establish themselves. Transparency of transactions through various Western organisations, which showed that our funding was going 100% to the orchestra, kept us credible and alive to our international partners over five years. The British Council and the German Friends played a huge role in ensuring that.

In contrast, the sheer resentment that Iraqis feel towards politicians and government officials living in Baghdad's international Green Zone, with full amenities and luxury conditions, cannot be underestimated. The rest of Baghdad, the Red Zone, has long suffered from lack of electricity, waste collection and water since 2003, while these same politicians siphon off money for themselves. The government shabbily rebuilt the Iraqi army after the US had dismantled it. Weakened again by corruption, incompetence and purely political appointments, they were poorly equipped to defend Iraq against ISIL.

The division between Sunni and Shia Arabs in Iraq is something I've never talked about in this book, as it simply isn't relevant to us. However, when the young pianist, Mohammed Ramsi, who I taught in 2013, lost his best friend to an explosion in Baghdad, he couldn't visit his grave because the cemetery is Shia, and he is Sunni. Most of the Arab players, having been students in the Baghdad School of Music and Ballet, were already familiar and comfortable with each other as musicians, in stark contrast to the city around them. United by love of classical music, everyone understood what it meant to be a minority.

However, during Saddam Hussein's rule, his Ba'ath party, which was Sunni, drove a wedge through the two sects of Islam, by brutally persecuting and killing Shia Iraqis. When he was ousted in 2003, Shia militias wreaked revenge on Iraqi Sunnis, filling the power vacuum left by the new Shia government, army and police. The wedge was driven deeper. When the Iraqi army confronted ISIL, corruption and nepotism had damaged trust and respect so much that the chain of command broke down. Iraqi Sunni soldiers facing ISIL, which is also Sunni, felt more strongly about not confronting their brothers than protecting Iraq.

So, in that window of opportunity between 2009 and 2014, the Iraqi Government could have chosen to spend their vast resources on improving amenities and restoring Iraq's diverse cultures, Arab, Kurdish, Armenian, Assyrian, Turkomen and

Yasidi to greatness. They could have chosen the path of South Africa, and installed a Truth and Reconciliation Commission. Instead, they chose a culture of greed bolstered by corporate and religious opportunism.

Will children's destiny in Iraq be steered by the family or religious sect they were born into? Yes. Will valuable education resources be strangled so that rich politicians and civil servants can get richer? Definitely. Will selfish old people continue to crush the young? For as long as they need to stay in power and feed their massive greed with money that should fund public services, of course. We can argue that this is simply human nature, but few places on Earth are as extremely afflicted as Iraq, a country already back on its knees with another war.

In contrast to all of this, it's great to see the Kurdistan Regional Government's *KRG Vision 2020* policy document state: 'By 2020, our government will be free of corruption and will fulfil all of its responsibilities fairly and efficiently.' They won't reach that goal, but at least they've named it.

And now, the blackest joke of all is that Iraq, brought into dire straits by ISIL, is pleading that it doesn't have enough resources to cope. If the billions that disappeared down politicians' back pockets had actually gone to the services they were meant for, would Iraq be in the mess it's in today? Where is that money now? If Iraq had invested wisely in cultural, security and municipal services that gave people a country worth fighting for, a country with a future, would ISIL, who now impose their own culture, deliver public services and brutally eradicate corruption in the areas they occupy, have been able to march in unopposed?

Incredibly, against this toxic backdrop, there are still young Iraqis trying to recover a sense of hope and dignity in the future, working to preserve some decency and structure in life. I have never experienced the power of hope and blind faith in humanity as strongly as I did with the players of NYOI. They have embraced generosity. They are my sisters and brothers. Without their incredible spirit, there can be no way out of the slow burning hell they're trapped in.

Index